*The Novels of
Charles Williams*

THOMAS HOWARD

The Novels of
Charles Williams

IGNATIUS PRESS   SAN FRANCISCO

Cover design by Marcia Ryan

© 1983 Oxford University Press
All rights reserved
Reprinted in 1991 by Ignatius Press
ISBN 0-89870-349-2
Library of Congress catalogue number 91-72757
Printed in the United States of America

For Joshua and Augusta Oden

whose measureless generosity,
encouragement, good humor,
and companionship
have made the weary old term
"in-laws" dance with vitality
and pleasure for me.

Contents

Preface

Any book about Charles Williams' fiction is bound to be a failure in some sense, for you cannot write about his novels without running onto one of various shoals.

On the one hand a complete commentary on these tales would run to many thick volumes, like rabbinic commentaries on the Mosaic Law, since almost every line of Williams' prose may be glossed and unpacked and cross-referenced to the tune of many pages' worth of comment. The shoal here, of course, is that this would be pedantry run amok. No author in the world is worth that sort of treatment.

But then short of that exhaustive method what do you do with this kind of writing? You have to be selective, and the shoal here is that you will leave something out. It is very difficult for readers coming to Williams for the first time to know what he is saying. There are two reasons for this. First, no one who is not already familiar with the dazzling firmament of images that stretches like a canopy over his imagination will have any way of knowing what he is talking about. Williams is like Blake or Yeats in this respect. Second, he writes with a kind of shorthand. There is nothing wrong technically with his prose: but, as with hieroglyphics or cuneiform, one needs to be taught how to read it. The almost universal cry from first-time readers of Williams is, "This is absolutely electrifying—but I haven't the least idea what it is about."

A third shoal might be called the critical one. That is, it is very hard to know just what tools of the literary-critical trade to bring to bear on prose like this. Any one of these tools—the psychoanalytic, the archetypal, the formal, the *exposition de texte*, the biographical—would do its own job on the material. But sooner or later one has got to come to terms with the fact that Williams was writing about Grace, really, and this eludes most art and all criticism. This is why it is hard for criticism to know just what to do with the work of people like François Mauriac, Flannery O'Connor, or T. S. Eliot without watering down the force of what they were saying. As long as you talk about them in purely literary terms you are to some extent whistling in the dark. What they write about is salvation, damnation, heaven, and hell, and they did not at all mean heaven and hell as colorful symbols of psychological states. Like Dante and Milton, these writers really thought that we are en route to either joy or wrath. Religious dogma determined their ideas of human behavior, and it is no use trying to translate this down into terms acceptable to a nonreligious era like ours. We are patronizing them if we do.

The rejoinder here would be that criticism has to do *something*, and one thing which it may not do is sail off into rhapsodies, any more than a surgeon may throw down his tools in the middle of an operation and shout, "This is the most sensational aneurism I have ever seen! Hurry up, everyone, and have a look!" The critic *as critic* may not gasp, "We had all better look to our salvation!" even though we had all better do just that sooner or later. Criticism's job is description and explanation. It is also appreciation, not so much in the sense of breathing, "Ah! Just look at that!" as of pointing out how the various elements in a thing work together to form a whole that has integrity, harmony, and significance.

It is possible to do this with Williams' prose. And no doubt it needs to be done one day. But that is not exactly what the present book sets out to do. My task here is the more modest and elementary one of helping readers to know what is going on in these novels. I will refer to these tales as novels for lack of any other convenient term even though I am aware that they do not fit very well into this category.

I have followed a somewhat peculiar procedure in the following chapters, and I should warn my readers. It will be noticed that in nearly every case a disproportionate amount of time and attention is given to the early pages of the novels, with the commentary then thinning out as though the commentator had got tired and was eager to reach the end. While that would be understandable, it was not my reason for doing things this way. Rather, my supposition was that once a reader was launched into a given tale, with the major images and complexities explained, it would be insulting to keep leading him by the hand too punctiliously. Hundreds of pages of explanation have been omitted, as it were. But then we are back to the first shoal mentioned above: no human author warrants that kind of endless scrutiny.

One other point about the following pages: there is a great deal of repetition from chapter to chapter. If one reads this book straight through he will find himself murmuring, "But this was explained in the last chapter." The point here is that this is not a book to be read straight through. I have tried to make each chapter as self-sufficient as possible so that if one is reading *The Greater Trumps*, for example, one will find the help he needs by reading the commentary on that novel alone without having to rifle back and pick up from the other chapters Williams' ideas on Exchange and Substitution.

Beverly Farms   T. H.
September 1982

Acknowledgments

One always has debts to pay, and I pay the following eagerly and gladly since they are debts of plain gratitude. Mary Ruth Howes sent me my first Charles Williams book in 1959, when I was at Fort Benning, Georgia. It was *The Place of the Lion*, and I sat in my office transfixed. I was like the Ethiopian whom Saint Philip found reading Isaiah in his chariot: I am not sure I understood much of what I was reading, but I was fascinated and moved. As it happens, that reading formed the start of a course of thinking that has shaped my whole imagination. Alice Mary Hadfeld, with her book *Charles Williams: An Introduction*, helped me understand something of this extraordinary figure. I regret only that her more recent study, *Charles Williams: An Exploration of His Life and Works*, did not appear before I finished the present manuscript. My student Sarah Winston, in a brilliant paper on *The Place of the Lion*, opened up a number of points of interpretation that twenty years of reading the book had not unplugged for me. In some ways I feel that I might have done better simply to include her paper as my chapter on that book (with proper acknowledgment, of course).

Most sets of acknowledgments end with "And lastly, to my wife, whose long-suffering and boundless good faith and cheer kept me going during the weary months of writing", and so forth. All that is quite true in the present instance. But there is more than that. My wife, Lovelace, is, quite literally, the embodiment for me of the Charity to which every line of Williams points. She is my Beatrice. I know something of what the expression *la carne gloriosa e santa* means because of her. I say this, I might add, after twenty-six years of marriage to her. The opinion is not a flash in the pan.

T. H.

Introduction

Charles Williams is a strange figure among twentieth-century writers. His work is hard to classify, since it will not fit any category of modern criticism. Is he a writer on the occult? Has he chosen worn-out themes for his poetry? May we call his narratives novels?

Lists of major British writers of this century will probably never include Williams' name. T. S. Eliot may have touched on at least part of the reason for this in his introduction to Williams' last novel, *All Hallows' Eve* (1948):

> What he had to say was beyond his resources, and probably beyond the resources of language, to say once for all through any one medium of expression. . . . Much of his work may appear to realize its form only imperfectly, but it is also true in a measure to say that Williams invented his own forms—or to say that no form, if he had obeyed all its conventional laws, could have been satisfactory for what he wanted to say. What it is, essentially, that he had to say, comes near to

defying definition. It was not simply a philosophy, a theology, or a set of ideas: it was primarily something imaginative [Introduction, xi, xiii].

If we find here a hint as to why Williams' work will never be included among the major works of our century, we may also have the key to its appeal. It was primarily something imaginative. Williams has nothing strictly new to say, but then neither did Dante or Shakespeare or Eliot. What all poets do is to take "the permanent things" (Eliot) and, by discovering fresh images for them or by refurbishing the old images and setting them out freshly, wake the rest of us up once more to the tang and bite of human experience just when we had almost slumped into ennui and torpor. In this connection we may recall that imagination, which is the poet's province, does not supply us with any fresh data. The poet's appeal, unlike the scientist's or the explorer's, can never rest on his bringing exciting new facts to light.

Williams' poetry, for example, stands outside the main currents of modern poetry. It cannot be understood at all without the reader's first having mastered the whole set of ideas and images that Williams presses into service, namely, the Byzantine Empire, Arthurian Britain, and human anatomy as an "index" or diagram of glory. His essays rush at you in a cascade of odd prose. The first three sentences in his brief Church history, for example, run thus: "The beginning of Christendom is, strictly, at a point out of time. A metaphysical trigonometry finds it among the spiritual Secrets, at the meeting of two heavenward lines, one drawn from Bethany along the Ascent of Messias, the other from Jerusalem against the Descent of the Paraclete. That measurement, the measurement of eternity in operation, of the bright cloud and the rushing wind, is, in effect, theology" (*The Descent of the Dove*, 1).

The subject of this study, however, is Williams' prose fiction. He wrote seven novels during the 1930s and 1940s. They have been described as "metaphysical thrillers", which is perhaps as close as we can get to finding a tag for them, although the phrase raises in us expectations of goblins and occult lore, and that is not what Williams is interested in.

What Williams is interested in is heaven and hell; or, to put the same thing another way, he is interested in human behavior.

This looks like a conundrum. How can we say that heaven and hell are the same thing as human behavior? If Williams really thinks they are the same thing, his imagination must be very far-fetched indeed.

It is. It is "far-fetched" in the sense that any great poetic or prophetic imagination is, in that it is fetched from afar. The noblest poetic imaginations have persisted in seeing the commonplace routines of human experience against an immense backdrop. Eliot spoke of "the fear in a handful of dust", referring to the enormous and alarming significance lying just under the surface of even the most ordinary things. Scientists see one aspect of this when they tell us about the subatomic activity raging and swirling about in the merest handkerchief. Prophets see another aspect of it when they tell us that modest items like casual oaths and cutting remarks and icy silences will damn us to hell. Poets see yet another aspect of it when they see the whole Fall of man in a fieldmouse's scampering away from a farmer's plough, or a world of hypocrisy in the fur trim on a monk's cuffs.

The ordinary stuff of our experience seems both to cloak and to reveal more than itself. Everything nudges our elbow. Heaven and hell seem to lurk under every bush. The sarcastic lift of an eyebrow carries the seed of murder, since it bespeaks my wish to diminish someone else's existence. To open a door for a man carrying luggage recalls the Cross, since it is a small case in point of putting the other person first. We live in the middle of all of this, but it is so routine that it is hard to stay alive to it. The prophets and poets have to pluck our sleeves or knock us on the head now and again, not to tell us anything new but simply to hail us with what has been there all along.

If anyone ever saw the fear in a handful of dust it was Williams. There was no detail of everyday life, no bodily function, no chance word, no bird or bush, no kiss or shaken fist, that did not signal Everything to him. Like all poets, he saw a correspondence between commonplace things and ultimate things. Everything supplied him with parables and images.

An image points to something beyond itself. The wave of a hand is an image of greeting, which is itself one aspect of courtesy, which in turn is a subdivision of Charity. The shake of a fist is an image of animosity, which is one aspect of anger, which is one of the Seven Deadly Sins. Everything keeps rising towards heaven or plummeting towards hell. The whole conflict of heaven and hell crops up at our elbow a thousand times a day.

Williams, being Christian, believed that this business of images is itself a clue to what everything is about. God himself, on this view, brought things to a point in the final image, the Incarnation. Christ was the image of God. A body here in the visible world manifested something beyond what you could see. Christians see this same principle at work in the sacraments: bread and wine and water become signs and bearers of Grace, which is invisible. In the Incarnation and sacraments we have not a disruption of Nature but a knitting back up of the seamless fabric of creation, which was ripped by us when we made our grab in Eden. In that act we introduced secularism, that is, the attitude that says, "This is mine." One of the tragic by-products of this tearing of the fabric is that we must now experience the whole as divided. We are obliged to think of things as spiritual or material, invisible or visible, immortal or mortal. But these are all divisions that would seem to proceed from the Fall. The fabric ought not to have a rip across it. There should be one unbroken pattern. Christians believe that it will be knit up again at the end of time, and that this knitting up has been begun in the Incarnation and is pledged and kept before us in the sacraments. Hence, for a Christian poetic imagination like Williams', we will find that imagery is more than a matter of powerful fancy: it is very close to theology.

It may seem odd to have strayed this far from the strict business of literary criticism. But we cannot read very far in Williams without becoming aware that almost every line summons the whole universe, so to speak. In this he has forerunners in Saint Augustine, Dante, Milton, and Blake.

But this would seem to be a shaky recipe for modern fiction. We might put up with the universe in Saint Augustine or Dante, but we are not sure we want it on every page of the fiction we read.

It is part of Williams' achievement that he made fiction go to work on a task usually undertaken only by certain

kinds of poetry. The stories he wrote are bona fide stories, and you can put your feet up in front of the fire and
enjoy one of these novels without having studied much
theology or poetry. On the other hand, if you are reading with the smallest rag of attention, you may be inclined before very long to leap from your chair in terror
or excitement. In that sense Williams' fiction does not
make for a quiet evening by the fire.

Williams' habit of seeing vast significance in commonplace situations is what accounts for the oddity of his
stories. They usually entail a clutter of situations, characters, and images. In one tale you find a chase for the
Holy Grail across the fields of Hertfordshire, and in another a blizzard stirred up by a pack of fortune-telling
cards, and in another the great Platonic archetypes in the
shape of lions and butterflies appearing in the countryside. There are satanists and doppelgängers and succubi
and wizards all rubbing shoulders with clerks and pub-
lishers and housewives. The picture may switch with no
apology at all from a policeman at a crossroad to the
Byzantine Emperor, the assumption being that in the
end they come to the same thing, says Williams, since
they all hint at the final pattern of all blissful order and
harmony, namely, the City of God.

An obvious objection to this would be that things do
not at all add up to any such pattern. What about all the
havoc and outrage and pain that mar things? Is not the
ghastly truth of the matter simply that we may wish
things were thus but that they never turn out to be so? Is
not the whole burden of modern fiction a testimony to
our discovery, following the breakup of the ancient and
medieval order in the Enlightenment, that there is not

any great and final pattern, and that things add up to nothing?

That is indeed the testimony of much modern fiction and painting. Williams' work, along with that of the later Eliot and many Catholic poets and novelists, would stand over against this testimony. They would all accept Dante's universe, as it were, not in the literal Ptolemaic sense of earth's standing at the center of things but rather of the universe's being intelligently ordered, and of there being a conflict between good and evil, and of our mortal life's participating in that conflict. On this view we are all en route to either heaven or hell, and the direction we travel depends on the choices we make and the attitudes and habits we form and every word we say.

The theme in all of Williams' works is order versus disintegration. In every one of his novels the evil that appears entails an attempt on someone's part to short-circuit the given pattern of things, defying the rules like a child at a party who grabs all the best pieces of cake, or a man cutting across in front of everyone in traffic: both are violating the rule of courtesy. Both are cads, and caddishness is an early straw in the wind blowing towards hell. In every Williams novel some attempt arises to defy the rules and to make a grab for knowledge, power, or ecstasy. The trouble is that the rules turn out to be far weightier than mere party manners or traffic regulations. They constitute the moral law of the universe.

The irony is that knowledge, power, and ecstasy are the very rewards that stand at the far end of this mortal pilgrimage for all who have obeyed the rules. They are the fruition of humility, purity, faith, courage, and generosity — of virtue, in other words. The quest for knowledge, power, and ecstasy is itself legitimate. We are made for that fruition. But the way towards it is a steep and narrow one, and you have to go along the appointed way. The Beatific Vision is for the pure in heart, not for the clever, the Machiavellian, or the lucky.

Shall a man bend his efforts to getting what he desires by any means at all? Or shall he try to discover the rules and submit to them in his quest? Neither Williams nor Dante nor Saint Augustine nor Saint Paul would seem to have any doubt in the matter; and they of course did not originate this way of seeing things. It is all in the Hebrew prophets and in the teaching of Christ.

The peculiarity of Williams' novels lies in the way he handled these questions. Modern novels ordinarily explore human behavior in terms of manners, as Jane Austen did, or Henry James; or by social protest, as did Dickens; or by satire, in the manner of Swift or George Orwell; or psychological analysis, like James Joyce. Williams, like Dante, tried to carry the exploration further in order to see what the end of it all might be, and in that end he saw only two alternatives: salvation or damnation.

This is not to imply that Williams' novels are religious novels or that a reader with Christian leanings will be in a better position to appreciate them than a nonreligious reader. Williams assumes quite unabashedly the whole Christian scheme, so that words like "salvation" and "damnation" appear quite naturally when you talk about his works (he himself does not much use them). But a man does not have to believe in heaven and hell in order to admit that these words conjure the most powerful pictures available to human imagination of states of being that manifestly belong to our human story. One may or may not imagine that we are all going to one of these places eventually, but one cannot deny that the picture of heaven represents all that seems planted most deeply in our desirings and that hell represents all that we most dread. Freedom, bliss, fullness, perfection, and peace are what we want, and heaven pictures them all. Solitude, bondage, impotence, ennui, and inanity are what we dread, and hell confronts us with them all.

It would be absurd to suggest that because Williams pursued his tales further than manners or psychology or satire, they thereby represent a higher achievement than that of Jane Austen or Dickens or Henry James. A novelist is not obliged to chase his tales across the border into that land from whose bourne no traveller returns. Indeed, such a chase would seem to remove the tale from the category "novel", since the modern novel has concerned itself strictly with the world of ordinary mortal experience. Ghosts, the occult, murder, intergalactic travel, and even high adventure—none of these seem to fit quite comfortably into the plain category of the novel. We have to find special names for them: ghost stories, murder mysteries, space fiction, thrillers, adventure, and so forth. On this accounting, we may only very loosely give the name novel to Williams' prose fiction. Literary criticism may someday supply us with a more exact category.

Williams was not interested in the occult at all except during a brief period in his early life. One might be pardoned for forming the impression from his novels that he was quite caught up in the occult, but this would be a mistake. His imagination was aroused by certain ideas that crop up in occult lore, but he remained a plain Anglican churchman all his life. He accepted the taboos that rule out forays into the occult. He wrote an entire book on witchcraft, but nowhere in the book can you find out how to say a black mass or any description of any ritual that might arouse inordinate curiosity. He confined himself in this study to recounting the Church's response to occultism down through the centuries.

Williams' concern in his fiction was the same as that of any other serious writer, namely, to give as true an account as possible of human experience. Like any artist, he brought all the resources of his imagination to his task, and since his imagination was full of all sorts of dazzling images, these are what show up in his work.

It might be helpful to have some sketch of his life, since the way he came at life was the way he came at his art.

His whole name was Charles Walter Stansby Williams, and he was born in London on September 20, 1886. His father was a foreign correspondent for a firm in the city. Both of his parents were devout Anglicans, and apparently the church nourished Williams' imagination from the start. He found in the liturgy and the sacraments not only orthodox doctrine but also the vivid presentation to his imagination of a world that was full of glory.

Williams had one sister, Edith, born in 1889. The family lived in a state of perpetual financial difficulty. His father's job was always in question because of his poor eyesight, and in 1894 he moved the family to Saint Albans and set up a shop selling stationery and artists' materials. Charles was sent to Saint Albans Grammar School and then to University College, London. After two years there he was forced to drop out and go to work to help make ends meet. He continued his education as well as he could by attending classes at the Working Men's College in London.

In 1908 he went to work at the Oxford University Press as a proofreader, and he stayed there until his death in 1945. Amen House, the office of the Press in London, became one of the "precincts" of his imagination, for he found there a company of people in whom he chose to see an idealized society in which obedience to the order of Charity results in joy. He wrote poems and little masques and pageants in which his colleagues show up as paragons of virtue and chivalry. He eventually dedicated one of his books "To H. M. [Sir Humphrey Milford, the London publisher of the Oxford University Press], under whom we observed an appearance of Byzantium", by which he meant that the atmosphere of order and harmony in the office under a good man is a case in point of the order and harmony that might be fancied as having been at work at least in the ideal, if not the reality, of the Byzantine Empire.

Williams was physically disqualified for military service during the 1914–18 war. This forced him to an idea which was to become central in all of his later work. He realized that the peace and well-being he enjoyed in England were due to the sacrifices being made by the young men in the trenches of France. In other words, everyone in England owed his life to these men who were laying down theirs.

It seemed to Williams that here was a principle. Everyone, all the time, owes his life to others. It is not only in war that this is true. We cannot eat breakfast without being nourished by some life that has been laid down. If our breakfast is cereal or toast, then it is the life of grains of wheat that have gone into the ground and died that we might have food. If it is bacon, then the blood of some pig has been shed for the sake of my nourishment. All day long I live on this basis: some farmer's labor has produced this wheat, and someone else's has brought it to market, and so on. These in turn receive the fruit of my work when I pay for the product. Money is the token and medium of the exchange that takes place: here is the fruit of my labor, which you need, and with this I purchase the fruit of yours, which I need. It becomes very difficult to keep all this very sharply in focus in a complex modern society where face-to-face transactions rarely occur. But the principle of exchange is at work in international commerce as well as in the village farmers' market. It is just harder to see.

Williams coupled this idea of exchange with two other ideas, namely, "substitution" and "co-inherence", but they all come to the same thing. There is no such thing as life that does not owe itself to the life and labor of someone else. It is true all the way up and down the scale of life, from our conception, which owes itself to the self-giving of a man and a woman to each other; through my daily life, where I find courtesies such as a door held open if I have a package; and laws obliging me to wait at this red light while you go, and then you to wait at the next corner for the other fellow; and commerce, in which I buy what your labor has supplied; right on through nature, with its grains of wheat planted and harvested and animals slaughtered for my food; to the highest mystery of all in which a life was laid down so that we might all have eternal life.

The point for Williams was that all life functions in obedience to this principle of exchange and substitution and co-inherence whether I happen to observe it or not, or whether I happen to be pleased by it or not. It presides over all life, so that to resist or deny it is to have opted for a lie. For Williams, hell is the place where such a denial leads eventually. To refuse co-inherence will reward me with solitude, impotence, wrath, illusion, and inanity. I will have reaped the harvest I have sown in my selfishness and egotism. I will have got what I wanted. I will be a damned soul.

On the other hand, the City of God is the place where we see co-inherence brought to blissful fruition. What we encountered in this mortal life as mere genetics, say, in our conception, or as agriculture in the bread we eat, or as law with its traffic lights and yellow lines, or as courtesy with doors being held open, or as economics with its buying and selling, or as theology with Christ's sacrifice—all this is unfurled in the dazzling light of the City of God. Saints experience as bliss the very same thing that damned souls hate. Vexing necessities like waiting at red lights or fetching cups of cold water turn out to have been early lessons in joy. For joy is the final fact. It is the way things are, whereas hell is the way things aren't.

If, for example, I can just try getting this cup of water in the middle of the night for my spouse, who is thirsty, even though God knows I am too sleepy to budge, I will have gone through a very small lesson in Charity, which is the name given to the principle of exchange and co-inherence when we find it at work in an intelligent creature exercising his free will (as opposed to a kernel of wheat, say, which has no choice). I may of course refuse, in which case I will have missed one lesson. The difficulty here is that this refusal turns out to be more serious than my merely having missed a lesson. I have *lost* ground. I am not where I was. I am a step back. Or, put another way, I am now less prepared to pass the next lesson since I have contributed by my refusal to an inclination, already too strong, to pass up the lessons. It is so much easier just to stay in bed here. It is much, much nicer. How comfortable and warm it is here. Let my spouse fend for herself. I'll just doze a bit more . . .

. . . and wake up in hell, says Williams. Not that he supposes I will be damned for a small thing like that. On that fierce accounting we are all lost. Rather, it is a matter of realizing that whatever I do is going to nourish either selfishness or charity in me. There is no third category. Williams might say that Lesson Two in this Cup-of-Water-in-the-Middle-of-the-Night section might be that I learn how to do it in such a way that my spouse will conclude that it is no trouble at all for me. A small self-deprecating jest goes a long way here. And of course the point for Williams would be that by my at least making the attempt to do it lightly and good-humoredly I will find that I have come upon one of the keys to joy. It may look rather small and doubtful right now, but it is a hint of what the City of God is made of. Selfishness and sloth, on the other hand, cannot even imagine, much less want, this joy. Williams might go on to suggest that Lesson Three could very well be my learning to *receive* such a cup of water, or to allow my spouse to get up and get one for herself without a lot of fuss and protestation, if that seems the best and least troublesome thing for both of us. Charity is not bondage and fuss. The giving and receiving fall into place when done properly, like the advancing and retreating steps in a well-executed dance.

This capacity to take the plain stuff of experience and discover in it suggestions of the biggest mysteries of all is at least part of the poetic gift, and it is this capacity that we find at work in Williams' novels and poetry. It would be hard to pick one experience as absolutely central in the development of his imagination, but certainly the experience of romantic love would be as close to the center for him as anything else.

He met Florence Conway in 1907, and it was she, he says in another book dedication, "by whom I began to study the doctrine of glory". By this he meant that this notion of glory, or ecstasy, stands at the far end of the lessons we are given the chance to learn when we love someone. Williams married Florence in 1917.

He began to experiment quite early in life with poetry, and by 1922 he had published four small volumes of poetry. Almost all of it had something to do with romantic love, but as he matured as a poet his poetry became less remote in its fancies and closer to the familiar realm where cups of water and other small tokens of unselfishness show up when love is at work.

During the 1920s Williams began lecturing on English literature at an evening institute in London. Besides his work at the Oxford Press, he was busy with editing and writing introductions for anthologies of poetry and editions of Dickens, Kierkegaard, Milton, and Gerard Manley Hopkins. He also wrote several small plays during this period.

The 1930s saw a prodigious output of work. During the decade, Williams published five of his seven novels, two theological works, six biographies, three critical works, and the first volume of his series of lyrics on the Arthurian legend.

In 1939 the Press was moved from London to Oxford to escape the German bombing, which seemed imminent. Williams at last found himself close to the scholarly atmosphere which he had never penetrated as a young man. He became part of the group comprising Tolkien, C. S. Lewis, and others, which called itself the Inklings and which met twice weekly to talk, read manuscripts aloud, smoke, and drink beer. He was eventually granted an M.A. by Oxford University and a lectureship in English. His health was never good, and he died unexpectedly after minor surgery in Oxford in May of 1945.

The 1940s had seen the publication of his last two novels, another volume of his Arthurian poems, his study of Dante, a history of witchcraft, and another biography, besides a torrent of reviews and criticism in both popular and scholarly journals.

Williams spelled out in his essays all of the ideas that run through his novels. Probably the clearest statements of these ideas appear in his two long essays published together, entitled *He Came down from Heaven* and *The Forgiveness of Sins*, and in his history of the Church, *The Descent of the Dove*. This latter is not a long book, but in it Williams scans the events of Christian history. Like all orthodox Christians he sees the Church as the embodiment here on earth of what is true outside of time. In this visible body of people the world may see a hint of the kingdom Christ was talking about, the paradox being that this hint glimmers through somehow, no matter how poor a showing this body of people makes. Of course the Church is as wicked as her worst enemies say she is. But in a great mystery this strumpet is called spotless by the Great King. A poor and spotty showing does not nullify the reality behind things.

For Williams this would obtain all up and down the scale. Glory is both cloaked and revealed in the stuff that we see about us, poor though that stuff may seem. When Williams refers, for example, to Byzantium as a beautiful, well-ordered scheme of things that may suggest the City of God to us, he is not blind to the murderous perfidy and intrigue that seemed to be the Byzantine specialty for a thousand years and more. For him, this discrepancy would merely have heightened the piquance of it all. Paradox flashes and dances all over the place. Expose Byzantium all you wish: there was nonetheless an *idea* at work there that was true, namely, that order and authority are, in the end, sacred.

This "nonetheless" is very close to the center of Williams' imagination: he was vividly and simultaneously aware of evil and chaos on the one hand and of the Good to which they bear perverse witness on the other. You could shout at him until you were purple in the face about the atrocities of which the Church has been guilty, and he would still insist, "Alas, yes, but nonetheless Christ calls her holy." Or you could flap the hair-raising pages of Byzantine court history under his nose for as long as you wished, and he would say, "Quite so. Quite so. But nonetheless the real thing was there under all that muddle. They ruined it to be sure, but that does not ruin my metaphor. I am talking about Byzantium as an image, not Byzantium as history."

We have to run hard to keep up with this capering, scampering imagination of Williams. To refer again to the policeman mentioned above who appears in his novel *The Greater Trumps*, we must not boggle if we hear a character say of him, " 'Behold the Emperor.' " As far

as Williams is concerned, a policeman and an emperor
are both cases in point of vested authority. Each must
carry his appointed burden of answerability, the policeman for this corner here, the emperor for this empire.
Both are uniformed, or vested, if we will, and those vestments, whether they are made of blue twill and brass
buttons or ermine and purple, speak of the office which
the mere man happens to be charged with, in the same
way that priestly vestments on a man say, "Christ's
priesthood", not, "Mr. Jones here, with his penchant for
dressing up".

This is crucial to Williams' whole vision. He saw that
the task or office was bigger than the man who held it.
The crown is there before King Arthur puts it on. Prophecy is there before Elisha receives the mantle. Poetry
is there before Dante picks up his pen. Fatherhood is
there before I take my son in my lap. I had better pay attention to the instructions that govern the office, for
I have been asked to serve *it*. It is not there to serve me.
"More than the voice is the vision, the Kingdom than
the king", Williams has his poet Taliessin say in one
place. The point for the poet or the prophet is not his
own voice, much less his personality or his preferences
or his inclinations, fears, rights, or anything else. The vision burning in him burns all to ashes. You must forget
yourself, it seems to say to him. There is nothing for it
but the complete immolation of yourself. That is the
way it is.

The paradox here is that this immolation is the very
thing which discloses the man himself in all of his dignity
and individuality. If he had tried to preserve some modicum of himself lest it get lost in the divine shuffle, he
would have ended up with no more than that modicum.

If it all seems too bizarre and contradictory, we need look no further than the nearest loaf of bread to see the same thing at work. "Breadness" was the office appointed for those kernels of wheat, the way prophecy was appointed for Elisha or poetry for Dante; and unless the kernels had fallen into the ground where the hard shell protecting the life in them could be broken open, they would still be there, little granules, inert, hard, useless.

This all hangs like a bright cloud over Williams' characters, the way it hangs over all mortals. A man may either assent to it, give himself up, and find his fullness, liberty, and joy; or he may reject it, try to squirrel away some little granule of himself, and end up in solitude, bondage, and wrath. Assent or rejection. Joy or wrath. Heaven or hell. A man may choose, alas. If it seems dreadful and life denying, we may recall the teaching of perhaps the greatest teacher ever to live and find the same thing taught. Williams did not make it up.

The slogan "This also is Thou, neither is this Thou" caught for Williams the idea of things both cloaking and revealing bigger things. The policeman, for example, stands for much more than himself, but he himself is not equal to the authority which he represents. The image is flawed. But even if it were an unflawed image, it would still be an image and not the thing it represents. Since all images refer us finally to the perfections found only in God, we may say of any image, "This also is Thou", thus reminding ourselves of That Which stands at the top of all the hints; but we must also say the second half of the slogan, "neither is this Thou", in order to avoid idolatry. The image is not the final perfection. The perfection, say, that a lover sees in his beloved is "Thou" in the sense of waking him up perhaps for the first time to see Beauty, which itself opens toward the vision of God. But the perfection that he thus sees is not quite "Thou". It isn't Thou at all, actually. If he stops short and says that it is, he is an idolator.

This way of understanding romantic love as the experience which above all other human experiences points us towards eternal felicity is what Williams called "the theology of romantic love". It may be called theology, he would have said, in that it is eventually about God. If it is not about God, what is it about? The exaltation that lovers experience, and the sublime beauty they see in each other, and the desperation of their efforts to become one with each other—either it is all a cheat eventually, or it really does point to something beyond the present situation.

In his study of Dante entitled *The Figure of Beatrice*, Williams elaborates this notion of romantic love as a true hint of a joy that lies beyond our mortal experience. The light in which a lover sees his beloved is a true one, not a false one. The glory which Dante sees shimmering upon Beatrice is the real truth about her. She *is* such a creature. We may not dismiss the lover as merely seeing his lady through the bright haze of his own passion. Rather, that passion in him has cleared the air that is hazy for the rest of us. It is a merciful thing, of course, that we are thus veiled from each other most of the time, since we could not sustain the vision of multitudinous unbearably beautiful creatures all about us. This "Beatrician" vision springs from the Christian doctrine of creation: man is the crown of creation; but his glory—the image of God—was dimmed at the Fall, not fully to be restored until the end of time. We all know theoretically that glory belongs to every woman and man, but when we love someone romantically we seem to glimpse this glory, and it overwhelms us.

But there is no question of the lover's lingering in a paralysis of ecstasy. This waking up to glory is what Williams calls the "Beatrician moment". The lover is given the chance to set out towards That of which her beauty speaks, namely, the divine perfection which is revealed only to those who have achieved sanctity. This does not mean that the lover will abandon his beloved for some spiritual quest. Indeed, if she is to be his spouse, it will be with her that he learns to walk in the way towards sanctity. The moment of bliss illumines the path ahead of them; and they will learn that kindness, attentiveness, forbearance, and courtesy are what is asked. They may assent, or they may refuse, but the moment has at least given them the chance to start.

The great temptation for lovers is to linger. But that is illusion. It is precisely this mere lingering over the ecstatic moment that shows up in Williams' novels as one of the possible doorways to hell. In the City of God we find the bright reality of which this moment was a hint, namely, that all other selves are glorious. But we only gain the capacity to see this by learning the rules first, and the rules do not permit us to dawdle in a voluptuous limbo. They boost us out into the world, where we must learn little by little to treat all other selves with the courtesy with which we love to treat our beloved, since the glory that rests on our beloved rests on every man and woman. Hell says that we need not bother with all this. We may indeed steal away, bar all others from our affection and attention, and revel in bliss. But this is false, says Williams. It is illusion. We may opt for this illusion and become selfish, or we may assent to fact and begin to learn Charity.

The frontispiece which Williams chose for *The Descent of the Dove* illustrates how he saw everything. It is a painting by Ludovico Brea entitled "Paradise". The Trinity appears at the top, with the Holy Ghost as a dove hovering over the figure of the Blessed Virgin. Around and below her we find the company of heaven; then, below a barrier of angels, the world of mortals. Along a margin at the very bottom we see the entombment of Christ.

Williams would have urged that this is a true picture. The mystery of the Trinity is the fountainhead of all things. The Holy Ghost imparts this life to our humanity, as when he came upon the Blessed Virgin at the Annunciation, making our human flesh the very bearer of the divine glory. Williams saw in the Virgin the type of what Dante called "the holy and glorious flesh", meaning not that the Virgin alone enjoys sanctity and glory but rather that in her we see focused what is to be true of all of us, namely, that we are hailed by Grace and invited to be bearers in our flesh of the Divine Love. What else can be meant by Saint Paul's teaching about Christ being formed in us? What is meant by our being temples of the Holy Ghost or of our being exalted and made to reign with Christ?

For Williams as for Dante the point here is that our flesh is to be the vessel of this mystery. What fell into corruption and mortality when we sinned in Eden is now redeemed and granted a dignity beyond Adam's, namely, that of being *theotokos*—God bearer.

This point of view is at a polar extreme from all efforts to make Christianity a merely spiritual religion. It was not Mary's *spirit* that was the vessel of the Incarnation. It was her body.

The Virgin stands in the painting as the focal point of redeemed humanity, both by virtue of her special role as Theotokos and because this role makes her the type of all redeemed flesh. The saints around her make up the company of all who have assented to the Divine Will as she did with her "Be it unto me according to thy word". In the entombment at the bottom of the picture Williams saw the harrowing of hell. This is the ancient Christian idea, only hinted at in the Bible, that on Holy Saturday Christ descended to the place of the dead and led forth the souls of the faithful who were in bondage there. Death and corruption were overthrown by our own flesh and blood, since this is what was taken on by God at the Incarnation, and this is what he wore in the battle at the Cross and what he raised at the Resurrection and Ascension.

Between the two extremes of heaven and hell in the painting lies "the great mass of created souls; those on earth, and, beyond a line of angelic beings, those 'in heaven' " (*The Descent of the Dove*, vii). The painting, says Williams, "is of the co-inherence of the whole redeemed City".

Williams derives his picture of the City from Saint John the Divine and from Saint Augustine. In its perfection of order and architecture it supplies us with a pattern (or what Williams also liked to call the "web" or "diagram") of glory. Things must be intricately worked out and interwoven. In any earthly city there are one-way signs, yellow lines in the streets, traffic lights, bus schedules, commerce, taxes, laws, police, a council, a mayor, and so forth. Every item forms part of the pattern without which everything would tangle, break down, and grind to a halt. If one car ignores the yellow line you have a shouting, hooting traffic jam backed up for blocks. The life of any city depends entirely on its obedience to the imposed pattern. The paradox, of course, is that this imposed pattern is the guarantee of everyone's liberty. The attempt to break free of the pattern results in chaos.

The difficulty is that all earthly cities are imperfect patterns. Corruption, sloth, inefficiency, stupidity, cynicism, and violence mar the pattern. But this only throws the thing itself into starker relief. There is no life that does not depend on this pattern of "co-inherence"—of you and me mutually submitting to the rules—for its sustenance, and where this is flouted you find anger, sorrow, and ruin, which is what you find eventually in hell.

There is one other image which we find in Williams' work. He called it "the index of the body". The phrase had struck him while he was reading Wordsworth's poem *The Prelude*, where Wordsworth says, "The human form / To me became an index of delight, / Of grace and honour, power, and worthiness" (cited in Williams' essay "The Index of the Body", in *Selected Writings*, 113).

On this view, human anatomy may be seen as a diagram, or index, of order, grace, and co-inherence, all the parts not only working harmoniously together but also mutually dependent. We all know this, but it takes a poet to keep us reminded of it. The body is one more commonplace thing that suggests to us the perfection of beauty and splendor that stands at the far end of all cities and all loves and all bodies and all acts of charity. Exchange, substitution, co-inherence, order, clarity, obedience, and joy are what Williams' imagination saw everywhere.

Evil stands over against all of this. If the final reality of the universe is good, as Christians believe, then whatever tries to destroy this is evil. Williams contrasts the City with the Infamy, and stresses that there can be no compromise between the two since the whole desire of the Infamy is to outrage the good. The choice between the two exists all around us all the time. Every act of courtesy, courage, generosity, or selflessness entails some assent to the good and some refusal of the Infamy. In every Williams novel we find the characters faced with the choice. By the choices they make, they proceed towards heaven or hell.

I

Shadows of Ecstasy

Shadows of Ecstasy is the earliest of Williams' novels. It was probably finished by 1926, although it was not published until 1933, after four other novels were already in print. The title points us to the idea Williams had for this story. We may put it this way: every good thing in our world is a sort of hint or shadow of the joy for which we were made in the first place and which is our destiny if we do not refuse it. It is possible to refuse, and this refusal is one of the main themes we find in Williams' work. Theology calls it damnation.

Plato says that what we see around us in this life is fleeting. The real things are eternal and unseen. A certain distrust of the visible world attaches itself to Platonism. Christianity agrees with this up to a point. The real things are indeed eternal, and everything that we now see will pass away. But, says Christianity, it is wrong to suppose that what we now see around us is an illusion. It is real and solid. It is the creation of God and is therefore good. It will all pass away, of course, but it will all be made new before its story has reached the final chapter. Then we will see that everything that surrounded us in this life was far more than illusion. It was all real, but after the Fall it lay under a curse. Every creature and thing strained at its fetters, as Saint Paul teaches in Romans. The great bursting through at the end of time to freedom and incorruptibility is called redemption.

Already we have four theological words before us: creation, fall, damnation, and redemption. It is impossible to read very far in Williams without finding these immensities crowding us. The oddity of his tales is at least partly to be attributed to the suspicion they arouse in us that they go beyond the sort of stuff that you can write a novel about. The tradition of the modern novel has drawn a circle around itself, excluding such regions as hell, purgatory, or paradise. Williams tended to step outside this circle, or at least to *look* outside it. His vision, like Eliot's, saw ordinary things as "hints and guesses".

The title suggests this way of seeing things. Nearly every religion and philosophy except for flat materialism takes some such view as this, and all art and poetry depend on it. There is no such thing as a poem that does not take something in the visible world (a crossroad, harness bells, an island, a beach, a Chicago stockyard) and say to us, in effect, here is a concrete thing that will suggest something bigger to us. The bigger thing may be an abstraction like fate, duty, solitude, despair, or love; or it may be some bright fixity like the City of God. But whatever it is, we seem to have no way of thinking about an abstraction without reaching for something concrete to help us picture it.

But it is not only religion, philosophy, art, and poetry that do this. We all do it all the time. "He's happy as a clam"; "Why do they lionize him that way?" "Well, that one fell flat", and so forth. In every case we are letting pictures of concrete things go to work to help make some abstract thing vivid.

The title *Shadows of Ecstasy* supplies us with a clue as to what we are going to encounter in the action. The trouble in the story is going to arise over someone's having got a wrong idea as to what we are supposed to do about these shadows.

Things start off thus: Mr. Nigel Considine, an explorer, is making a speech at a dinner given by the Geographical Faculty in the University of London. He is suggesting that Western civilization, with its enlightened tradition of science and logic, may have missed something. On the other hand, cultures like those found along the Amazon and Zambesi rivers, with their darker traditions of witchcraft and mumbo-jumbo, may be in touch with mysteries that lie at the bottom of everything.

Considine goes on: by looking to external things like food, sex, music, and so forth for nourishment and pleasure, we mortals fritter away the energy that we might otherwise channel into keeping ourselves alive. He is proposing, in a word, the conquest of death by the gradual and disciplined weaning of ourselves from our need of these externals and the focusing of all the energy thus conserved into the imagination of ourselves as being alive. This very imagining, says Considine, will win the victory over death. Williams never quite makes clear just how this effort is linked to tribal rituals rather than to European scientific rationalism. He simply assumes that his readers will share the general idea that mumbo-jumbo may reach deeper than logic. All religious points of view, of course, would encourage some such idea, Christianity included.

The thing which Considine is trying to achieve is the breakthrough from this realm of shadows in which we mortals live to the realm of pure and undying ecstasy of which all these shadows are merest hints. As long as we feed on shadows (food, music, sex, etc.) we will never make the passage to that bright realm, he believes.

It is easy enough to see how close all this is to certain Platonic and Christian ideas. The idea is ancient and widespread that this sublunary world is not our final habitat, and that we are en route to a region where peace and fulfillment await us, and that we must wean ourselves from too fierce an attachment to things here since they are all going to fade anyway. Considine's mistake, Williams implies, is to insist that this world here is an illusion and that it can be overcome by one's own powers of imagination. But what begins as a mistake becomes evil when Considine goes the next step. He has set himself up, it turns out, as a sort of messiah not only to preach this gospel but to force it on the world, by murder and war, if necessary.

These alarming designs do not show up in Considine's speech at the dinner, of course. We hear only his general theory intimated. Listening to his speech are several of the characters whom we will follow through the action. Roger Ingram is a young professor of Applied Literature in the university. His wife, Isabel, is there with him. Sir Bernard Travers, a famous surgeon, is also there. Presently, back at Sir Bernard's house, we meet Philip, his son, who is engaged to the dyspeptic and fidgety Rosamond Murchison, and also Sir Bernard's great friend, Ian Caithness, an Anglican priest from Yorkshire.

We discover soon enough that the action arranges these characters like the figures in a medieval morality play, or a masque, where each one's significance is proclaimed as plainly as though he wore a placard announcing his role and identity.

Things begin to get odd when we find Sir Bernard, who is a complete sceptic about all religion and superstition, reflecting as he rides home in a taxi from the dinner, that he recognizes Considine. The odd thing is that he recognizes him from a photograph which is many decades old and that Considine has not aged a day in the interval.

So: Considine is Exhibit A of what he is preaching. Perhaps this talk of overcoming aging and death is not just an idle fancy.

At this point we find ourselves presented with the pattern that Williams follows in all seven of his novels. Things are going along fairly normally in modern England when suddenly some peculiar thing crops up and all is thrown off balance.

In this story the thing is Nigel Considine and his idea. In another it is the Holy Grail turning up in a country church, in another it is a pack of Tarot cards, in another it is Platonic archetypes, in a fifth it is a small cube of the original matter of the universe with the Hebrew name of God inscribed in it, in a sixth it is death, and in yet another it is a pageant being produced during the hot summer months by a group of local theatrical amateurs. In each case what happens is that the common routines of ordinary life are flagged down, as it were. Ultimacy muscles in. From then on nothing may be taken for granted.

But it is not quite a case of "anything can happen". Rather, we are suddenly permitted to see the characters under a very searching light. How does each one react to the situation that has cropped up? Long-standing habits, attitudes, personality traits, words, and actions stand out very starkly. Nothing appears merely commonplace any more. Every gesture, remark, and pose betrays all. And just as we are about to accuse Williams of raising the stakes too high and of falsifying experience by casting this eerie glare on everything, we recall that every novel, drama, short story, and poem in the world attempts to do some such thing as this. What is art, after all, if it is not a matter of our trying to get some distance and some fresh angle of vision and some perspective on ordinary experience, thereby vivifying and sharpening things so that we can see what is otherwise blurred by the murk of the commonplace?

Any story in the world entails *something* that flags things down. For Peter Rabbit it is Mr. McGregor; for Henry James' characters it is Europe; for Tolstoy's it is love or war; for Dostoevsky's it is crime or madness. In ancient tales the interruptions tended to be garish: Adam and Eve were interrupted by a serpent, Noah by a flood, Jacob by a wrestler, Moses by a burning bush, the Virgin Mary by an angel, Saint Paul by a light. And for all of us, if we miss all our other cues, the Last Trump. One way or another it seems necessary to flag everyone down.

Williams arranges everything very neatly in this tale. Each character has some interest, inclination, habit, or vocation, which does two things: it gives him some way of responding to Considine's appeal, and it also represents one of the "shadows" that Considine would like to have us reject.

Roger Ingram, for example, loves and teaches poetry. It is almost his whole life. Well, says Williams, is not the whole point of poetry to wake us up and to hail us with the beauty that is there if we will only rub our eyes and see it all around us? Poetry testifies to something greater than itself. To that extent poetry is one of the shadows. Roger, because he has been taught by poetry that there is bright reality beyond poetry itself, finds Considine's invitation appealing. Perhaps it is worth pursuing. Late in the book he has a sort of vision in which he sees Wordsworth running towards him holding a shell high in his hand. Like a conch shell which seems full of the voice of the sea, poetry reverberates with the sound of that which is infinitely bigger than itself.

We see Roger mulling over this early in the story. Considine has entertained a group at dinner, and now they have adjourned from the table and are listening to some chamber music. Since poetry and not music is Roger's first love, he picks a line at random from Milton—"And thus the Filial Godhead answering spake"— and allows his imagination to drift along it while the music plays. He wants to see whether it might be true, as Considine has suggested, that all great art holds simultaneously in itself both death and new life. Roger, understandably enough, cannot quite grasp this complicated idea. But as his reverie proceeds he finds that such contrasts as "filial" and "godhead", with their respective suggestions of subordination and authority, and even such contrasts as the Latin "filial" with the Anglo-Saxon "godhead" are somehow vivified by the music, which has its own contrasts—slow and fast, loud and soft. He seems to find himself nudged along towards a state of affairs in which all contrasts turn out to be in the service of the ecstasy that is the fruition of all combining and resolving of apparent contradictions and opposites. It is the humble task of all art to point beyond itself. And yet it also partakes of the very reality to which it points. Roger himself, in one of his university lectures, has suggested to his class that the two lines "The single bliss and sole felicity, / The sweet fruition of an earthly crown" not only spoke of the majestic mystery of kingship: "they grew by their very sound into something of the same enormous royalty" (61).

Isabel, Roger's wife, does not seem at first to have any particular specialty. She is not a poet or a scholar or a priest or a king. She is "just" Roger's wife. But there it is: she is woman and spouse. In her very marrow and womb she already knows that ordinary stuff like bodies and sexuality hint at bright and joyous mysteries. To be a spouse in a good marriage is to have entered into that mystic relationship where giving and receiving become indistinguishable, and where knowing another person turns out to be joy. Anyone who has ever loved knows at least something about this. Isabel's own love for Roger has "initiated" her quite naturally into realms that Considine seems to think are the special province of the illuminati.

Trying to explain this to Roger, Isabel says at one point, " 'I mean—perhaps it's nothing very new, this power your Mr. Considine talks of—perhaps women have always known it, and that's why they've never made great art. Perhaps they *have* turned everything into themselves. Perhaps they must' " (125). And, echoing another story in which a woman is at the center of the mysteries without her having to move an inch, Considine says to Isabel at one point when she demurs about joining his side: " 'You are perhaps a wise woman . . . but if you are you shall be a centre of our wisdom in London, and all the women of England shall learn from you what it is they do' " (148). Isabel is not hereby an allegory of the Virgin Mary: rather, all women, including the Virgin, embody somehow some hint of this being-at-the-center that we see in Mary's role in the Christian mystery.

With Isabel we run into a quality that baffles readers about Williams' fiction. On the one hand, we are clearly head over heels in great terrors and splendors in this fiction. But on the other, every line seems to shrug slightly with a wry, hurried detachment, as though to say, "Ah. Great mystery there. How droll of the universe. Well, buzz along—let's not get tremulous and starry-eyed. Here—have a cigarette." The note struck in all of Williams' prose is this demurral and doubt and a certain embarrassment that hides its blush behind a mask of haste. Or to change the metaphor, where a composer might resort to shuddering glissandos in order to catch some soaring feeling and impress us, Williams keeps up the staccato, even the pizzicato. It is always business, brisk business, even if that business is Eden, Sodom, Gethsemane, or the City of God.

We can see this in Williams' treatment of Isabel. We never really see much of her, and she does not have many lines in the book. But Williams briskly assumes that we will see in her all the mystery of womanhood. We will see her in these London streets and parlors the way we might see Venus trailing clouds of glory drawn from all the myths, or even the Blessed Virgin herself. What else? Come (Williams seems to say): If this is not what woman is, what is she, then?

For example, when Sir Bernard asks Isabel at one point why she has told Roger to go ahead and follow Considine, she says, " 'Because I wanted him to, since he wanted to. . . . More: for I wanted him to even more than he did, since I hadn't myself to think of and he had' " (162).

Sir Bernard blinks and reacts as we would: " 'Isn't it a little risky deciding what other people want?' "

" 'Dear Sir Bernard, I wasn't *deciding* . . . I was wanting. It isn't quite the same thing. I want—whatever he wants. I don't want it unselfishly, or so that he may be happy, or because I ought to, or for any reason at all. I just want it. And then, since I haven't myself to think of, I'm not divided or disturbed in wanting, so I *can* save him trouble. That's all. . . . It's the way things happen if you love someone' " (162, 163).

Now this may be true, but it sounds like the language one might encounter in a Saint Teresa of Avila. It is a very exalted order of affairs, and even the keenest and most saintly of us mortals glimpse it only dimly and intermittently. The reader tends to share Sir Bernard's mumbling incredulity. What Isabel says defies all plausibility and prudence so violently that we have no stomach even to expostulate, and yet we suspect that what she is saying is infinitely truer than the routine plausibilities and prudences of everyday life.

We find ourselves wondering whether even with the convenient device of Sir Bernard's doubt Williams is not asking too much of his readers here. What he so blithely capers past has had saints and sages, not to mention poets like Dante, rubbing their chins and peering into the murk for millennia. At the very least the following questions are at stake: What is the nature of the union of which marriage is the sacrament? What unique contribution does femininity make to this? How can this submission of Isabel's be the very precondition of real freedom and peace? What is this realm of perfect love, so immeasurably beyond logic and plausibility and argument and self-interest?

The difficulty is not so much what the answers to these questions might be as whether any conceivable story can bear the weight of them.

Williams' reply here might run thus: of course not—no story can bear such weight. No art can bear the weight of all that it evokes. But is not that the point? Painting and poetry and narrative do not *bear* the bright mysteries: they *hint* at them.

But then remembering, perhaps unfairly, Homer and Dante and Shakespeare, we may reply with the point that Williams himself has had Roger make about poetry: it not only speaks of majesty; it also grows by its very sound into something of the same enormous royalty". On no accounting may this be said of Williams' prose. But if it is objected that it is not fair to compare his prose with Shakespeare's poetry (who of us could sustain that?), then we may at least say that whatever power may lie in Williams' stories lies just beyond the perimeter, flashing again and again into the circle of the prose, so to speak, but never quite resting on, much less in, the circle itself.

It is a hard thing to say of a man's achievement that the best thing about it always just barely eludes it. But perhaps this is what T. S. Eliot meant when he commented in his Introduction to *All Hallows' Eve*, which we have already alluded to, "What [Williams] had to say was beyond his resources, and probably beyond the resources of language, to say once for all through any one medium of expression" (xi). Williams' narratives have neither the sheer sublimity of Dante, nor the sheer size of Tolstoy, nor the sheer grace of Henry James. They are bound to seem, if not flimsy, then at least rickety. Will the structure hold up? we keep murmuring anxiously, all the while dazzled by the fugitive immensities appearing there.

Turning to another of the figures on stage, we may consider Sir Bernard Travers. He is a "mere intellectualist", in his own words. Where Roger's love for poetry has given him a foothold in things bigger than himself, and Isabel's identity as woman and spouse does likewise for her, it is Sir Bernard's sheer good sense and integrity that are "counted unto him for righteousness", if we may borrow this biblical comment on Abraham's faith.

From the very start Sir Bernard is the voice of prudent and charitable scepticism. His disbelief never takes the form of carping, however. Rather, we find him always interested in getting things clear and in getting everyone to think intelligently. Furthermore, he seems to be naturally inclined towards what is decent. He smells a rat in Considine's proposals, and there is never any question which side he will take. His attitudes and actions are animated by this inherent integrity and goodwill rather than by any inclination to poke into the preternatural, for which he has the strongest distaste. Sometimes we find him embroiled in situations very foreign to him, but in every case he does the decent thing, as when he helps the priest, Ian Caithness, push the hypnotized Zulu king,

Inkamasi, out of Considine's house towards a waiting rescue car. The narrative adds, "For a moment Sir Bernard could have believed that they were drawing Inkamasi out of its influence and depth, could have wondered whether indeed he were doing well thus to interfere on behalf of one magic against another" (94).

And, in an allusion typical of Williams, we hear Sir Bernard saying to himself, " 'What doest thou here, Gehazi?' " The reader, unless he has kept up with his Old Testament, has to rake back through his early schooling and haul up the story of Elisha, whose servant Gehazi was. The point becomes clear: Sir Bernard sees himself as a sort of attendant on truth, even if he disclaims any prophetic insight for himself. This sort of thing nettles readers, and by its airy cleverness siphons off something of the force of the narrative. One wants to say to Williams at every third sentence, Come: if you want us to stay with you and trust your narrative, you will have to stop waving us down these rabbit holes.

We find presently that Caithness wants to have a Mass said at Lambeth, the archiepiscopal palace in London, in behalf of this Zulu king, Inkamasi, who seems to have slipped into a torpor under Considine's malign influence. Sir Bernard "gravely put his telephone at Ian's disposal" (98). In a Williams narrative, even a detail like this is significant. The point here is that while the sceptical Sir Bernard can attach no significance to rituals like the Mass, yet because he is a good man and is attached by the virtue of plain friendship to the priest, Caithness, he is prepared to assist at good men's efforts to oppose what is clearly evil. If he cannot pray the Mass, he can "put his telephone at Ian's disposal", so that Mass can be arranged.

Sir Bernard reflects on all that is going on and finds that "all these things shook his sedate and happily ironic brain. . . . He felt obscurely alone—his own house, his own friends, were grown alien to him; nowhere in all the world was there one intimate with whom he could mock at the monstrous apparitions that loomed on the outskirts of his mind, closing round the slender spires and delicate gardens, in which of late its chosen civilization had moved. Not so much the facts, though they were grotesque enough, but the manner of the facts, disturbed him—the triumph, the fanaticism, the shadows of ecstasy" (97, 98). As he reflects, other familiar sights that seem to hint at the same disquieting unmanageability of things flick across his memory: "An insane political hotgospeller in Hyde Park, Caithness vestmented in an ecclesiastical ceremony, the antique faces of the Jews in the crude reproductions of the papers, a look in Philip's eyes as he watched Rosamond" (97). Each of these memories pierces the scrim of reasonableness that Sir Bernard has drawn across the world, and opens a peekhole through which he may glimpse all the mysteries that lurk beyond the surface of things. Political passion, priesthood, Judaism, romantic love—where does it all come from? Certainly from sources deeper than any which Sir Bernard's reasonable irony can plumb. "Where was detachment, where was contemplation there? . . . Darkness was to be exiled, not embraced", thinks Sir Bernard.

At the risk of floundering straight into the "personal heresy" here in which we turn from the true business of criticism to the more titillating business of speculating about the chimaeras that might have raced through an author's brain, it does seem that something ought to be said here, not so much by way of peering into Williams' psyche just for the sake of peering as of tracking down a quality in his prose that is both ubiquitous and unsettling. Some readers will consider this quality to be a great strength in Williams' prose, and others will write it down as a weakness. It is an extension of the rather elliptical quality that we observed in his handling of Isabel.

An amateurish and quasi-psychological way of getting at this quality would be to guess that Williams never could make up his mind which image of himself he liked better: the audacious and unabashed believer or the sceptical ironist. He obviously was enthralled with everything preternatural, from the black arts and the Cabbala to the Mass; and there is something electrifying (and you get the impression that Williams enjoyed being electrifying) about a literate man in modern London and Oxford who makes no bones about believing all sorts of unclassifiable things like Virgin Birth and so forth that ordinary moderns balk at. On the other hand, there is something slightly eager, even fevered, in what looks like the wish on Williams' part that we see him as an easy member of the urbane and donnish fraternity of sceptics. He had not himself been to university, least of all to Oxford, and he cannot have been indifferent to the stigma. If it comes to kindred minds, we seem to hear him saying to himself, give me the Sir Bernards of this world. He has a whole section in his brief history of the Church on "the quality of disbelief", and he cannot conceal his fascination with Voltaire and company.

Williams himself was squarely on the side of the orthodox believers, as his books and his circle of friends at Oxford testify. But his prose seems bedevilled with an intermittent uncertainty of tone. To avoid the stickiness that often lards religious sentiment, Williams seems to

dance to the other extreme, flicking his wrist at sanctity,
as it were, and giving the shortest possible shrift to mystery, but all the while flapping sanctity and mystery in
our faces.

Those who see this as a strength in Williams' fiction
will argue that this is the very quality he sought. Irony
saves belief from the quagmire; scepticism salts the loaf
of faith. We might say that Williams caught "the very
note and trick", as Henry James put it, of modern experience. What *about* this chiaroscuro of modern life, where
the lights and shadows play over things in such a way
that we may be fooled into supposing that there is nothing beneath the surface, only to be unnerved by fleeting
glimpses of the dragons and great deeps? How shall fiction be faithful to this quality of experience? We have lost
the warrant that Dante had to talk plainly of heaven and
hell, so we must come at it along the oblique route of
doubt, the characteristic attitude of the modern world, as
belief was of Dante's.

There is a sense in which Sir Bernard's point of view
controls the whole story, or at least hovers over the action. In the middle of the chaos brought on by Considine's final assault on London, we see Sir Bernard
watching "as if on a rocky island—one of a scattered ar-
chipelago of such islands—a lingering child of a lost race
watched the sea overwhelm his city" (161). Caithness
and Roger have gone off as either guests or prisoners of
Considine, and Sir Bernard stands "surveying the room
. . . the general disarray that had meant companionship
and now meant desertion. . . . It wasn't *whom* you lost;
it was *what* you lost, what centre of what concern or
quality of yourself was torn away, so that your own ca-

pacity moved helpless in the void. Something very like stability had been torn from under him" (162).

Sir Bernard contemplates Isabel, who seems to have lost so much more than he, namely, her husband, whereas he has lost only his friend Caithness. He "wished he could have heard Considine and Isabel arguing—not that Isabel would or could have argued. So far as he could see, she was saying exactly the opposite of Considine, and yet they curiously agreed. They were both beyond the place of logic and compromise, even amused compromise. They were both utterly, utterly— well, they were both utterly" (163). Earlier Williams has shown us Sir Bernard seeing

> the intellect and logical reason of man no longer as a sedate and necessary thing, but rather a narrow silver bridge passing over an immense depth, around the high guarded entrance of which thronged clouds of angry and malign presences . . . this capacity of knowing cause and effect presented itself nevertheless to him as the last stability of man. Always approaching truth, it could never, he knew, *be* truth, for nothing can be truth till it has become one with its object, and such union it was not given to the intellect to achieve without losing its own nature. But in its divine and abstract reflection of the world, its passionless mirror of the holy law that governed the world, not in experiments or ecstasies or guesses, the supreme perfection of mortality moved [121].

A double difficulty arises in connection with the matter of Sir Bernard's point of view. For one thing, it does not seem to be sufficiently assimilated into the texture of the narrative. We do not so much see it as *hear about* it, even if it is included as one of Sir Bernard's own reveries. But deeper than this, if Williams wishes us to believe that this is Sir Bernard's limited and somewhat mistaken notion and not Williams' own preference, then we must protest that Williams does not establish enough distance between himself as author and Sir Bernard as one of his characters. He never forces us away from the suspicion that *he* thinks this scepticism is the best frame of mind. But there is a further blurring. We never see the dramatic resolving of two good things that Williams has set over against each other in this story, namely, the way of vision that we see in Roger, Isabel, Caithness, and Inkamasi, versus the way of scepticism that we see in Sir Bernard. Williams never obliges us to abandon Sir Bernard's vastly attractive idea that the supreme perfection of mortality does indeed move in the intellect's divine and abstract reflection of the world. Or rather, he forces us to abandon it on one page and then leaves it intact on another. Indeed, he leaves it apparently intact in the last pages of the book, where Sir Bernard says that what he has wanted has been " 'justice and proportion which is the daughter of justice, knowledge and abstraction which is the daughter of knowledge. This dreadful tendency to personify and [therefore] mythologize I attribute to you [Caithness] and the late Mr. Considine . . . behold the history of religion!' " (222).

This, however, is not the place where Williams wishes the drama to come to rest. We finally see Sir Bernard through the prism of Roger's thoughts. Roger has dreams of great deeps, with octopuses and sharks and Considine's body floating in the deep. The body is spoken of as "that advancing humanity" and the "shining lucidity". This was the vast of experience, currents and

tides, streams and whirlpools, restless waves and fathomless depths, absorbed by man. The salt that tinctured
it, as the salt of Sir Bernard's amusement tinctured life,
was absorbed also. Valuable as that preservative salt was,
in the end it was infinitely less than the elements of which
it was part, and to prefer it to the renewed body would
be to prefer the means to the end, detachment to union.
Irony might sustain the swimmer in the sea; it could not
master the sea. A greater than Sir Bernard did that now"
(223, 224).

We have to say that the thing which we are asked to
believe to be greater than Sir Bernard's luminously charitable and civilized intelligence may well be greater, but
the events in this story do not oblige us to reach that con-
clusion. The narrator seems too dazzled by his villain
Considine and too sympathetic to Sir Bernard, whose
point of view he asks us to believe is too limited. He has
not got our *feelings* quite squarely on the side of Isabel
and Caithness, who are patently in the right. The difficulty here is that the drama is too pageantlike for any
very complex subtleties like this. The whole thing is like
a masque, one of those stiff and gorgeous seventeenth-
century court pageants, and things have to be stark in a
masque. If you want the subtleties of a Henry James
novel, then you cannot have your characters lined up
holding placards the way they do in *Shadows of Ecstasy*.
"Priest", "Woman", "Poet", "Sceptic", "Villain", they
all proclaim. Well, then, they had better be lined up the
way you want them lined up when the curtain rings
down. We need to know just what has been vindicated.

But then we are back at T. S. Eliot's comment, which
was not so much a stricture on Williams' achievement as
it was an explanation. There is no literary form that will

quite do the job. A masque will do one sort of job and a novel another. But what conceivable form will hold all of *this*?

Given the masquelike array of characters and what they all represent, we may say that Caithness is obvious enough. He is a priest. As such he will bring to the story the reminder that there are bright or dark immensities lying very close on the far side of things as commonplace as bread and wine and that these things themselves may be not only shadows of those immensities but also bearers of them. Like Roger and Isabel and Considine himself, Caithness knows something that will always elude the scientific rationalism of Europe. His presence in the drama supplies a certain plausibility to what might otherwise seem to be merely primitive sorcery. Sober Western men, from Augustine to Aquinas, Erasmus, Pascal, and Eliot, have supposed that powers are abroad that will not yield to mere scientific inquiry.

Caithness does not develop as a character other than to reach the end of the story a sadder and wiser man. He does, however, furnish us with an example of the difficult task Williams set himself in trying to tell a tale like this. Here is part of one paragraph about Caithness:

> The nature of his intellect and the necessities of his office had directed his attention always not towards things in themselves but towards things in immediate action. He defined men by morality; it was perhaps inevitable that he should define God in the same way. The most difficult texts for him to explain away had always been those which obscurely hint at the origin of evil itself in the Unnameable, "the lying spirit" of Zedekiah, the dark question of Isaiah—"Shall there be evil in the city and I the Lord have not done it?" He was

always trying to avoid Dualism, and falling back on the statement that Omniscience might permit what it did not and could not originate, yet other origin (outside Omniscience) there is none [196].

This is a heavy burden for fiction to carry. It would even be a heavy one for poetry to attempt. Whether we may ever speak of evil as originating in God is a nice question at the best of times, but the story sags under its weight, even if we permit some connection between the question and the theme of the story. It is hard to know whether the staggering weight of this account of Caithness' thoughts is an aside which Williams could not resist, since his own thoughts continually flashed along lines like that, or whether it really is germane to the drama here. It does furnish us with some understanding of the sort of person Caithness is and hence of the sort of contribution he will make to the events of the story, and to that extent we may say that it is germane. But we must also say that it plants in our minds the uneasy suggestion that room might be found in the darkness of the Unnameable for Considine and his way. If Williams wishes to glance at this possibility, he has done so here. But in so doing he has shifted the ground underneath the drama ever so slightly, so that we are forced now to wonder whether it is not so much a question of good and evil that are at war here as of pedestrian goodness over against exciting possibilities that might be permissible to a few illuminati but won't do for the ordinary run of mortals. But if we grant this, we have granted Considine's case, and the drama is in ruins. It may, of course, be urged that part of the force of the drama derives from this very attractiveness of Considine's case. But let us grant that: still, Williams somehow manages to make us wonder if *he* is not toying with Considine's ideas. He does not succeed in keeping us inside his story the way a good narrator should do. We keep having to look up to see the expression on Williams' face, as it were.

The Zulu king, Inkamasi, we simply have to grant at whatever cost to our willingness to believe the story. He is an African king rather than the more believable scion of some Russian or Albanian royal house, since Williams needs to have an opening into African imagination as opposed to the flat rationalism of Europe. There is in any event some rag of plausibility about Inkamasi since such minor tribal kings do exist and are as likely to find themselves washed ashore in England as anywhere. This would have been especially true during the days of Empire, when the story was written.

Inkamasi's royal station supplies another shadow of ecstasy. An anointed and crowned head suggests to us at least two great mysteries, namely, vicariousness and majesty.

If a king is a good king and fulfills what kingship is supposed to be about, then his life is a vicarious one in that he bears in his person the whole burden of his people. He exists for the kingdom, not vice versa, no matter how often actual kings have got this backwards. The mystery of vicariousness casts a particularly vivid shadow in the figure of the king.

This brings us to the second of the mysteries illustrated in Inkamasi, namely, majesty, which itself turns out to have a twofold significance. First, humanity itself, being the *imago Dei*, is majestic. But since when we lost our innocence at the Fall, we lost also our freedom to wear the real robe of our majesty, namely, our naked-

ness, we have now to try to remember and acknowledge
that majesty by second-best tokens like crowns and scepters and gold. These say as best they can, "Behold the
glory of man." Solomon is as glorious as all the panoply
that surrounds him, but then so is every other human being. Since we cannot all walk caparisoned that way,
however, we have to crown one representative figure
who will stand for us all. Solomon's glory is the glory of
Israel. The Queen's majesty is the majesty of England. A
crown is the heaviest hat of all, made as it is of gold. The
sovereign wears it *for* us. Which brings us to the second
aspect of majesty, namely, vicariousness, and we are
back at the original point. That is, the most noble thing
a human being can do is to lay down his life for another.
This laying down may take the form of actually standing
in for another's death, or of bearing on one's shoulders
the weight of a nation, or of nursing one's child in the
middle of the night. But in this laying down of life, mere
mortals seem to rise, transfigured and majestic. There is
some connection between vicariousness and majesty
—or there ought to be. When we find indulgence and
tyranny and mere luxury in a court, we know that something is rotten.

In the figure of Inkamasi all this is implicit. He constitutes what Caithness calls "a presented moment" (96),
that is, a small case in point on display, or a momentary
glimpse presented to us, of the whole mystery of majesty.

Also in the array of characters is Philip Travers, Sir
Bernard's son. He is an engineer and works for a firm
with interests in developing things along North African
rivers. We find that his superior, Munro, is already in
Nigeria reconnoitering, and Philip is to follow. Two

men called Stuyvesant run the London offices of the company, but a certain Simon Rosenberg seems to be the financial power behind it all. Very early in the action Rosenberg is reported shot, and it is not clear whether it is murder or suicide. Whichever it is, it turns out that the only legatees of his enormous wealth, and especially of his jewels, are two second cousins of his, Ezekiel and Nehemiah Rosenberg. Mr. Patton is Rosenberg's solicitor.

This jumble of personages never comes to much. It is as though a murder mystery is dragged across the stage, complete with butler, and then disappears. Its connection with the main action is tenuous at best. It turns out that the elder Rosenberg had a passion for decking his wife with jewels. Sir Bernard explains to Philip, " 'In fact, she was a creation in terms of jewellery, the New Jerusalem turned upside down so that the foundations showed' " (26). There is our clue. Rosenberg's jewels are one more shadow. " 'Tiaras and bracelets and necklaces and pendants and earrings . . . she looked not merely like the sun, the moon, and the eleven stars, but like the other eleven million that Joseph didn't know about' ", says Sir Bernard (26). And they were being collected *for her*. " 'He saw them *on* her, you see; they existed in relation to her. And when she died they fell apart—he couldn't find a centre for them.' "

Rosenberg, then, unwittingly as far as we know, had a foothold in the great mysteries of adoration and generosity. He did not want the jewels for himself the way a miser does. He wanted them for his wife. He adored her and wanted to honor her perfections by decking her with jewels, as Dante and Petrarch decked Beatrice and Laura with poetry.

It is Considine who points out Rosenberg's limitations. " 'He had externalized in that adorned figure all his power and possession; it was his visible power, his acknowledged possession' " (28). So far so bad, we might say. Rosenberg's foothold in adoration is on a very low level, since it is all adulterated with what looks very much like cupidity. But nonetheless a foothold is a foothold, Williams always implies, and where is any of us to start?

As for the legatees Ezekiel and Nehemiah, we find that they have one passion, which is the rebuilding of the Temple in Jerusalem. All the money from their inheritance will go to that. The jewels, Considine tells the assembled company at one point, " 'These they will take as they are, "an oblation to the Holy of Holies, a recompense for iniquity and for that one of their house who has touched the unclean thing." I repeat their words' " (69).

So. Another shadow. More mysteries touched upon by visible things. Holiness. Oblation. Atonement. Before the story has finished, both brothers are violently dead, but in them we have encountered men who love things not as ends in themselves but for what lies beyond them. Jewels for a beautiful lady, jewels for the Temple—things *for* something else. That is enough for the moment, Williams seems to say. This idea of a rudimentary gesture or attitude, not yet purified in itself, yet nonetheless being *for the moment* enough, runs like a motif through all of Williams' novels and echoes God's receiving Abraham's obedience in a small matter like getting out of Ur of the Chaldees as a token worthy to be called the fountainhead of all faith until the end of the world.

Jewishness in Williams' tales always represents the notion of "the Unity". Jews are custodians of the ancient revelation of God as one. The deeper mystery of the Triune Unity came later. Williams wants to keep us reminded that at the source of all things in heaven and earth stands the Unity. His Jews have no other function in his stories. They may be noble, but they are blind to the idea of co-inherence, which derives from the Three Persons constituting the Unity. Williams' handling of Jews is excessively clumsy though: hooked noses, secretiveness, and extravagant Old Testament names, unless they appear in a full-dress Dickensian narrative, do not assist our willingness to suspend disbelief.

It will have been noticed that we somehow got shunted into the Rosenberg subplot in speaking of Philip Travers. This underscores one of the difficulties with the story: it is hard to find the center. Or, if Considine is the undoubted center, the focus keeps getting blurred. Is this a murder mystery or not? There is more than one violent murder before things have finished, and we get bits and pieces of Agatha Christie scenario. But then the story sweeps on, and all the *names* we have been trying to keep track of (Simon, Nehemiah, and Ezekiel Rosenberg; Patton; Stuyvesant; not to mention Mottreux and Vereker and Nielsen, who are Considine's lieutenants; and Suydler the Prime Minister) turn out to be not worth keeping track of. We feel that we have run into a ditch somewhere between Agatha Christie and Dickens. In either of these two writers we expect and welcome quite a crowd of characters. We know that Agatha Christie will work them all into the thickening plot quite neatly, and we know that Dickens will regale us with the sheer oddity and color of his ragtag and bobtail cast besides

working them with infinite finesse into his plot. But
with Williams we catch glimpses of figures who *represent*
something, as we would in a masque; but things are
much too tangled and hugger-mugger for us to be able to
settle in to the leisured sumptuousness of a masque, and
much too hastily sketched for us to think "Dickens", and
not really murder mystery enough for us to think "Agatha". Where are we? We scamper along with Williams
as best we can, as everyone who knew him had to do all
the time anyway.

Philip Travers is the lover. It is Rosamond Murchison
whom he loves, but that does not really much matter.
We come to her presently and find her to be a bore,
which does not help things at all except perhaps to emphasize Williams' idea that romantic love will see the
beauty in its beloved no matter what ugliness mars her.
We are told that "by that secular dispensation of mercy
which has moved in the blood of myriads of lovers
[Philip] had felt what he did not know and experienced
what he could not formularize" (46). He does know a bit
about Dante and Beatrice and Tristram and Iseult, but he
is "ignorant of the cloud of testimony that had been
borne to the importance and significance of the passion
that was growing in him" (46). The passion is his love
for Rosamond. But "he had hardly heard, he had certainly never brooded over, that strange identification of
Beatrice with Theology and of Theology with Beatrice
by which one great poet has justified centuries of else
doubtful minds" (46).

Here we are head over heels in Williams' idea of romantic love as the most dazzling shadow of all, if we
may speak of dazzling shadows. Williams would insist
that it is not his idea; it is Dante's. What on earth is ro-

mantic passion about if it is not a bright light, giving all lovers in the world the chance to see and believe that another being is glorious? The lover is the only one who sees clearly. Far from his eyes having been enchanted with the gold dust of illusion, they have been opened to see what the rest of us must strain at, namely, that this creature does reflect the image of God. Beatrice's connection with theology is that the sharp eye of the poet saw beauty in her and realized that this beauty was itself a summons to glory, a shadow of ecstasy. Pursued for itself, it would turn into an idol and destroy Dante. Followed obediently all the way to That of which her beauty was the merest shadow, it would be a great and joyful gift. Philip has only the dimmest apprehension of all this.

We come upon him at one point in the London Underground, reading Considine's proclamation about Africa and the end of the age of intellect. It rings bells with Philip, not because he has the slightest interest in what the proclamation says but because words like "adoration" and "vision" and "apprehension of victory" and "conquest of death" occur: "Never before, never anywhere, had any words, printed or spoken, come nearer to telling him what he really felt about Rosamond. . . . He knew it was silly, but he knew also that he had felt through Rosamond, brief and little understood, something which was indeed apprehension of victory and conquest of death" (47). To Caithness' later remark that the proclamation is just a matter of thrills and that thrills are not safe things to live by, Philip reflects that "his sensations about Rosamond were not—no, they were not *thrills*; and he wasn't at all clear that they weren't things to live by" (48).

He also wonders, in an aside more believable of Williams than of any possible character he might create, whether whatever happened about the proclamation could alter "the terribly important fact of the shape of Rosamond's ear" (48). This is bizarre, but anyone who has ever loved knows that the smallest feature of the beloved seems more real and important than such marginal matters as international politics and war. Williams would urge that this "seems" might just possibly turn out to be "is". People who have tried hallucinogens tell us that an ear or a chair or a blade of grass will take on almost unendurable significance, even glory. And it may be that they are seeing something true which the rest of us are mercifully prevented from having to cope with all the time, even though they have paid for their peek with the bogus currency of drugs. Saints and lovers seem to bear witness to somewhat the same sort of vision.

Philip, reflecting on Considine's invitation to the conquest of death, realizes that "though Rosamond would die the thing he had seen in Rosamond not merely could not die but had nothing whatever to do with death" (99).

But what about Rosamond herself? She hates Inkamasi, for a start. " 'It was the way he talked, looking like a god . . . I hate him to look like that . . . I hate him' " (60). Rosamond has no imagination and thus cannot cope with this sudden "presented moment" of something so unmanageable as majesty. Presently we find her spitting out even the name of her fiancé. Everything and everybody in the world are hateful to her because she is wholly selfish. Isabel remembers an incident from their past, "How her small sister, who had always carried herself as if she pretended to disdain chocolates, had once secretly and greedily devoured a whole boxful" (63).

Because Rosamond wants no part of anything at all, she wants no part of Considine, or of Inkamasi, or even of Philip, "for Philip to her agonized mind was at once a detestable parody of what she wanted and a present reminder of what she longed to forget. . . . The shadow of ecstasy lay over her life, and denying the possibility of ecstasy she fled through its shadow as far as its edge. . . . She was alive, and she hated life" (134, 135).

What she longs to forget is that joy lies on the far side of giving ourselves generously and helpfully to other people. The last we hear of Rosamond, she is recuperating at a cottage in Dorset from a collapse, in a sort of purgatorial pause before being given another chance to go on with her pilgrimage towards joy under Philip's tutelage. (Similar pauses befall various characters in C. S. Lewis' Narnia tales, most notably the tiresome Uncle Andrew, whom we last see having been put to sleep like a child; and the strutting Rabadash, whom we last see changed into an ass for as long as might be necessary for his redemption.)

The figure of Nigel Considine looms over the whole drama, and we do not get very far before we encounter language about him that obliges us to acknowledge that he stands as a diabolical parallel to Christ. Considine proclaims the conquest of death. Considine says, " 'Because I live, men shall live also. But they shall do greater works than I' " (74). Again, in a scene where police arrive to arrest Considine, we see them staggering back before the sheer force of his presence, like the soldiers at the arrest of Christ in Gethsemane, and Considine passing through the midst of them, as Christ did at one point when the mob threatened to lynch him. In yet another scene, unmistakably reminiscent of Peter attacking Malchus in Gethsemane, Considine says to his servant, who has fired a shot rebuffing an attack from Inkamasi, " 'Mottreux, Mottreux, is it necessary?' " (47) and orders the healing of Inkamasi's superficial wound. Considine's entry into riot-ridden London is almost an exact echo of Palm Sunday, with cries of " 'Glory to the Master of Love! Glory to the deathless one!' " (150). It seems a little labored, not to say embarrassing, for Williams to have Negroes doing all this shouting, but his point is doubtless that it is from Africa that Considine has drawn his own arcane knowledge and also that a prophet is without honor in his own country, or at least from his own countrymen.

Again, we see Considine sitting at the head of the table, breaking a piece of toast (172). Or, "Considine was in the room . . . he might have materialized out of the air" (191). Again we hear him saying, " 'Whom do men say that I, a son of man, am?' " (208). And, in an ironic switch that suddenly casts him in the role of Judas Iscariot he says, " 'What we do we do quickly' " (208).

If these parallels seem too forced, we may remember two things. First, this was Williams' earliest novel, and we very often find certain elements in the early works of an author which do not seem to have quite found their way very comfortably into the fabric of the work. They obtrude. One has only to read an early Shakespeare play to see this. The sumptuous poetry and speeches at times bulge like cannon balls in a fabric of gossamer. The drama hardly seems tough enough to hold them, much less absorb them into some overall pattern. *Romeo and Juliet* and *Richard II* might be examples here.

Second, if we were disposed to defend these stark and frequent parallels which Williams sets up between Considine and Christ, we might say that they do fit quite naturally into the special material Williams is working with here, since the whole fabric is spangled with brilliants. As with a masque, we not only excuse bright color and elaborate costume but also demand them. Part of the bright effect which Williams seeks here is brought about by simultaneous surprise and recognition: he surprises us with a new or sudden idea such as that poetry and majesty and romantic love all witness to the same thing, or that Considine resembles Christ in unnerving ways, but at least half of our surprise lies in our realizing that we recognize the thing at once. Of course! we are obliged to say. What else? I knew that. Or, if I hadn't ever quite thought of it, it is simply because I hadn't ever quite thought of it. If we have any criticism it might be that we do not want the effect too often. A motif has got to be an organic part of the whole pattern. We must not suspect that it is just cropping up.

Considine is defeated in the end, and the characters return to their ordinary lives. It is as though great possibilities of good and evil have sailed near and have passed on their way. The characters are either destroyed or chastened or ennobled in the process. Arcane lore has borne perverted witness to the ecstasy that stands at the far end of love, duty, honesty, courage, and obedience. What the perversion omitted to mention was that you cannot get to that ecstasy by any shortcut. All black arts, like all greed and power mongering and pride, represent attempts to dodge through such a shortcut to bliss. Damnation is at the end of that attempt.

Certain specific images besides the major thematic ones of poetry, majesty, womanhood, kingship, priesthood, and irony present themselves in the narrative, and it is worth our being aware of them.

There is the image of darkness, which we come upon in the first five lines of the book. It needs no explanation, since Williams uses it in the traditional way to suggest the unknown, the unconditioned, the perilous, the mysterious. In *Shadows of Ecstasy*, darkness stands over against all that can be illumined by the light of common day or by Sir Bernard's reasonableness. What Considine is pursuing is dark, not only because it is evil but also because it is vast and remote and uncharted and alarming. The forests of the Amazon and the Zambesi, from whence Considine has fetched his lore, answer by their very density and dimness to the thick darkness into which his vision peers. And we find Roger, full of poetry as he is, mulling over the notion of encountering darkness as a bride—even hugging it. The sense that the thing which frightens us most may be the very thing we want most is an ancient and universal one and haunts everyone from saints to devil worshippers.

Another image which occurs is a set of immense blue curtains in the room at Considine's house where he takes his guests to listen to music after dinner. Williams speaks of this blue as "a blue so deep that though it had not the blaze it had the richness of sapphire" (75), and we see Roger looking at Considine "against the immense and universal sapphire of the draperies . . . the vast azure" (81). Indeed, for a moment it almost seems to Roger as if the curtains might be Considine's own priestly, "hieratic" vestments, held up by an attendant who has just taken them from Considine and is about to fold them up. The point is that what Considine is proposing to them all has an appeal as immense and glorious as the universe itself, and what but sapphire will quite catch this notion of celestial glory? Considine seems somehow to *wear* the very glory of which he speaks.

The house by the sea to which Considine summons everyone in chapter eleven looks this way to Roger:

They came into a hall which opened round them as if into distances. The walls were hung or covered with

some kind of deep grey from which light shone, almost as over a landscape. Its furniture was not merely
furniture but natural to it: a chest showed like an antique boulder on a hillside; a table was a table certainly,
but it had grown in its place, and had not been set
there, a chair or two glowed darkly as if shrubs of glis-
tening leaves reflected the sun. Roger walked after his
guide with a sense of perfect proportion such as no
room he had ever entered, however admirably deco-
rated, had given him; the best had been but arranged
art, pleasant to his judgment, while this was an art
which answered his human nature and contented his
blood. It communicated peace [167, 168].

Clearly, art and nature have become one here. It is a
place where the ancient struggle of mankind to bring
about that harmony has been rewarded. It is as though
Considine summons them by his teaching to a realm in
which everything is knitted back together again, especially the disjuncture between man (art) and his world
(nature). Seamlessness. Unity. Peace. Harmony. What
else is it we long for? What else was it that we know we
lost in Eden?

We may observe several things about the state of
Williams' art as of the writing of this first novel. There is
the problem which T. S. Eliot touched on, that no conceivable art form will quite assimilate Williams' vision.
He needs the densely packed texture of poetry, plus the
splendor of pageant, plus the closely analytic capacities
of the novel, and all of it caught up somehow by music.
As it is, his narratives seem to creak under the weight
they bear.

Further, it is not only the sheer weight of the vision
that burdens the narratives. The elements in the action it-

self seem to jostle one another, or worse, to have almost
nothing to do with one another. The war and the riots
seem to exist in one tale, and the jewels and murders in
another, and Sir Bernard and Roger in yet another, with
Considine's shadowy presence somehow touching and
not touching everything. We may of course show how
all these strands in the plot work together. But they do
not work together very successfully.

Moreover, the reader is asked to accede to all sorts of
implausibilities: the African attack on London, for example, which never convinces us in the smallest degree; and
a Zulu king; and a *submarine* suddenly showing up like a
deus ex machina at just the right moment to spirit Considine away at the end; and Philip's finding his way mag-
ically through the rioters right into the Rosenbergs'
house. There are also elements that worry us on a deeper
level, such as the jeering of the mob at the "niggers" and
Jews. Somehow Williams has not set enough distance
between the voice of the narrator and these raucous
voices. It seems abrasive.

Implausibilities are essential to certain kinds of fiction.
We do not shy at Swift's Lilliputians and Brobdingnagi-
ans, or at Merlin, or even at Kafka's poor Gregor Samsa,
who turns into a bug. With these the oddity seems as inevitable a part of the design as scrolls on an Ionic column
or leaves on a Corinthian. But we find ourselves in difficulties with Williams because, on the one hand, he has
set a certain brisk and sceptical narrative tone that is too
impatient to try to convince us of the "realistic" implausibilities such as the war and is ill at ease with the preternatural implausibilities such as Considine's powers. But
on the other hand, there they all are. We have no objection to marvels, but the narrator must convince us that *he*

has no objection either. Williams always seems simultaneously fascinated and embarrassed by the djinn that has loomed out of the pot at his summons.

Again, we are not quite sure about Williams' attitude towards Considine. This uncertainty can be fruitful if it is handled rightly, as in *Richard II*, where Shakespeare seems to prod and needle us from all sides, no sooner convincing us that Richard is a bounder and cad and must be thrown out than he overwhelms us with a speech by the Bishop of Carlisle or the Duke of York, convincing us that the king's person may never be touched. Williams' attitude towards Considine, on the other hand, seems almost to invite the sort of speculation that arose some decades ago about Milton's Satan, namely, that Satan was Milton's real hero. There is no question at all that Williams is enthralled by Considine. This may be very well, but it then leaves the reader with the suspicion that the author was not entirely in control of things and that the drama which he started out to write somehow slipped out of his grip. The djinn was not entirely submissive. In order for this drama to be what it purports to be, Considine must be bad in the end. But we are bothered by Williams' sheer admiration for him. It is not enough to say, but that is just the point: the devil and all his works *are* admirable, and it is this that must be overridden in the struggle between good and evil. Sooner or later the drama itself has to come to rest in the serene conviction that evil is evil. The Gospels, *Oedipus*, the *Divine Comedy*, or *Macbeth* do not leave us looking wistfully back over our shoulders like Lot's wife: *Shadows of Ecstasy* does, somehow.

Finally, there is Williams' elliptical prose. How is a new reader to make anything of this: "The moment of vision in Isabel's kitchen, when Rosamond's ear had lain like a bar of firmamental power across the whole created universe, dividing and reconciling at once" (99)? It makes perfect sense once you have mastered Williams' ideas and his technique. But it is this sort of thing that discourages new readers. Who will keep going in the face of this: "She could almost have desired to find it in her to pretend to be in need . . . to indulge by her own goodwill the spiritual necromancy of Gomorrah" (*Descent into Hell*, 209).

The difficulties we stumble over in this earliest of Williams' novels gradually diminish as his art becomes increasingly sure of itself in the later narratives.

2

War in Heaven

The thing that controls everything in *War in Heaven* is
the Holy Grail—or, as Williams likes to spell it, Graal.
This is the cup that is thought to have been used by
Christ at the Last Supper, and its story has come down
through the centuries of Christendom with strange and
unflagging force.

It is an obvious image for Williams to use, since it is always attached in our imagination to that Supper, the
whole point of which was what Williams would call Exchange, or Substitution, that is, someone's giving up his
life for the sake of others, which is the simple and fathomless principle of love.

As is the case in every Williams novel, the thing that
shows up (in this case the Graal) turns out soon enough
to be judging everyone simply by being itself and by calling forth responses from the characters which reveal the
sort of people they are. It is a bit like a heap of gold in a
fairy story: you can tell straight off which the good and

which the bad characters are by the way they react to the pile. If their eyes light up with plain and open astonishment and uncovetous delight, it is a fairly safe assumption that they are decent folks; if a beady light of covetousness flickers in their eyes, and their eyelids narrow to scheming slits, you have a fairly strong cue as to how far you can trust them. And of course what you see at this moment of discovery when they blunder onto the gold flashes back and forth along the line of their character: it gives you a glimpse of the sort of people they have been all along or at least of some undiscovered weakness in them, and it also hints at what you might expect from them in the coming adventures. Put into moral or psychological terms, it is nothing more than the truism that what we are all making of ourselves every day all day by the habits we cultivate and attitudes we adopt and choices we make is going to show up when the test comes. Put into theological terms, it becomes very frightening: "From thence he shall come to judge the quick and the dead", says Christendom. How will we show up at that sudden accounting?

The story starts out like a good murder mystery. A phone is ringing in an office, but the man under the desk does not answer it for the very good reason that he is a corpse and therefore cannot hear it.

The office is that of the publisher Gregory Persimmons, although he himself has retired and passed on the management to his son Stephen. The corpse is discovered by one of the editors, Lionel Rackstraw, and we very quickly find out the sort of man Lionel is. He has an overwrought imagination, so that he must constantly fend off wild fancies that loom in his mind about the havoc that is no doubt gaping at his very feet with every step he takes. He is what we might call a pessimist. This is, oddly, a point in his favor in Williams' scheme of things, since whatever honest and unselfconscious inclination a man has may sooner or later be turned to his benefit, since it may give him a toehold into the truth of how things are. A poet because he loves poetry; a lover because he loves a woman; a king because the holy oil is on his head; an honest sceptic because he sees the ambiguity in things; a priest because he lives in the presence of the Ineffable; and even, perhaps, a pessimist, if only because he is keenly aware that things are, in fact, fragile and perilous, which is quite incontrovertibly true if we take a cold look at things. Lionel's reaction to the corpse is, more or less, "Of course. What can one expect under one's desk but a corpse? And whose desk rather than mine?"

Apparently the corpse, a smallish man, has been strangled. During the preliminary questions being put to the office staff by Inspector Colquhoun, we learn from Stephen Persimmons that his father had been interested in, among other lines of publishing, books on the occult, mesmerism, and astrology. One of the firm's current authors is one Sir Giles Tumulty, whose book *Historical Vestiges of Sacred Vessels in Folklore* is being published by Persimmons.

In the second chapter, "The Evening in Three Homes", we see more of Lionel Rackstraw's dire imagination at work, and it seems to be the touch of his wife Barbara's hand that in some way steadies him very often. He has been telling her about the murder at the office, and as he does so he catches her hand in his, "and felt as if his body at least was sane, whatever his mind might be. After all, the universe had produced Barbara. And

Adrian [their small son] . . . was at least delimited and real in his own fashion" (19).

This is a major theme in the story, and in all of Williams' work. Over against whatever swirling fantasies, horrors, allurements, and even principalities and powers there might be stands the solidity of the Creation. This good, solid flesh of men and women and children is an undeniable witness that *something* is good, no matter what denials may come from the crannies of evil, whether in one's imagination or from sorcerers, demons, or heretics. When my mind and my imagination have lost their footing, then let me hang onto my wife's hand, or my friend's voice, or even the good, crusty texture of bread if nothing else—just something outside myself and manifestly good. (Readers of C. S. Lewis' stories will recognize this theme: when Mark Studdock is about to lose his grip altogether at Belbury, it is his memory of his wife, Jane, that stands as a lodestar for him; when Puddleglum and the rest of them have almost succumbed to the Green Witch's powders and charms, it is Puddleglum's dogged attachment to the real sunlight above ground in Narnia that tells him this is all a ghastly cheat.) If we wish to hear theological echoes here, as we are so often obliged to do with Dante or Milton, then we may hear in all of this the ringing affirmation of the creation and the Incarnation, which are "products", we might say loosely, of pure Good, or, more accurately, of God, who is pure Goodness. It is always and everywhere the effort of evil to undo the bright solidity of goodness. Hell is vacuous. Sin leeches away the good thing that was a man or a woman until you have only a wraith left: all we need do is look at the pitiable sight of some old lecher, or some bitter old person dried up from years of petulance and self-pity, and we know that that detritus is not what was meant when God made Adam and Eve.

We will find, during the course of the novel, that it is precisely these two, Barbara and Adrian, embodying as they do real external sanity and goodness for Lionel, who are the targets of the assault of evil. That assault, like the murder in the office, disregards the plain physical life of people in its pursuit of its own ends. They are expendable for the sake of an experiment in knowledge and power which the evil Gregory Persimmons is pursuing. Readers of Williams' other novels will recognize an exact parallel here to the situations in *Shadows of Ecstasy*, with the evil Nigel Considine prepared to sacrifice people for his ends, and in *The Greater Trumps*, with Henry Lee prepared to go as far as murder for the sake of knowledge and control which he seeks, and in *All Hallows' Eve*, with Simon the clerk slowly draining the vitality away from Betty Wallingford in the course of his own experiments in knowledge and control. It is always the same: no matter what its claims are, evil has for its net effect destruction. Stalin and Hitler both claimed to be building something great. All tyrants, and all vivisectionists and inquisitors, and all seducers who are prepared to pillage the shrine of the other's personhood claim to be seeking some good: a classless society, an Aryan society, better medicine, your soul's eternal salvation, a beautiful night of bliss.

On this same evening we learn a bit about one Kenneth Mornington, Lionel's colleague at the publishing firm. If Lionel is a pessimist, Mornington is something of a cynic, although not a bad one. He is described thus: his "slightly scornful mind pointed out to him . . . that the shock which he undoubtedly had felt was the result of not expecting people to murder other people, 'Whereas they naturally do,' he said to himself. . . . 'So silly not to be prepared for these things' " (19, 20). What saves Mornington, however, is a trait which we learn of presently. He must pop round to the vicarage of his local parish with some papers he has been (voluntarily, we should note) working on with respect to parish finances: "He had never been able to refuse help to any of his friends" (20). Therein lies his salvation. His cynicism, like Lionel's pessimism, may have to be modified or turned upside down before he is through, but he has a strong safeguard in this generosity of his against any bid that evil might want to make for him.

At the vicarage we meet, besides the local vicar, a visitor, one Julian Davenant, the archdeacon of Castra Parvulorum, a hamlet down in the country. He turns out to be in some sense the principal character in the story, and we note in him a certain pensive insouciance. He is, clearly, not easily upset by things and takes a sunny attitude towards life in general, but this is the result of some very deep inner tranquillity in him rather than of any flippancy. He makes the offhand comment, when Mornington complains that the murder at the office made him forget to get some advertising copy in to some journal, " 'After all, one shouldn't be put out of one's stride by anything phenomenal and accidental. The just man wouldn't be' " (21). If this sounds unconscionable, as though the Archdeacon would put a small matter of advertising copy over a murder in order of importance, this is not quite the thrust. Rather, we might think of some perfectly free and holy soul—Christ, say, or even a mortal like Saint Francis—who would not be sent flapping about by calamity. Some great anchor holds the holy soul in complete steadiness, no matter what the tumult. We find that the Archdeacon is one of these.

One aside which might be noted here is that the Archdeacon's account of how the name Castra Parvulorum eventually ended up as the modern English Fardles is not quite accurate from the standpoint of history of the language. He refers to "Grimm's Law", but he has it somewhat mixed up. This is a pedantic point, though, and does not affect the story in the slightest. Indeed, both names are appropriate, since the Latin name means "the camp of the children", and "fardles" is an archaic English word meaning "burdens" (the only place we run into it nowadays is in Hamlet's speech about whether to be or not to be). In the story at hand, the village does furnish a place where the child Adrian is defended, and great burdens are borne by the Archdeacon before it has all finished.

The third home which we visit on this evening is a flat in the Ealing section of London where old Gregory Persimmons is listening to his son Stephen tell about the murder. He stuns Stephen presently by telling him that it was he, Gregory, who did the killing.

Since the suspense in the book does not at all hang on the discovery of either murderer or the motive, and since this murder and Persimmons' motives for it flit in and out of the action in a rather confused way, it is as well that we sketch in here this component of the story. It is a possible criticism of this novel that Williams never makes up his mind whether he is writing a murder mystery or just what. Certainly readers will find it nearly impossible to keep the threads clear. The murder part of the story goes something like this: Gregory Persimmons' wife has been shut away in a lunatic asylum, and he tells

Stephen that this is unfortunate, since he wants another child to be his heir. Apparently old Persimmons is something of a sadist. He enjoys tormenting the nervous Stephen with mockery and threats of disinheritance. He also puts in at this point that, besides another child, he wants the Graal, although we have no idea why. Later in the action we find that his victim was one James Pattison, who had been somehow in Persimmons' employ and had once been caught stealing something. Persimmons thus had the man in his clutches, since he could always threaten blackmail. Hence, Pattison would do whatever Persimmons wanted, and this seems to have included forgery along the line somewhere. But then Pattison got himself "saved" under the influence of Wesleyan preaching and became troublesome, wanting to make his misdeeds right and wanting to testify to Persimmons. Persimmons saw that he was going to have to get rid of Pattison one way or another and thought that perhaps sending him to Canada would do. But then the chance to murder him presented itself, and, being wholly devoid of any human feelings at all, Persimmons took this quick way of ridding himself of the pest, choosing the publishing office as a convenience. Inspector Colquhoun, in the course of his investigations later, comes upon a well-annotated Bible which Pattison had left in the house of Mrs. Hippy, his landlady, and in Pattison's marginal notes Colquhoun discovers that Pattison knew that he was going to be killed, probably by the devil, who is not pleased with Pattison's change of heart. Still later, we learn that Persimmons seems to have had a threefold motive for Pattison's murder: first, simply to silence him, since who knows what he might do by way of going to the police in his effort to cleanse his soul; second, for "mere amusement", as he says to Stephen; and third, "partly as an offering to his god" (243).

Within the next day or so, further developments complicate the action. It is worth our noting the following items. Sir Giles Tumulty, the author of the book on sacred vessels which the publishing firm of Persimmons is about to publish, wants a certain paragraph removed from the page proofs, namely, the one which reveals that the vessel reputed to be the Holy Graal now rests in the parish church of Fardles in England. It turns out that Tumulty is in league with Persimmons in occult pursuits entailing the Graal, and it would not do for people to know that the Graal is anywhere about lest it elude the grasp of these two gentlemen. But the Archdeacon has been permitted by Mornington to read the unexpurgated manuscript just as a matter of interest, and he sees this item. It is of course most intriguing for him, but we see the Archdeacon's inner freedom once more in his reaction to the news: " 'In one sense, of course, the Graal is unimportant—it is a symbol less near Reality now than any chalice of consecrated wine' " (37). As far as he is concerned, the main point about the Graal is that it was once a humble token of the Divine Mercy; and nothing can touch or violate that Mercy, so why should one worry about this vessel? Honor it, to be sure; and protect it if possible: but the Mercy from which this vessel draws its honor is omnipotent, and one may rest in this.

We see the Archdeacon the next day taking the Graal out of its shelf in the church and wondering what harm would ensue even if it were stolen, saying in a reverie, " 'Ah, fair sweet Lord . . . let me keep this Thy vessel, if it be Thy vessel; for love's sake, fair Lord, if Thou hast held it in Thy hands, let me take it into mine. And, if not, let me be courteous still to it for Thy sake, courteous Lord' " (42). We also see the Archdeacon from time to time during the course of the story humming quietly to himself various tags from liturgy and Scripture such as "for his mercy endureth forever" and so forth. This attitude is where the Archdeacon's freedom, strength, and fearlessness come from.

Presently we see Persimmons' scheme closing in. He has taken a country house named Cully, near Fardles. On the grounds is a cottage which Persimmons seems uncharacteristically eager for the Rackstraw family to take for the month of July. It will be recalled that Lionel and Barbara have a small son, and that Persimmons has told his son Stephen that he wants another child.

When the inevitable attempt is made to pillage the parish church and steal the Graal, we find the Archdeacon carrying the Graal back to the church from his house, where he had decided to put the Graal against just such an attempt as has been made on the church. Here is how the narrative goes:

> Carrying it as he had so often lifted its types and companions, he became again as in all those liturgies a part of that he sustained; he radiated from that centre and was but the last means of its progress in mortality. Of this sense of instrumentality he recognized, none the less, the component parts—the ritual movement, the priestly office, the mere pleasure in ordered, traditional, and almost universal movement. "Neither is This Thou," he said aloud [50, 51].

The "types and companions" of the Graal, if it is the Graal, are, of course, all the chalices that ever get used at Communion for Christians. And the Archdeacon knows that in the mystery of this Communion Christians *do* become "part of" what they handle: as the paten and the cup bear the Body and Blood, or, more, as the bread and wine themselves "bear" that Body and Blood, so the very souls and bodies of the faithful, priest and laity alike, "become" the Body of Christ, as Saint Paul points out in his teaching about the Church's being Christ's body here on earth. The Archdeacon, again like all Christians, "radiated from that centre and was but the last means of its progress in mortality", in the sense that he *moves out*, or is *sent out*, from that center of Love. His mortal flesh becomes the "last means of its progress in mortality", the final way in which this Love has chosen to move in the world of men, namely, in the personal presence of men and women who consent to being bearers of that Love. The Archdeacon recognizes the sense in which he is a mere "instrument", and as such he is set free from the anxiety and torment that would be his if the guarding of the Graal (or of Omnipotent Love) were up to him alone.

The maxim "Neither is this Thou", which he murmurs to himself, is the second half of Williams' favorite maxim, "This also is Thou; neither is this Thou", which catches the paradox that we may say that *any* "this"— any lovely and good thing in the world—is "Thou", not in the pantheistic sense that all things merge into the Creator but rather simply that this is a pointer to his perfections; but it is necessary always to add immediately, lest we slide into either idolatry or pantheism, "neither is this Thou", no matter how good or glorious or perfect the "this" may be—a beloved face, Mozart's music, the Graal itself. These are not, really, Thou; but they may be vivid and piercing pointers to Thou.

Gregory Persimmons does, in fact, manage to carry off the Graal, not without some violence to the Archdeacon, and the plot is off and running.

There is an interesting sample of what we might call "typically Williamsian" prose at the start of chapter five, in which we see something of the irrepressibility of Williams' imagination. Indeed, it is this quality which will doubtless keep Williams' prose forever in the category of "special" or "peculiar" and never allow it to take its place comfortably on the shelves of twentieth-century novels. It is too much like poetry, not in the sense of rhythm and rhyme but rather in the sense that it flashes in all directions with virtually every word or phrase, obliging the reader to scamper hither and yon, all over psychology, theology, legend, and domestic ordinariness all at once in the attempt to stay with Williams' meaning. Like the poets, Williams sees similarities and correspondences where the rest of us miss them. Hence this *discordia concors*, where he packs together items and suggestions that would seem on the surface to have little to do with each other.

Passages like this one are very close to being diversions, although it could be urged that what we are seeing is the Archdeacon's frame of mind and that this is, in fact, essential to the action. But one's overriding suspicion is that it is Williams being ebullient.

In the passage in question we find that the well-intentioned Mr. Batesby, the actual vicar of the local parish at Fardles, comes to the rectory to visit the convalescing Archdeacon, who has been hit on the head in the course of Persimmons' theft of the Graal, and stays for some weeks. He quotes for himself, by way of validating this visit, Christ's words about "I was sick and ye visited me." But, says Williams, he neglected another maxim of Christ, namely, "Be wise as serpents"—that is, be shrewd enough to remember that not everyone wants a visitor for three weeks. Further, he imagines that the Archdeacon is greatly enjoying their chats, which mainly consist of Mr. Batesby's pontificating about all of his favorite (and tedious) topics. The Archdeacon always seems to see in these topics "a high eternal flavour which savoured of Deity itself", which is quite true, since a saintly mind like the Archdeacon's can see glory in a mud puddle, for that matter. The operative thing for the Archdeacon is the phrase in the Athanasian Creed that the Incarnation was a matter of taking the manhood into God more than a matter of converting the Godhead into flesh. Hence, with that cue, the Archdeacon is able to take all of these routine concerns of manhood which so occupy the good Mr. Batesby and raise them to God, in the sense of being thankful for Mr. Batesby's amiability and good intentions and so forth, and of believing that no doubt even these dull topics may be somehow re-deemed and glorified. On the other hand, it is hard for him to believe that Mr. Batesby is not all the while "rather firmly and finally" converting the Godhead into flesh—that is, taking life and making it as boring as pos-sible. " 'The dear flesh' ", the Archdeacon says to him-self, like Saint Francis taking a wry and merry view of this odd humanness of ours that gets itself knocked on the head, and must sit through horrible parish meetings, and was also dignified by being made the bearer of the Godhead.

If all of this appears to be diversion from the task at hand, three comments might be offered here. First, a reader who comes to a paragraph like this for the first

time is going to have trouble attaching all of Williams'
asides to the progress of the story. Second, to speak at
this length about a mere paragraph is to indicate the very
nature of Williams' prose. Third, the whole point of the
struggle in this novel is the clash between the mind of
hell, which defiles and profanes everything, and the
mind of heaven, which is "Athanasian". This is another
way of saying that the clash is between evil and good.

Presently we find Gregory Persimmons paying a visit
to Sir Giles Tumulty and securing from him the address
of a chemist shop in London. Apparently this shop will
supply Persimmons with a certain ointment that he
needs. We also discover that the shop is kept by a Greek
named Dmitri Lavrodopoulos, who, instead of asking
payment from Gregory for the ointment, says, " 'It is a
gift, but not a gift. . . . Give me what you will for a
sign' " (68). It turns out that one of the legends about the
chalice at Fardles is that it may have been in Ephesus at
one point in its history. The implications here are apparent only if a reader happens to have the New Testament
at his fingertips. The Greeks seek a sign, says Saint Paul:
their reasonable minds will not believe these scandalous
wonders that make up the Gospel. The only thing that
will impress their sceptical minds will be marvels such as
you might get in the mystery religions. But nothing bare
and simple and plain like Love will impress them. The
Cross (or the Graal, or for that matter people like the
Archdeacon) is not nearly marvelous enough for those
weary and blasé and civilized minds. Ephesus, of course,
is the city where Saint Paul's preaching of the gospel
stirred up a riot among the silversmiths whose trade was
largely the making of silver images of the city's patron-
ess, Diana. To the mind of Ephesus, the only thing

worth noting about a cup like this Graal is how much silver is in it. The mercenary mind finds anything beyond the question of monetary value to be opaque.

Persimmons takes the ointment back to his house, and we witness a strange ritual in which he smears his naked body with it. This is apparently the agency which will in some sense enable him to get on with his whole aim in life, which is to destroy everyone with whom he comes in contact. He seems to be a pure sadist. This is the only picture in all of Williams' fiction of this particular manifestation of the destructive tendencies of evil. All Williams' other villains have some ulterior purpose to which they are prepared to sacrifice people. But Persimmons has only the glee of destruction in mind. He loves to torment Stephen, he tormented his own dying father with pictures of a diabolically vengeful God, he murdered Pattison gratuitously, and now he will advance his cause by these occult means.

In this ritual he finds himself drawn into union with something which turns out to be the "that" which stands behind all witches' sabbaths and secret revels. He concentrates all of his attention, and intention, on union with this destructive that, and his experience is described with the vocabulary of sexual bliss. He is being married to, and ravished by, this evil. Like the exiled Satan in *Paradise Lost* he is saying with all his will, "Evil be thou my good," and evil is rewarding him.

But he senses some check, some blockage. What is it that keeps him from the final, orgasmic marriage with hell? Suddenly the figure of Adrian drifts into his memory. There must be a sacrifice. All deities, evil and good, demand sacrifice and oblation. Very well: it shall be the innocent Adrian.

Upon Persimmons' assent to this, his union is complete, and the description makes the picture an unmistakable parallel and parody of both sexual bliss and crucifixion. (This imagery has widespread precedent in the poetry of the Renaissance, in which to be united sexually was to "die".) Persimmons is now "nailed" to the bed on which he lies. His pangs bring him ecstasies beyond his wildest dreams. At this moment of his complete marriage to hell, he is "divorced from the universe; he was one with a rejection of all courteous and lovely things" (76).

By his willingness to pursue his sadistic inclinations, even to the point of sacrificing an innocent, he is indeed "wedded" to hell, which has no intention other than the destruction of all that is good. Insofar as he is united with hell, he is divorced from the whole world of courtesy and mutual exchange and the enjoyment of all good things.

Persimmons' experience upon the fading of this spell is of desolation and anarchy, which is what he has sought in any case. In the next chapter we even see him performing what amounts to a black mass in his attempt to dragoon Adrian into his power. Readers need not know their Latin vocabulary to know that what is being attempted is a diabolical reversing of the intention of the Christian Eucharist, which is to unite people with life and joy.

We presently meet the Duke of the North Ridings. He is Roman Catholic. As such his attachment to the Graal is somewhat different from that of the Archdeacon, who is Anglican. Both of these churches are sacramentalist in the sense of seeing that the eternal touches time at real physical points. But the Duke, being Catholic, is stoutly attached to the vessel itself. He will go to any lengths to rescue the cup, whereas the Archdeacon, with his typically Anglican demurral on questions like this, is prepared to let the physical item go if that must be, so long as the Love of which it is the token still rules his own heart. This would be in keeping with the Anglican refusal to work out just how the bread and wine at the Eucharist may be held to the Body and Blood of Christ, whereas the Roman Church has formularies that spell it out fairly rigorously. (Williams himself, it might be noted, remained Anglican all his life, but his appreciation of the Roman vision of holy things was probably more lively and exquisite than that of many Catholics themselves.)

Things come to the point where the Archdeacon seizes the Graal. He and the Duke take flight with it in the Duke's car. Mornington, Lionel's colleague, happens to be with them in the great chase that follows. He thinks of the Graal drama in terms of the King Arthur stories, and this, Williams implies, is good enough for the moment. Mornington is noble and trustworthy and well disposed towards things being set to rights, and he will find out all in Love's good time what it is that he really serves with these generous attitudes.

When a second attempt is made by Persimmons to seize the Graal, this time by long-distance mumbo-jumbo, it happens that the Archdeacon, Mornington, and the Duke are together with the Graal in a room in the Duke's London house in Grosvenor Square. They sense that some attack is being made on the cup, and in the ensuing scene, when they have all been enjoined by the Archdeacon to pray, we see their different understandings of what is going on.

Then we find this: "Unimportant as the vessel in itself might be, it was yet an accidental storehouse of power that could be used, and to dissipate this material centre was the purpose of the war" (141). This does not seem to me to be entirely clear, since readers might take this to mean that both sides in this war had it as their goal to "dissipate" the Graal, whereas there is one sense in which neither side wants this. Evil would like to hang onto the Graal as long as it proves useful. Good, although its final trust is in the Maker and not the thing, is unwilling to see any obscenity or desecration take place in any realm. The struggle centers upon the question as to whether power is going to be used for good or evil.

There is yet another character whom we must meet, one Manasseh, a Jew. Two things are worth observing here. Manasseh was the Old Testament king of Israel who perpetrated the killing of infants as sacrifices to idols. Second, Williams at times invites the suspicion of anti-Semitism, since at least two of his villains are Jews. But anti-Semitism is very far from his intention. He uses *all* facts and characteristics in a highly "visionary" way, and his sole point about Judaism is that it never accepted the Incarnation. Hence, theologically speaking it has opted for a divided world in which the restoring of the fabric of creation, torn by us in Eden, has not yet been inaugurated by the union of the Maker of all things with the flesh that he made. If there is a quarrel between Williams and the Jews it is not racial. It is solely theological and does not differ from the questions that have always stood between Christian and Jewish theology (as opposed to the passions that have sometimes stood between Christians and Jews).

Manasseh is a cohort of the Greek Dmitri. It is as though we have here the array of opponents recognized by Saint Paul in his comments about how hard it is for the gospel to be understood: to the Jews it is a stumbling block, and to the Greeks it is foolishness.

We find that Manasseh has only one passion: to destroy the Graal, as he desires to destroy everything in the universe. It is a sort of final, savage passion in a disenchanted and angry soul. If things won't be as I want them, then I will find my sole joy in destruction. The attitude shows up every time a child smashes a toy or kicks down a sand castle. Dmitri, on the other hand, exhibits a different face of damnation. He is utterly vitiated. He has no desires at all, no passions, nothing but an infinite weariness and ennui. He does not really care about the quarrel between Manasseh and Gregory, the one of whom wants to destroy the Graal and the other to use it. It all comes to the same thing in the end, says Dmitri. Evil has only one goal anyway, and that is nothingness. It is, of course, these three who have made the second attempt on the Graal which was sensed by the Duke and the others at Grosvenor Square.

One final character who figures in the drama is a stranger who shows up in a vague sort of way and says his name is John. He turns out to be Prester John. Here Williams is drawing on one of the remote aspects of the Graal legend. From very ancient times there has been said to be a king-priest from somewhere in the East (sometimes it was thought to have been Ethiopia) who does not die and whose task it is to keep watch on the Graal. This is who this stranger is, and on Persimmons' first encounter with him Prester John seems to see him and neglect him all at once. This is a way of hinting at the old notion that evil hardly exists at all when you come down to it, since its whole effort is to destroy things. Next to the titanic solidity and splendor of the City of God, hell dwindles to insignificance. (C. S. Lewis catches this same idea in *The Great Divorce* when it turns out that the whole gray world from which the lost souls have come seems to have got itself lost between the floorboards of heaven.) Prester John also seems to smell an objectionable smell. It is the decay embodied by Gregory. Williams uses this same idea in *The Place of the Lion*, where a stench running through most of the story turns out to be the rotting mind of Damaris Tighe.

In the course of Persimmons' further attempts to pursue his sadistic ends, he manages to see to it that Barbara Rackstraw's finger is pricked as they all work over a toy train with Adrian. He offers some ointment, apologizing profusely for his clumsiness, and we watch the effect of this ointment on Barbara, who seems to be nothing more than a sort of experimental lamb of sacrifice on whom Gregory wishes to try out and observe the effects of this ointment en route to his real conquest, namely, Adrian. But whereas for Persimmons the ointment brought about a closer union with the destruction which he had chosen as his native realm, for Barbara it turns out to be an alien invader. She is sent into paroxysms, and Williams describes her wild movements as those of a dance. But it is the dance of evil—not because Barbara is evil but because she, having "drifted through the world like most people, 'neither for God nor for his enemies' " (160), has no defense against this assault and is obliged to leap to the motions aroused by the ointment, whereas Persimmons, advanced in evil as he is, and therefore more controlled, had been able to remain motionless in his body while his soul went out to the ecstasy of evil.

The thing that saves Barbara is that she screams out for Lionel and for God, as anyone in this sort of extremity would be likely to do. In Williams' scheme, no cry like this goes unheard by the Mercy. Barbara will be saved.

As a sort of postscript to this frenzied scene, we find Gregory playing "pictures" with Adrian with a small black disc that is not otherwise mentioned in the story. Apparently it gives the gazer certain powers of clairvoyance, and, upon Gregory's questions to Adrian, it becomes clear that Adrian is seeing Prester John—not just in his inauspicious garb as a wayfarer as he has recently been seen around Fardles but as warrior and king and priest. Gregory is perplexed. Later he is warned by Tumulty, who recognizes from Persimmons' description who this is, that he had better give over the whole scheme, since if Prester John is looking out for the Graal, all heaven is against them, and their chances of success in the war are no better than Lucifer's.

Lionel sees in the apparent overthrow of Barbara's sanity the confirmation of all his worst fears about life. With the loss of whatever remnants of comfort she was able to bring to his pessimism, all seems lost. His despair is so black, in fact, that Persimmons experiences it as an obstacle, since he must believe that there is joy (or whatever the joy of demons may be called: glee, perhaps) even in horror. But Lionel's ferocious denials of this are so implacable that it seems as though Gregory has come upon iron gates, or a stone wall, in his schemes. The point here would seem to be that *any* honest reaction or emotion, if it has nothing more to be said for it than that it is honest—and Lionel's pessimism is certainly honest—may be put to good use. There is at least the rag of truth in Lionel's attitude that horror is horror; and truth in any form, no matter how little of it, is an obstruction to evil.

In the third attempt on the Graal, Persimmons manages to reacquire it from the Duke by promising Lionel that a doctor friend of his, who turns out to be Manasseh, can help Barbara. The price will be the Graal. It seems that this doctor would like the Graal instead of money. Lionel, of course, has no particular view in the matter and rings up the Duke's house to see what can be arranged. It is the Archdeacon who persuades the guardians of the Graal to bring it down from London to Fardles, since "I would give up any relic, however wonderful, to save anyone an hour's neuralgia' " (184). Once more, the only crucial thing for the Archdeacon is mercy. The Omnipotent Love will look after its relics. Our job is to tend the sick and so forth, which is what relics are all about in the end anyway, since they are "nothing more" than remnants and tokens of love and holiness.

Things go as Persimmons hopes, and Barbara is quieted—with the one oddity that Manasseh seems to notice that she quiets down just *before* his ministrations could take effect. Something else seems to come to her aid. But in any event, they have got the Graal once more.

We learn something more of Sir Giles Tumulty presently when he encounters Prester John at the railway depot at Fardles. Prester John gives Sir Giles a strange warning, the thrust of which seems to be that perhaps the very thing that Sir Giles prides himself on—namely, his scholarly objectivity, which has not only made him detached but clearly has also led him to a frame of mind where he does not care a fig one way or the other for goodness, evil, or anything else—that this very refusal to take sides may meet him in the end, and that he may find himself, under the serene gaze of the universe, scrabbling at the universe like "an ant against the smoothness of the inner side of the Graal, and none shall pick you out or deliver you for ever" (190). Prester John prefaces this by saying that "one day when you meet me you shall find me too like yourself to please you". This is a way of putting the ancient notion of damnation as souls' meeting and having to endure in each other the very thing that they have been. The sense in which Prester John may say that this will be Sir Giles' meeting *him* is that Prester John is the guardian of the Graal, and hence of Love, so to speak, and hence "stands for" Love, and for all that Sir Giles abominates; but, like every soul ever born, Sir Giles is going to have to encounter sheer reality, which turns out to be synonymous with Love; and hence he may be said to be destined to meet Prester John one fine day. On that day, Prester John (or the universe) will gaze dispassionately on Sir Giles' scrabblings with the same detached serenity with which Sir Giles has gazed upon all things here during his life—with what he has been pleased to call objectivity. In that sense Prester John will be too much like Sir Giles for Sir Giles' comfort.

We also see a brief encounter between Mr. Batesby, the local vicar, and Prester John. Like the Graal itself, Prester John merely by showing up stands as a sort of judgment on people, bringing out the real truth about them. Mr. Batesby becomes more and more bland and windy and sententious as he talks with Prester John—a betrayal of the blandness and windiness of Mr. Batesby's religion. He is, in fact, Williams' picture of a modernist: "He became more than ever a guide and guard to his fellows, and the Teaching Church seemed to walk, a little nervously and dragging its feet, in the dust behind him"

(191). Mr. Batesby's effort, like that of all modernist theology, is to explain things so that they dwindle to innocuous platitudes (e.g., God is so loving that he would never be angry with us—that sort of thing) rather than to be the steward and herald of all the stupendous tidings of the gospel, alarming as well as consoling.

But the most revealing encounter with Prester John, which amounts to a full-dress epiphany, comes presently when the Duke and Mornington and Lionel and Barbara find themselves talking about what happened to Barbara when the "doctor", Manasseh, was present. Manasseh had noticed that she quieted down from her fit before his treatment was actually applied. It turns out that they had all noticed this. Her account of it is that, just when she seemed about to fall over some edge into a pit, she recognized someone, and suddenly everything became all right. " 'I fell into safety. . . . I knew him at once' " (201). Just at this point Prester John himself comes along, and she recognizes him immediately as her savior. Indeed, they all recognize him; and as they each grope about to recall the times and places where they might have known him, it becomes clear that they have met him wherever they have encountered love and sanctity. Barbara before her marriage, and since then too; Lionel can't think where; Mornington thinks Prester John is a priest he has met somewhere; and the Duke thinks he has met him at Oriel, which, readers will recall, is the college at Oxford associated with the name of John Henry Newman, the nineteenth-century Anglican priest who became the great Catholic theologian and cardinal. In a wry aside, Prester John remarks, " 'Not so very much lately' ", referring to the idea that he might be encountered at Oriel, the implication being that the fervor for holiness that blazed at Oriel in Newman's day has perhaps cooled a bit and that it might not be a place where one would run into the likes of Prester John.

Prester John speaks to each one of them, much as the Risen Christ spoke to his disciples and others, giving a word of consolation, promise, or prophecy to each. It is not that he is Christ: rather, like John the Baptist and Mary and Galahad and others, indeed, like the Graal itself, he is the herald and bearer of "the things which are to be". His word to Mornington is simply, " ' "*Surely I come quickly*. To-night thou shalt be with me in Paradise" ' " (203).

This comes to pass soon enough, when the Duke and Mornington attempt to raid the chemist shop in London and rescue the Graal from Manasseh, Lavrodopoulos, and Persimmons, who are proceeding with their black arts. Mornington dies in the struggle, and the Duke is overpowered and obliged to write a letter to the Archdeacon telling him to come to the shop, since he, Mornington, and the Graal are all there, and the Archdeacon's help is needed.

There is an interval in the action, in which we accompany the police as they search for the chemist shop, having been put onto this trail by various bits of evidence involving the murder and now the disappearance of the Duke from his house in Grosvenor Square. They cannot find the shop: it seems to have disappeared in a dense fog, right out from between the two houses that adjoin it on each side. Just as they have reached a point of near madness over this absurdity, the fog thins, and Gregory Persimmons presents himself, saying, " 'I wish to give myself up to the police for murder' " (233).

What has been happening in the shop in this foggy interval is Persimmons' final attempt, with Manasseh and the Greek, to effect their destructive purposes by means of the Graal. The Archdeacon has come; and Adrian has been brought by the housemaid from Cully, since Lionel and Barbara are planning a short seaside holiday, and the kindly "uncle" Persimmons has generously agreed to look after his small friend Adrian. Although it is never entirely clear just what the nature of the nefarious plan is which the three villains have in mind, it is one of pure destruction, involving domination over souls. Pattison's soul is to be called back and forced into the Archdeacon's body (presumably the Archdeacon will have to die in the process); the Graal will be the agent of passage; Persimmons' desire will be the catalyst; and Adrian, before all is over, will be sacrificed as an appropriately pure and innocent lamb to whatever dark god is asking for these rites. Persimmons and Manasseh periodically refer to their own eventual journey to the East with the Graal: readers of Williams' poetry will know that the Far East—the "Antipodean Sea"—exists in Williams' imagination as some sort of final locale of evil, the polar extreme from Logres, which is Arthurian Britain, the place where the Graal was kept, and which came very near to being a kingdom of goodness and love, if it had not all been spoiled by the squabbles that wrecked the Round Table fellowship.

In any event, the Archdeacon is bound, and the attempt on him begins. Insofar as he is the embodiment of love and goodness undergoing this assault from evil, this is his Gethsemane and his crucifixion, and the narrative makes this plain. His strength derives from his having learned, in good times and bad, simply to consent to being at the disposal of the Divine Mercy, who, after all, is in control. He experiences dereliction, as Christ did on the Cross; and senses the presence of a threefold evil in the assault: the anger of old Persimmons, which, oddly, turns out to be a harbinger of Persimmons' salvation, since he "trembles still with desires natural to man" (241) and is hence not wholly gone into the posthuman region of the damned; the hunger of old Manasseh, which is the predatory hunger "with which the creation preys upon itself, a supernatural famine that has no relish except for the poisons that waste it" (241); and third, Dmitri's attitude of "rejection absolute . . . of every conceivable and inconceivable desire this was the negation". These are all variations on the theme of evil, with this final negation of the Greek's being perhaps the most infernal.

The Archdeacon's experience during this onslaught is parallel to what we saw of Persimmons in his early experiment of giving himself over to the dark powers by means of the ointment. There are a sinking, and a darkness, and then an approaching "marriage" with Pattison's soul, as opposed to Persimmons' nuptials with Satan, as it were, and finally what threatens to be a death: Persimmons is almost worn out with the energy he is putting out in beckoning Pattison's soul from the realm of the dead into the Archdeacon and would be glad to leave things there, but Manasseh and the Greek see that only a "haunting" has been achieved and that "something more" is needed.

But they have gone too far. That something more turns out to be too much. It arrives, but it is not what they have anticipated. It is Prester John, like an archangel blasting in to the rescue and destroying the works of evil. All that can be saved is saved: the Archdeacon; the Duke; Adrian and the maid; Mornington, who is now "with" Prester John; and even Gregory—who must give himself over to the law, presumably to be executed for murder and thereby to be saved. The Jew and the Greek we last see shaking and crouching, awaiting whatever fate will be assigned them. We see them no more.

The final scene is of the restoration and consummation of all things, so to speak. All are safe back at Castra Parvulorum, "where tradition said, Caesar had restored the children to their mothers" (252). It is no longer Fardles—burdens. In a talk with Lionel, Prester John manages to hint to him that his very fears may be the pointers towards his salvation.

Then they all go to church. Prester John is the celebrant at the Mass, and Adrian serves. Each one sees, in a vision, as it were, what he is capable of seeing. The Duke, being Roman Catholic, cannot actually participate in this Anglican Mass, but, standing in the door of the church, he sees all of his ancestors, so fiercely loyal to the Mysteries which are being celebrated here; and, though this Mass is being said in English, he hears the Latin words of the Roman rite: "*Introibo . . .*" (I will go [unto the altar of God]), and it seems that Adrian answers with the ancient response, "To God who is the joy of my youth."

Barbara, not a churchgoer in recent years, recognizes nonetheless the familiar phrases of the Anglican liturgy: "To Whom all hearts be open, all desires known", from the Collect for Purity; and, at the end of the Gospel reading, "Behold, I make all things new", which readers of Williams will recognize as one of Williams' favorite biblical texts, passed on, as it were, by Dante in his great vision where he hears the words "*Ecce, omnia nova facio*", which sum up the entire enterprise of Redemption, as opposed to the destruction of all things sought so sedulously by evil.

The Archdeacon, having just experienced the horrible and deathly division threatened by the assault of evil on him, experiences the knitting up of all things—rite and reality, word and sacrament, vision and act—as a unity, or *the* Unity, rather.

Presently we become aware that the pronouns being used for Prester John are being capitalized. Christ himself is now the celebrant, as is true in any Mass in any case; and all glory seems to be unveiled—which also is true in any Mass. The Archdeacon is called to the steps of the altar, where he dies; Adrian is restored to his mother and father in the safety of the family; and the Duke goes across to fetch the Poloniuslike Mr. Batesby, who can only hurry to the church from the rectory babbling the flat platitudes of his modernism.

It is as though the Cloud of Glory, like the cloud that accompanied Israel in the wilderness, has come very close to the characters in this tale and then has passed on its way, leaving them chastened, sobered, even transfigured. And this, of course, is exactly what any experience ought to convey to us in any case, Williams always implies. The Mass, since it is the exact diagram of how that Glory touches our ordinary experience, is an appropriate climax to the events we have witnessed in *War in Heaven*.

3

Many Dimensions

Readers who have heard about the oddity of Charles
Williams' novels very often ask which of them might be
the least daunting one to start with. *Many Dimensions*, although far from being Williams' best novel, might be a
candidate here, for the simple reason that, even though
it is an extremely bizarre tale, there seem to be fewer of
the cursory dashes into allusive asides that Williams is so
fond of, and that leave so many readers panting and bewildered. Partly because the tale is so peculiar, Williams
is obliged to keep us abreast of just what is occurring.

What is occurring is that the crown, or what is left of
it, of one Suleiman ben Daood, King in Jerusalem, better
known to most of us as Solomon, has shown up in London. The man who has got hold of it is the villain of the
piece, one Sir Giles Tumulty, whom readers of *War in
Heaven* will recognize as the traveler, archaeologist, and
student of the occult who played a role as accomplice to
the archvillain, Gregory Persimmons, in that tale. Like

all Williams' villains, Sir Giles is prepared to ride rough-shod over all questions of human decency, let alone charity or goodness, in his hot pursuit of knowledge, power, and ecstasy.

The center of attraction about this crown is not just its great antiquity, nor even its interest as a relic. Rather, it contains a small, cubical stone, milky in color and flecked with gold. Engraved on this stone, or rather in it, are some jet-black Hebrew letters which turn out to be the four letters of the Tetragrammaton, the unutterably holy name of God which we commonly transliterate into English as Jehovah or Yahweh. Sir Giles has apparently come into possession of it by bribing a member of the Islamic family in Persia which had been custodians of the stone for centuries.

This might seem to introduce a confusion, since most readers will associate Solomon with the history of the Hebrews, not the Moslems. But it will be recalled that the Moslems honor all the great figures of the Old Testament and also that eventually the Islamic conquests overran all the Hebrew holy places, and that hence it might be supposed, at least for purposes of the story, that they came into possession of many of the holy relics of Old Testament events.

A certain vocabulary surrounds this stone—or Stone, we should say, since we find the word capitalized throughout the story, like the name which it bears. The Persian family which has been its custodians through the centuries have been known as the Keepers. God, or Allah to the Persians, is often spoken of as simply "the Permission", the idea being that when you have a relic this holy, the power which stands behind it will not ignore its fate or abandon it, but will watch over it, never permitting it to be engulfed by the obscenities and sacrileges of such men as Sir Giles and his ilk. Nothing happens outside the circle of this Permission.

Williams is always shy of using such terms as "God" or "the Lord", and this shyness is itself very much part of his whole frame of mind, and hence of his prose style. It is as though we mortals find our small routines of life being carried on under the looming arch of the Infinite—and not just the vacuous infinity of space research, nor even the impersonal infinity of the Transcendentalists, but rather the Infinity whose name is Holy. The Ineffable. The Holy One of Israel. Perhaps it is best not to speak this name trippingly on the tongue too often. Perhaps there are oblique ways of mentioning this Ineffable One, not because he (and Williams almost never uses the pronoun "he" when speaking of the Deity) is unknowable, but because he is holy. Williams prefers such guarded terms as "the Omnipotence", or "the Mercy", or "the Unity", or, sometimes when referring to the Son of God, "the Incarnacy" or "Messias". Anything but the routine vocabulary of theology and piety. Here again we may see at least two reasons for this in Williams' prose: first, part of the artist's job is to boost us up out of all that has come to seem merely routine and platitudinous—to jolt us awake, as it were, and thus to enable us once more to see the stark glory and terror behind the routines and platitudes, not by way of denying the platitudes (they are always true), but by way of revivifying them. And second, Williams himself seems to have embodied the tension between the sceptic and the believer in a way that is very rarely found with such peculiar tautness in one man. The "believer" part of him, if we may put it this crudely, was intensely conscious of the majesty, inscrutability, and holiness of the Most High, but the "sceptic" in him preferred not to be indulging in too much talk that smacked of routine piety. Or we may carry this admittedly finely tuned analysis half a step farther by guessing that it was the very believer in Williams that was shy of routine pieties, or at least of the vocabulary ordinarily associated with those pieties, since the One referred to in all the pious talk is, precisely, the Ineffable. To be sure, on the Christian view, he has shown his face in the face of Christ (Williams would never in a thousand years put it this way, but we may be pardoned for reaching for New Testament phrases here); but our eyes had perhaps best be averted in the presence of imponderables like this.

Another of the attributes of the Deity which seems specially attached to the Stone from Solomon's crown is the Unity. This brings us very close to the center of the drama. This Unity is, of course, the fountainhead of all creation. The universe is not a clutter or a jumble or a mistake. No smallest gnat, mote, or forget-me-not is without its place in the great design; and not only this, but every gnat, mote, and forget-me-not, along with seas, mountains, dragons, nebulae, and seraphim, speaks directly and eloquently of the glory of that Unity. Another way of putting this is that everything that exists has its place in the great Dance; and since the name of that Dance is Love, we may say that love, or goodness, in a man, will always recognize, or at least guess at, the pattern of the Dance, and honor it; whereas egotism, or evil, will care nothing for the pattern so long as it gets what it thinks it wants. Hence, the tendency of evil in any Williams novel is to tear things apart, whereas the tendency of goodness is to submit humbly to the pattern, on the assumption that if you tear it apart you will have committed both an obscenity and an outrage. Evil either fails to recognize the Unity or cares nothing for it; goodness worships the Unity and obeys it. We might see examples of this in a ballet or a symphony: the good dancer or violinist cares about the whole lovely pattern of which every step or note is one part; the careless or rebellious performer has no fidelity to the whole and is prepared to spoil it for everyone to gratify his own whims or grudges.

The history of the Stone is recounted by one Hajji Ibrahim, a faithful descendant of the Persian keepers of the Stone. Legend, he says, suggests that this Stone was perhaps the first created thing made by the Merciful One, and that the universe came into being when the Shekinah (an Old Testament name for the glory of God) gazed on the Stone. It is in some sense, then, the "First Matter" from which all things, both material and spiritual, were made. It came somehow to be in the crown of "Iblis the Accursed", whom Jews and Christians would call Lucifer, or Satan, and when he fell, the Stone dropped from his crown. Adam possessed it in Eden, and it was the only thing he brought with him out into history when he and Eve were exiled. Thence it passed to Nimrod the mighty hunter, and on to Solomon, and eventually to the Caesars, then Muhammed, then through seven khalifs to Charlemagne, who put it in the hilt of his sword "Joyeuse". Then it disappeared into the keeping of the Hajji's family.

The point about the Stone is that it is a source of tremendous power. If we were disposed to translate Williams' tale into merely psychological or political terms, we might say that the Stone was a "symbol" for what is obvious, namely, that all rulers do, in fact, possess a thing called power, and that this power is something that won't quite yield itself to our attempts to analyze it. When a paper hanger or a haberdasher becomes ruler of a great nation, something happens to him. Some mantle seems to cloak him, and the coldest and most pragmatic of us must admit that some mystique surrounds the personage who wields power. Our imaginations balk at calling the head of state by some nickname like Jimmy.

But power is not the only attribute of the Stone. It is somehow "the End of Desire". Apparently whatever it is that is embodied in this Stone is itself the fulfillment of all longings and strivings. The man who is mad for power, for example, Alexander the Great or Napoleon, finds that when he has got what he thought he was after, the joy and satisfaction that he supposed would attend this state of affairs are as far away as they were when he was nobody. Apparently this Stone represents the Reality of which all the sham and trumpery of politics and military conquest and all other sorts of powermongering are the counterfeits.

But it will not be had for the grabbing. A man, or any number of men as we find out soon enough in this tale, may seem to possess the Stone or even a copy of the Stone, but in the end the thing he thought he would gain by making his grab for the Stone will elude him, as well the Stone itself. It is only the Permission which allows the Stone to be taken, and in the end it will always return to its appointed Keepers who, far from seeing themselves as possessors of it, look on their office strictly as one of stewardship.

Once more, if we were to translate all this into psychological or moral terms rather than the superficial political or military questions of power and desire, we would see that Williams has found an image for a riddle that lies close to the center of human experience and that bedevils us all. We all want *something:* that much is clear. But exactly what it is and how to get it are what elude and madden us. All strife—the shrieking struggle for the toy shovel in the sandbox, the fevered passions of the lecher, the lethal, icy, and barbed darts that fly through the air in respectable social situations; or lawsuits over inheritances and damages, fisticuffs on the street, the tense and murderous plotting of the miser or the Mafioso, and thermonuclear war itself—what is it all but our frantic attempts to snatch and keep what we think we want? But no one who has ever won any of the above struggles will bear very blithe testimony to the quality of satisfaction gained thereby. The very sweetness of victory is somehow salted with a poison that shrivels the soul.

Well, then, who can ever hope to find satisfaction and repose—the End of Desire? We learn from Hajji Ibrahim that the way to the Stone is in the Stone itself. Apparently, then, if one truly desires the good of which this Stone is somehow the repository, it will not be so much a matter of possessing the Stone as of being possessed by it. "Resignation" is the word that Hajji uses in describing this mystery to Chloe Burnett, and that word carries us straight into the vocabulary which crops up again and again in the testimony of the saints: somehow they have found the End of Desire, not by scrabbling and clawing and scheming for it but rather by submitting to what it seems to ask of them. The freedom and serenity and bliss

that we observe in the saints are the fruit of their resignation—crucifixion, if we wish to carry it all the way
into the teaching of Saint Paul and of our Lord himself.

But, to return to the mere events of the story in question: Sir Giles Tumulty has got hold of this Stone, and
his nephew, Reginald Montague, is very keen that they
reap all possible dividends from it. The Stone has certain
other peculiar properties, among which are the fact that
it is infinitely divisible without ever diminishing: that is,
you can cut it with a knife as many times as you wish, but
each piece, or "type", will be an exact and whole replica
of the original, and the original will still be intact. Furthermore, it turns out that the Stone has the power to
transport people through both space and time. Experiments in testing these powers of the Stone and its types
account for a good deal of the action in the story. Indeed,
the prolonged speculations on the part of Sir Giles and
his scholar friend Palliser on this point in connection
with their attempts to send the unfortunate Elijah Pondon through time by means of the Stone seem to point
to the notion, important in Williams' vision, that *any*
wrenching and violating of the appointed pattern of
things, including even such a pedestrian business as the
ticking along of time hour after hour, is a transgression
and an outrage, with consequences that will certainly
bring on havoc. Or, put in a positive rather than this negative way, we may say that all the conditions and limitations that we find in the pattern of our world (such as
our not being able to flit from place to place instantly, or
to hurry up time, and so forth) are part of the pattern of
which we too are a part, and to submit to these conditions gladly and obediently is perhaps to be in a position
to learn something that will altogether elude the sorcer-

ers, tyrants, and supermen who attempt to raid the pattern by main force.

In this connection, we find that the Stone is also able to illuminate a man's mind, so that he can know what is going on not only in another place but also in another man's mind. But perhaps its most unnerving property is that "it will do nothing for itself of itself", as the Hajji explains to Lord Arglay, the Lord Chief Justice of England, who is wondering whether the Stone itself might not simply undertake to reamass all the proliferating "types" back into the original one cube. Somehow or other all this apparently infinite power attaches itself to the choices that men make. It would seem to be somehow subject to their will. This would seem to be an anomaly, which it no doubt is, except that any Jew, Christian, or Moslem must keep some such anomaly alive in his own view of how things happen in this world, since we are obliged at one and the same time to worship God as omnipotent and also to affirm man's freedom. No formula or equation is of the smallest help here.

The Hajji points out that there is one condition under which the Stone will act to reverse the mercenary and sacrilegious proliferation of types planned by Montague and others. If some person were to will, quite unconditionally, that both he (or, as it turns out rather significantly, she) and the Stone were to be "with the Transcendence", then the Stone would act. Our bewilderment over this vague phrase does not last long, however. We find that this self-offering on the part of some person must be quite without strings. Prince Ali Mirza Khan, who is attached to the Persian embassy in London, is very anxious to save the Stone, but he wants to do it for the Moslem faith. That is the condition which he stipulates as a prerequisite for any self-offering on his part. The Hajji wants the same thing, but it would be for the ancient honor of his house, the Keepers of the Stone. Again, a condition. Other Persians would be willing to offer themselves, but in every case it would have some condition—even such august considerations as glory, or peace—and " 'we dare not bring these things into the Transcendence' " (59).

The point, of course, is that the Transcendence (God, in other words) is such that it (he) is infinitely above *all* conditions, even high and holy things like faith, honor, glory, and peace. No mortal may bargain with the Most High, no matter how costly and venerable the tokens he brings for barter. Unconditional obedience is the sole condition under which any mortal may make his approach to these precincts, and the Hajji knows this.

What he cannot know, because he is a Moslem and therefore does not accept the real union with our flesh which has already occurred when that Transcendence "was incarnate by the Holy Ghost of the Virgin Mary and was made man", is that such an unconditional act of submission can indeed be made and has been made by a woman once already in our history. The woman in the present story turns out to be Lord Arglay's assistant, Chloe Burnett.

Lord Arglay cannot at the moment take in all that is suggested in what the Hajji says, but a faint hope stirs in him, long since laid aside in his preoccupation with law, that perhaps "the nature of law was also the nature of God. But if so, it was not in the Transcendence but in the order of created things" (59). In other words, law is a sort of tag end, or hem of the garment of the Transcendence, which supplies us with the barest hint, down here in the world of created things, of what exists as impenetrable and transcendent mystery for us mortals. Law is for this world of created things. It is the name we give to the order that must preside over things. But the Transcendence knows no "law". It is not "under" any order. Law is perhaps the knotted underside of a great tapestry which, seen from above, turns out to be a pattern of such beauty and perfection that our bliss at seeing it too soon would overthrow us entirely.

But to return to the interested parties: all is not going to be smooth sailing, of course. For one thing, this Prince Ali Mirza Khan has found out that Sir Giles has the Stone and is attempting to persuade him, at almost any price, to return it to the Persians, who are the rightful custodians of it. He, like his uncle Hajji Ibrahim, has a proper respect for the powers of the Stone and is afraid of what will happen if infidels get to tinkering with it.

Lord Arglay turns out to be an uncle of Reginald Montague's by marriage on the other side of the family from Sir Giles. Lord Arglay is an eminently sensible and decent man whose instincts seem to be just right. He is writing a *Survey of Organic Law*, which suggests that his Lordship has a deeply rooted commitment not only to law as a sort of artificial grid imposed on societies to keep them running but as itself an unfolding of principles rooted in nature itself. Not only society but also psychology, morals, biology, zoology, and the universe itself all function by law, which is another word for the Dance—that lovely choreography that weaves all things into its joyous pattern. Lord Arglay is also a sceptic, not in the sense of refusing to believe anything beyond what his senses can discern but in the sense of being disposed towards giving things their readiest and least preternatural explanation. This, however, does not at all blunt his perceptions, and it is this very habit of caution and hesitancy in the face of the inexplicable that dignifies his opinions and beliefs when he does grant the presence of the marvelous. If *he* is convinced that we are in the presence of things beyond our ability to manage or explain, then we had all better sit up and take notice. For example, he is not really sure what is meant by the Stone being called "the end of desire", but he can see the force of the notion that the way to the Stone is in the Stone itself, since (he reflects) this is true everywhere anyway: "For as you cannot know any study but by learning it, or gain any virtue but by practising it, so you cannot be anything but by becoming it" (49). Arglay himself is a vivid case in point of exactly this, since he not only holds the office of Lord Chief Justice of England: he *is* justice, in the sense that with every impulse of his being he embodies the goodness of which the laws of England are the merest diagrams.

There is a rather wide array of marginally important characters crowding the stage of the story, but as is always true of a Williams novel, most of them tend to be like the two-dimensional figures in a pageant, embodying some virtue or villainy, but hardly existing in the three dimensions which we have come to expect of characters in modern novels. The only ones worth noting, besides those whom we have already met, are: Frank Lindsay, who is wooing Chloe and who must learn that she has been chosen for something other than marriage to him; Angus and Cecilia Sheldrake, American millionaires who think they can buy the Stone for 73,000 guineas from Montague and who represent worldliness in its most banal degree; Oliver Doncaster, who finds the

Stone which the Sheldrakes have lost in a hedge in the country and who takes it back to his rooming house, where it seems to exhibit healing powers on the land-lady's old mother; and Eustace Clerishaw, the mayor of the town of Rich, who feels strongly that the Stone ought to be used for the good of the populace generally. The others, including the various ministers of government and other attendant figures, only come on stage as they are necessary to peripheral incidents in the main action.

That action entails the return of the Stone to itself by means of Chloe Burnett's offering of herself to be the means of that return. If we translated this suddenly into very high theological terms, we might say that this is very much like what has happened in our own history. Holy things were profaned when mankind made its grab for power and knowledge in Eden, saying, "This shall be ours", and the unity was ripped. Not, of course, the Unity of the Godhead itself but the unity that bound all creation, both matter and spirit, into one seamless pattern. Thereafter we were doomed to experience things as divided: profane and sacred, matter and spirit, mortal and immortal, visible and invisible. Sir Giles, Montague, and the Sheldrakes are prepared to rifle and pillage the unity for their own ends of knowledge, power, and, grubbiest of all, money. In the chaos that attends every-one's scramble to have a bit of the loot (and what else does the sad record called history record?), there will be some quiet soul somewhere who will know that the chaos is just that—chaos—and that it might be possible to offer oneself in response to the bidding of the Unity as a vessel for the rescue of things from this unnatural frag-mentation.

The Virgin Mary appears in the Christian Gospel in this role, with her "Be it unto me according to thy word"; and, in the Incarnation, in which she was "partner", if we may speak thus, with the Holy Ghost, there occurred that rescue of things from the unnatural fragmentation into which they had been plunged when we profaned it all in Eden. Similarly, in this story, we find Chloe eventually offering herself as the human means whereby the Unity may be restored.

It must be she, and not the Hajji or the Prince, for perhaps two reasons at least. For one thing, as Moslems they fervently honor the Unity, but they do not accept the notion that that remote Unity has united itself with our flesh. That is a scandal to Islam. Hence their loyalty is only partly useful. This shows itself at one point when Lord Arglay observes to the Hajji that the Hajji cares more about the Stone's being divided than about the harm that may come to people from Sir Giles' toying with it. Hajji admits this, since the former is an offense against the Holy One and the latter "only" an offense against man. Lord Arglay, the embodiment of human justice, as it were, can only demur, saying that he knows nothing of Hajji's Unity and so forth but does know something of man. The implication with which Williams is plucking our sleeve here is that in the end the two are one: to offend man is offend God, since God became man. There is the real Unity. But neither Islam nor human justice can quite carry things this far.

For another thing, Chloe is a woman, and in Williams' vision, as in nearly all ancient mythic ideas, womanhood embodies the whole notion of response to the approaches of the divine. From Ge, the earth-mother, to the Virgin Mary it has been woman who has somehow borne and nurtured the seed planted by the god which will bring life and salvation. If we imagine that this is all too embarrassingly prescientific and arcane, we must nonetheless grant that Williams was not cobbling up a novel idea here: he drew it directly from a universal story—and, Christians would say, from The Story which actually came true on the stage of our history.

From the beginning we see in Chloe a certain hesitant and bemused detachment about the Stone. She is certainly interested in it and all that concerns it, but we never see her trying to *organize* it. Her reaction to Montague's chipping at the Stone to derive a replica of it is that such an act is not decent. She seems to have an almost innate awareness of the holy that the mercenary Montague completely lacks. She also seems to be plagued with a restlessness that will not be satisfied by any human means, even the attentions of her suitor Frank Lindsay. The point about Chloe, of course, is that she, alone among the characters, is entirely devoted to the Stone without the least rag of self-interest. At one point this devotion may take the form of leaping at Sir Giles in a fury not unlike Christ's with the money changers: the disgust of purity in the presence of sacrilege. At another it may take the form of utter submission, as when she and Lord Arglay make their first attempt to retrieve Pondon from the past in which he seems to have got stuck by Sir Giles' machinations with the Stone.

In this incident, several items are worth noting. For one thing, at the same time as Lord Arglay and Chloe are at his chambers at Lancaster Gate attempting to see what they can do for Pondon (they have one of the copies of the Stone with them), Sir Giles and his friend Palliser are attempting to use the Stone to discern what Lord Arglay may be thinking. All they can conjure, as they strain to peer into his thoughts, is the image of Chloe. This leads them to conclude the obvious: he is obsessed, presumably sexually, with his secretary, and Chloe is all that is in his mind. The thought occurs to Sir Giles that surely the Lord Chief Justice of England can't be *that* obsessed—but then why can they only conjure Chloe as they try to read his mind? The one thing that cannot be true, in Sir Giles' opinion, is that whatever this concentration on Chloe may be which he discerns in Lord Arglay, it certainly cannot be altruism. Here is a case in point of the ignorance and stultification of evil: evil simply cannot *see* into pure goodness. Altruism is opaque and incomprehensible to it. Tolkien touches on this same idea in his saga *The Lord of the Rings*, when the evil lord Sauron, for all of his diabolical insight, cannot at all guess the one, simple thing that is animating his enemies, namely, altruism. Evil cannot even imagine selflessness. " 'Do you mean to tell me Arglay can read my mind and I can't read his?' " (132) demands Sir Giles. It would seem to be so.

Further, in this incident it is worth noting the differing experiences that Lord Arglay and Chloe have as they each offer themselves, so to speak, to the Stone, in behalf of the unfortunate Pondon, trapped in the past into which Sir Giles has sent him. The experience is a dark one for both of them, as any serious experience of self-giving, or of bearing another's burdens, is bound to be at one point or another; but Chloe is sustained in the thick of it by the memory of Frank Lindsay, who, as her suitor, has been an embodiment of love to her. His kisses have been real, tangible tokens of the strongest power in the universe, namely, love. But then, gradually, these tokens themselves seem to be supplanted somehow by a hand and voice which turn out to be Lord Arglay's. It is as though his encouraging words to her, " 'Go on, child' ", are not mere articulated thoughts, but have the solidity and firmness of a man's hand—and that hand the hand of the Chief Justice of England. It is as though she is being helped further along on the way of love on which she has embarked, to lonelier regions where it will not be for her to have the delights, good and rich in themselves, of romantic love but rather to go alone, sustained by another mode of the same thing, namely, pure justice, which in the end is, of course, virtually synonymous with love.

She recalls the words in the title of Lord Arglay's work: *Organic Law*. It is organic law—the nature of our flesh-and-blood humanness, if we will—that she grow older and pass beyond the delights of youthful, physical dalliance. But love itself has not evaporated with the passing of dalliance, and she, apparently, is one of the ones chosen for the virginal way of proving and embodying and exhibiting what love is. Because she has known the attentions of a man, she knows something of what she will be forsaking, but she is also reminded that whatever this organic law may be that makes us grow older and less desirable physically, it is not a bad thing. If it exists at all, it is synonymous with the law of the whole pattern and is therefore joyous. She is sustained, on the immediate level, by Lord Arglay now, but even he appears in her vision as merely a present case in point of all the protectors of justice down through the centuries— all good rulers and magistrates. The suggestion in all of this, of course, is that in the end justice and love are one and the same thing but that in the ordinary run of things we do not always see this and that justice must commonly appear to be a colder and more abstract thing than love. Hajji has predicted of Chloe that " 'Allah shall bring you to the Resignation' " (45). In a vision he has seen Allah's name in Chloe's forehead and knows thereby that she is a vessel chosen for the return of the Unity that even he, for all of his loyalty and integrity in defending that Unity, cannot be. The Resignation of which he speaks is of course that resignation so abhorrent to the worldly mind but which is spoken of by all the saints as the key to bliss. It refers, apparently, to the act of assent that one makes with one's own will, which says, in effect, "The pattern is perfect; the Dance is joy; the Will of God is my delight." In other words, "Be it unto me according to thy word."

Lord Arglay, for his part, is sustained in his experience of offering himself to the Stone in behalf of Pondon by what we might call his sheer generosity of spirit, and even his scepticism. He is by now prepared to acknowledge that indeed some power does rest in the Stone, and his lifelong habit of serving justice rather than wresting it about to make legality serve his own ends disposes him now to a similar attitude towards the Stone and whatever it might represent. The thing paramount in his consciousness is rescuing Pondon from the injustice that has been done to him, so that even though he has no disposition towards "faith" that might assist him in doing some generous act in service to this mysterious Stone, yet this inner commitment to justice brings him to the same point as though he had faith in the Stone, or as though he loved Pondon. The act which results is the same. Somehow faith and justice and love seem to be running together in the same channel.

A preliminary but sharp test of Chloe's pure fidelity to the Stone rather than to anything it can do, much less anything she can do with it, comes when Frank asks her to use it to help him with his exams, since it clearly would be effective in recalling things to one's mind. She refuses. That would be to traffic in something holy. Frank is understandably offended, but there is nothing he can do. Presently, in a vision which seems to be granted to Chloe as in some way a consequence of this test, she sees all of history and religion and nature (chiefs, priests, gods, and beasts) and sees that what appears tumultuous and bloody is actually all crying out in praise to the Eternal One. Above the jumble sits a king on a sapphire throne, and on his head is the crown with the Stone. He lifts his hand, and "there leapt upon her from it a blinding light, and at once her whole being felt a sudden devastating pain and then a sense of satisfaction entire and exquisite, as if desires beyond her knowledge had been evoked and contented at once, a perfect apprehension, a longing and a fulfillment" (169). In our own story we would call this the Annunciation. For Chloe, as for the Virgin Mary, the power of the Most High has set her apart and filled her. But it has been preceded, as it were, by a crux in which she is tested to see whether her resignation to the Stone can be modified by her natural wish to help her suitor Frank. She passes the test. She also passes a further one in which the General Secretary of the National Transport Union, Mr. Theophilus Merridew, tries to get Frank to persuade Chloe to sell him her copy of the Stone in the interest of instant and cheap national transportation. But again, she will have nothing to do with these vastly plausible but worldly consider-

ations. Plausibility and efficiency and common sense
pale and flee in the presence of whatever it is that Chloe
is keeping and pondering in her heart.

A grimmer test comes presently when Lord Arglay refuses to use his copy of the Stone to rescue Chloe from
a savage assault of temptation brought against her by Sir
Giles. We witness her coming very close to turning into
a vixen as the desire to possess and control the Stone
grows upon her, but she is helped and delivered by Lord
Arglay's presence and words. Williams even refers to
Lord Arglay as "a Joseph" sheltering and sustaining a
Mary, and watching Chloe's progress towards the end of
desire. She may not be "his", any more than Mary could
be Joseph's for the time being: but his task is to shelter
and sustain her.

As the action progresses, the sense in which this Stone
may be said to be the End of Desire becomes gradually
clearer. It entails a notion that is all too frighteningly suggested, not only in Williams' scheme of things but also in
the Christian scheme, namely, that we will all get what
we want in the end. Whatsoever a man soweth, and so
forth. We will be judged according to how we have re-
sponded to whatever light we did have. We might see
this Stone, then, as a sort of focusing, for purposes of the
tale here, of the Destiny that hangs over us all—not in the
dispassionate and crushing sense in which the Greeks understood Fate but rather in the sense, certainly implicit in
the Gospel, of our being rewarded with the fruit of the
choices we have made. It is the very same Destiny (or
Judgment, or Will of God, or End) that results in bliss for
one man and wrath for another. Sir Giles will have what
he wants, but what he wants, because it is predatory, will
turn and gobble him up. Lord Arglay will have what he

wants, which is real justice: he may not, as an agnostic, yet see the connection between justice and anything that could be called Divine Love; but nevertheless, every act and attitude and choice of his is on the side of equity and generosity and integrity, and so he will find himself rewarded with the fruit of all this when he comes to the End of his desire. "End", of course, is to be understood here in the sense of *telos*, that is, fulfillment, or goal, or purpose. It is as though this tremendous and awesome canopy of potentialities that religious people call Judgment, and that Christians believe to be synonymous with the Divine Love, has been dropped into the laps of the people in *Many Dimensions* in the form of a small stone. How they react to it, and the effects of their reactions, are disquietingly close to what we would all suspect to be the case in our own story. As in every story he ever wrote, Williams manipulates what on the surface appears to be the occult or the bizarre, and we find that it is nothing at all but a flawless mirror of our own existence. Whether the reflections we see in this mirror look more like Sir Giles, or Angus Sheldrake, or Lord Arglay, or Chloe is, alas, up to us.

A further and most severe test comes to Chloe when Prince Ali Mirza Khan is persuaded by Sir Giles to burgle her house and take her copy of the Stone from her by force. The scene is in the best tradition of burglary thrillers: the darkness, Chloe in her bed, the doorknob turning, the sinister presence moving stealthily closer and closer, Chloe's hand grasping the Stone. Her experience, both of sheer fright and of temptation to use the Stone to bring about some rescue, grows more and more intense until this is the language we find: "And being in an agony she prayed more earnestly" (218). This language, lifted verbatim from Gethsemane, did not appear here by chance. Just as the Servant of the Divine Will once upon a time found himself in an agony of earnest prayer as evil drew near in its assault on him, so Chloe is being taken more and more into the mysteries of the fellowship of that suffering which attends this offering of oneself for the good of others.

What happens at this point might, in a lesser story, be accused of being a case in point of the *deus ex machina*. There is a flash of light (we suppose it must be the Prince's torch being switched on), and a note of music, as though the trumpet at Solomon's palace gate had sounded. What is happening in London is that the local police constable is blowing his whistle upon finding the body of a man, scorched as though by lightning, lying at the gate of the house where Chloe lies. The Stone is its own custodian. The Holiness of which it is the token has indeed intervened to ward off this assault.

We learn presently a bit more about the Stone from Hajji Ibrahim. He speaks to Lord Arglay and Chloe about a union between Chloe and the Stone "by which the other Hiddenness is made manifest" (227). This turns out to refer to a speck of light in the Ring of Solomon. It is "that Light which is the Spirit of Creation, the Adornment of the Unity, the Knowledge of the Loveliness, the Divine Image in the mirror of the worlds just and true" (227). Apparently this Light resides somehow in the Stone and in all the copies of the Stone, and its power "is in the soul and body of any who have sought the union with the Stone" (228). This, of course, is the language of the occult, or at least the remotely arcane; but we hardly need to translate it at all in order to see that some such language might be used to refer to anyone at all who will do what the plain teaching of the New Testament enjoins on all Christians, namely, to submit to the Divine Will as Christ did, in an act of self-giving. What follows upon such an act is our initiation into "the fellowship of his sufferings", or our "baptism into Christ", or our "crucifixion" with him. The New Testament does not spell out just exactly what this experience will feel like; but certainly, if we take note of the language which the saints have reached for, we will see no oddity in any single one of the phrases that Williams uses to describe this Light supposed to have rested in Solomon's Ring.

We do come upon one oddity at this point, however: the Hajji has recognized that Chloe has gone beyond the rest of them somehow, because of her total submission to "the Will of That which is behind the Stone", and he pronounces woe on her if she ever reneges. She cries out in fright, but Lord Arglay encourages her by saying, " 'I am at the moment, as you say, the Light that is in the Stone' " (229). This confuses the Hajji, naturally enough; but Lord Arglay's point is that at least for the moment the thing of which he is the custodian and the embodiment for England, namely, justice, will support and protect Chloe. He personally will do this, of course, as Saint Joseph watched over the Virgin during her months of strange union with the Most High, but he recognizes that it is not so much he as the Justice whose name he bears for the time being for the sake of England.

The pace of outside events picks up as the narrative moves towards its climax, with the murder at Brighton of Reginald Montague, and Mr. Garterr Browne, the Home Secretary and a thoroughgoing secularist, attempting to discredit the Stone at the same time as he secretly wonders whether it might not be a nice talisman to have after all. It is Sir Giles Tumulty's experience, however, which presently stands out in stark and appalling contrast to Chloe's. He too is drawn into the Stone—or rather, "sucked into the convolutions of the Stone" (244). He is granted power to see because he possesses one of the types of the Stone, but his vision is a horrifying one. The same light that Chloe experiences as ecstasy leaps out at him, and he screams in pain, not bliss. It divides "nerve from nerve, sinew from sinew, bone from bone. Everywhere the sharp torment caught him" (245). The point is the obvious one: to good souls, the light of Truth is nothing but joy; to evil souls, it is destruction. It is the same light, of course; but how we experience it depends on what we are made of. Sir Giles is found in his room, twisted, pierced, and burnt all over, "as if by innumerable needle-points of fire" (246).

The last we see of Chloe's suitor Frank Lindsay is his shabby act in stealing Chloe's copy of the Stone from her handbag and then trying to sell it, like Judas Iscariot, to the Transport Union. The scene in which Chloe asks him to give it back to her reveals a great deal about Lindsay. He has known Chloe and has loved her, so there is a poignance about how narrowly he misses the reward that real love would have given him. He and Chloe have been intimate, but have never "known" each other in the ancient sexual sense of that word. There is a long and difficult paragraph in which Williams seems to be saying that Chloe has now passed beyond Frank to another mode of knowing the fullness of love, and that Lord Arglay is now her protector and guardian (not her lover) as she enters into union with the Divine Will. Frank cannot know what is happening, since his motives are all jumbled up with selfishness and weakness and deceit, and this is not permitted in the sacred precincts where this union takes place. (We recall that only the pure in heart see God.) The sexual act—"that full and sovereign union", as Williams calls it here—is a sort of type and concentrating of all beauty and blessing and liberty, and Williams' language here could very easily be taken in an antinomian sense—that is, the notion that when lofty souls have reached a certain point of initiation or illumination, then nothing is denied them. In religious history this notion has with tedious regularity translated itself into lechery. But Williams himself, both in his writings and in his personal life, gainsaid this. It would appear that he means no more than what the New Testament means when it says that to the pure all things are pure, or what Saint Augustine meant when he said, in effect, love God and do what you want. The crucial thing here is that it is the *pure* who are being spoken of. It is those who *love God* who know things the rest of us cannot imagine. It is not a warrant for indulgence.

In any event, this is the last we see of Frank. He refuses to return the holy thing to Chloe and attempts to sell it for money to the union. But somehow it disappears, and the transaction breaks down in quarreling and recrimination.

Meanwhile, at Lord Arglay's house at Lancaster Gate, Chloe makes a final offer of herself to be the vessel of the Stone's return to itself, or, put another way, to be the vessel of the restoring of the Unity. Inevitably the language Williams reaches for in this part of the narrative echoes the language we all know from that other narrative in which a woman consented to be the vessel of the restoring of the Unity—the knitting back up of the fabric torn at the Fall and now to be restored at the Incarnation when we see Godhead and manhood perfectly united. We hear Chloe saying, in answer to his question as to whether she will be the path for the Stone, " 'That is as you will have me' " (257), an almost direct echo of the Virgin's " 'Be it unto me according to thy word.' " It is interesting, but not odd, that the great task must be done by "the weaker vessel", the woman, and not by the man—even the Lord Chief Justice of England. He can only be a watcher and a guardian.

At the point when Chloe actually begins her act of self-offering, we find that the way Williams describes things echoes Christ's self-offering as well as the Virgin's. Remembering Frank Lindsay's perfidy, she says, " 'Poor darling . . . he didn't, he couldn't, understand' " (250), and she offers him and his failure, along with all others who have thus failed, including Sir Giles, in an act of intercession to "That which" the Stone represents, namely, the Divine Mercy. "Her heart gathered all." We do not mistake things if we seem to hear "Father, forgive them for they know not what they do", and "Mary kept all these things and pondered them in her heart." It is not a question of Williams having blundered into a confusion, with Chloe standing as a blurry allegorical figure for either Mary or Christ. Rather, Williams would point out that both at the Annunciation and at the Cross, complete submission and self-offering were asked. And, to carry it half a step further, Williams would also hope that we could see the experience of every good soul here, not just that of one select soul picked out for a bizarre transaction with the Divine. Nothing happens to Chloe that does not happen to any human being who is willing to be the vessel of the Divine Love. The act of submission turns into an immolation, which has the double effect of joy for the soul making the offering (the saints tell us this) and joy for those for whom the offering is made (any one of us who has ever been helped in any way by someone else's kindness or generosity or "going to bat" for us will testify here). The "death" turns into life all around. Easter follows Good Friday. The Assumption is the climax of the Virgin's story, according to very ancient and widespread Tradition.

The four men watching Chloe exhibit the reactions proper to their character. The Hajji rejoices at the return of the Unity he has so nobly worshipped for so long. The mayor of Rich, also present, is still thinking of the people who might have been helped if they had cut up and distributed the Stone—but the hint here is that at least his interest, misbegotten though it might be, is somehow generous. Oliver Doncaster, the young man who had found Mrs. Sheldrake's Stone in the first place, concentrates on Chloe, like one of the shepherds at the manger looking at this mother in this odd place. Lord Arglay alone *sees* the return of the Unity, as though all aspirations of all men, and all their desperate efforts to find and seize power and joy, now flow back to the source through the vessel offered for this purpose. Indeed, it seems to Arglay's watching eyes that "what the Stone had been she now was" (261). What had been enshrined in a bit of rock (a tablet of stone, we might venture) now appears at work in living human flesh. What mere Stone had proclaimed and heralded is now unfurled and incarnate. Lord Arglay seems to see now what the Hajji had earlier seen, namely, the Tetragrammaton appearing on Chloe's forehead. She bears the name of God, as do all the sons of God restored through the operations of his mercy.

The ordeal, for it is an ordeal, requires Chloe's life. She falls into a sort of trance, or coma, for nine months (nine months), at the end of which she dies. The conversation between Oliver Doncaster and Lord Arglay as they go to and from the cremation stresses what we all know by now: " 'May not this child have found a greater thing than either you or I could give her?' " (268).

In what might seem a melancholy anticlimax, we find Lord Arglay in the very final few lines hunting up the telephone number of a typewriting agency. He needs another assistant and typist for his manuscript on organic law now that Chloe is dead.

We might protest that this is a petty and superfluous detail for Williams to have tacked onto the end of so haunting a narrative. But the whole point, of course, is that if anything Chloe has done has any rag of legitimacy, and if there is anything true about all law—mere legality, *or* the "organic" law of the universe—then the best thing anyone in the world can do is to get on with the work he is supposed to be doing. Our life and our work have been hallowed and glorified, if any of the story is true. Things did not come to a halt with the haunting narrative of the Gospel: they began in earnest.

4

The Place of the Lion

The obvious question with which to begin an inquiry into *The Place of the Lion* is, What does the title mean? To answer this, we must follow Williams as he picks up an idea as old as Plato.

Plato taught that behind the visible world lies the invisible world of "Ideas". That is, behind every chair that we might come upon, regardless of whether it is a gilded and damasked Louis XV affair or a stump used by a hillbilly, lies the *Idea* of "chairness". There is, so to speak, an eternal Chair from which all chairs proceed. Every chair is simply a case in point of that chairness.

This applies to everything in our world, on this Platonic view. A table is an instance of the Idea of tables, or of the Table. An alp, a crag in the West Highlands, a knoll in the Cotswolds, are all instances of "mountainness". A man and a woman are cases in point of maleness and femaleness. The visible items in front of our eyes keep pointing us to the reality that lies behind them.

A point of view like this will affect a man's whole out-look. It will reverse his natural inclination to suppose that what we see about us is the real world and that if there is an unseen world somewhere it is slightly less real, or at least thinner and more ill defined. On the contrary, says the Platonist, if there is anything that may be called unreal, it is this transitory world of mere appearances that we live in. This is all mortal and to that extent "unreal". The realm of reality, and incidentally our own final homeland, is eternal and invisible.

Williams, like any Christian, shared Plato's notion of the eternal lying behind what we see, but like any Christian he would have argued that doctrines like the creation and the Incarnation prevent Christians from quite sharing Plato's notion that this visible realm is not quite real. God did not create an illusion at the creation, says Christianity, nor did he involve himself in a mere masquerade or apparition at the Incarnation. Somehow this visible world *is* real, on the Christian view.

This is all somewhat beside the point for us here, since a poet or a novelist is free to use any picture of things he wishes so long as it helps him to get the exact effect he wants. He appeals to our imagination. This does not mean that he presents a false world. It means that he looks at the everyday world of our experience through a lens of his own choosing. You choose a lens, not to falsify the picture you are trying to get but to get a special angle or distance or color so that people will notice what they had stopped noticing because they had got used to it.

The picture which Williams chose for *The Place of the Lion* is this Platonic one. The special thing he does with this picture is to have the Ideas (or "archetypes", or "principles", as Williams prefers to call them) suddenly push through the scrim that separates appearance from reality and land out here where we can see them.

We get our first clue about this in the story when we find a lioness sniffing the air of Hertfordshire from behind a hedge. This is very unsettling, but we are still on believable ground: some careless travelling circus might have let one of its cats escape.

The ground presently begins to seem less certain when Anthony Durrant and his friend Quentin Sabot, who have been out walking in the country, spot the lioness in the road and take refuge in the porch of a cottage behind a nearby gate. By the time we get through the next few minutes the whole stage is set for the drama. As with all opening scenes, if we pay attention we will amass a great number of cues as to where the author is going to take us. The curtain goes up on *Macbeth*, for example, and we find witches on stage. *Hamlet* opens with news of a ghost. The scene may take only a few moments, but we may be sure the author did not stumble sideways into his story. He designed that scene with the greatest care, the way a composer chooses the opening for his symphony. All follows from this.

After giving us our initial glimpse of this lioness, Williams has shifted his narrative to the two friends. The transition occurs quite neatly when we see the lioness stiffen as though she scents some prey or enemy, and "almost a mile away Quentin Sabot jumped from the gate on which he had been sitting" (9). It will turn out that Quentin is very much a prey and an enemy of all that this lioness represents.

In the conversation between Anthony and Quentin in the opening scene we will probably not pick up anything special on a first reading. It is only when we turn back to these pages after having watched the whole drama that we can see what Williams has been up to.

Quentin is the more nervous of the two young men. When a posse of local men come along with lanterns, pitchforks, and rifles and announce that there is a lioness roaming about, Quentin's first reaction is, " 'The devil there is!' " (11). Anthony's is, " 'I see—yes. That does seem a case for warning people.' " When Anthony asks Quentin presently what he would do if the lioness showed up, Quentin says " 'Bolt' ".

This all seems normal enough. The trouble is that in a Williams novel we are deprived of the luxury of supposing that things are ever at all "normal" if by that we mean safe, manageable, and unimportant. The blanket of the commonplace is whipped away, and suddenly everything is exposed, all jutting and stark where it had just now been shrouded and softened by ordinariness. The fact that Quentin is nervous may appear harmless enough ordinarily, but it is very far from appearing harmless in the glare of this tale. Like psychoanalysis and the Last Judgment, Williams' fiction exposes with terrible clarity small things like someone's being highstrung.

Quentin is jumpy because he is running away from things. Worse, he has always run away from things, and in Williams' world this route lands in hell since hell is the vacuity that drops away at the end of all flight from sheer fact. All the illusions and dodges that we throw up to shelter ourselves from the plain truth have the effect finally of unfitting us to cope with that truth; and if the

City of God is the final Fact behind all facts, then we had better get ourselves accustomed to coping with facts as they come to us rather than warding them off or flying from them. So might run a summary of what happens to the characters in Williams who refuse even to attempt the courage and candor demanded by reality. I am a coward? Then let me at least make a beginning by naming this bald fact: I am a coward. To that extent at least I will have made a brave attempt to face reality. Let me not muffle it with euphemism and tergiversation.

We may see this tendency growing and hardening in Quentin when we listen to him later in the story giving an account of what he and Anthony saw that first evening in the countryside. The lioness had come along the road to the gate of the cottage where the two friends were hiding, and at the same time a man had paced out onto the lawn from around the corner of the cottage. The lioness leaps over the gate, there is a scuffle, and when the dust settles they see the man lying quietly on the ground, "and standing over him the shape of a full-grown and tremendous lion" (14). The lioness is no-where to be seen. Quentin blurts out presently, " 'O my God, Anthony, let's get out of it. Let's take the risk and run' " (15). Anthony, on the other hand, feels bound by the concern all decent men ought to feel for the prone figure on the ground. " 'We can't leave him like this.' "

In his account of this later, Quentin says, " 'We were not frightened: I am not frightened: but we were startled. And the old man fell. And we did not see clearly.' The sentences came out in continuous barks" (51). Quentin is acting like all the jackals and hyenas in animal fables: devious, skulking, defensive. When Mr. Foster, the one listening to his account, says, " 'And will you see clearly?' " Quentin cries, " 'No! . . . I will not. I will see nothing of it, if I can help it. I won't, I tell you. And you can't make me. The lion himself can't make me' " (51).

This throws rather a bleak light on Quentin's agitation and timorousness. He *won't* see? This is serious.

The frightening implication in Williams' picture is that when these small natural tendencies harden by someone's refusal of various chances to be set free from them, they become like prison bars, and then the man cannot get free. But the bars are of his own forging. They started out soft and malleable. We watch Quentin quail further and further into his prison of fear, away from the bright Reality that is breaking through around them all. What was a bark a moment ago turns into a howl when Mr. Foster asks him if he actually thinks he is going to escape from the lion if the lion is really on his track. " 'It isn't on my track, I tell you', Quentin howled. 'How can it be? There isn't any—there never was any. I don't believe in these things. There's London and us and the things we know' " (52). What was understandable fear a moment ago has turned into a frenzied denial of almost everything, and the denial of everything is eventually hell in Williams' scheme.

We see something of Anthony's frame of mind when he observes at this point, " 'That is at least true. . . . There is London and us and what we know. But it can't hurt to find out exactly what we know, can it?' " (52). What might seem a slight difference in style or inclination between the two friends here is really a continental divide. Anthony's willingness to accept plain facts and proceed from there leads towards joy: Quentin's flight leads towards wrath.

But this is to dilate too much. Perhaps the single most noticeable characteristic of Williams' prose is its "emblematic" quality. Like those complicated symbolic picture-and-text combinations called emblems, so popular in seventeenth-century England, Williams' prose almost compels a phrase-by-phrase commentary ranging over the whole field of morals, theology, and psychology. Suffice it to say of Quentin that as the narrative unrolls we watch him go from bad to worse. He goes from hardly noticeable anxiety to fear to anger to frenzy and finally to cringing and skulking in a ditch under a hedge. He is saved by a woman who is the main character, herself badly in need of salvation, and who can only barely bring herself to put up with his snivelling. She saves him: herself she cannot save.

The candor, modesty, courage, and agility that we begin to see in Anthony in the opening scene burgeon and leap until we rub our eyes in the final scene at the spectacle of Anthony appearing like Adam in Paradise. He is not an allegory of Adam. Rather, Williams would seem to say that the authority exercised over the creation by Adam in Eden is the patrimony of all men. Adam undoubtedly enjoys a primacy of dignity by virtue of his appointment as father of the whole race; but all his sons are his heirs. It is evil that has trapped us into the poverty and impotence visible in Quentin, but this is precisely the *loss* of the inheritance. We come into our own only when we come into that inheritance again. Anthony seems to be well along the way when we first encounter him.

For example, Quentin suggests in the opening lines that they keep walking and let the local bus overtake them rather than waiting for it, since, says he, " 'That's our direction' ". Anthony says, " 'The chief use of the material world . . . is that one can, just occasionally, say that with truth' " (9). It turns out soon enough that the material world does appear to be overtaking them and that unless they are to be overwhelmed by it they had better know what its "use" is, and to say, "that's our direction". At least one of its legitimate uses is to carry us towards Reality, even if that Reality ramps upon us like a lion.

Presently we see more of Anthony. He greets the news of the lioness with curiosity and equanimity, and his first instinct, unlike Quentin's, is to offer to help the posse. It is only a straw, but it is a straw in a very big wind, namely, the wind of Charity. Quentin is all for saving their own hides. That does not occur to Anthony.

After the posse has gone on, Quentin, referring back to something the two friends had been talking about at lunch just before the narrative opens, says, apropos the peril that has suddenly risen, " 'I hope you still think that ideas are more dangerous than material things' " (12). It is all very well to advance that notion in an easy discussion in a safe place. But when a lioness appears things appear in a somewhat different light.

Anthony replies, " 'Yes, I do' " (12).

This brings us to the crux of what is happening in this odd tale. Who is this lioness? Or, more importantly, who is this lion who appears to have swallowed up the lioness herself?

He is one of the Platonic Ideas, or principles. Here is the most succinct statement about them in the book. Mr. Foster is speaking:

This world is created, and all men and women are created, by the entrance of certain great principles into aboriginal matter. We call them by cold names; wisdom and courage and beauty and strength and so on, but actually they are very great and mighty Powers. It may be they are the angels and archangels of which the Christian Church talks. . . . And when That which is behind them intends to put a new soul into matter it disposes them as it will, and by a peculiar mingling of them a child is born. . . . In the animals they are less mingled, for there each is shown to us in his own becoming shape; those Powers are the archetypes of the beasts. . . . Now this world in which they exist is truly a real world, and to see it is a very difficult and dangerous thing [53].

The man whom Anthony and Quentin have seen pace onto the darkened lawn at the cottage, and who has been left lying on the ground after the scuffle with the lioness from which the lion emerges, is one Berringer. He is a cult figure in the neighborhood, and the matter of these archetypal Platonic principles has been his "specialty". He thinks about it all the time. We find out what has happened as Mr. Foster continues:

But as I told you just now, since these powers exhibit their nature much more singly in the beasts, so there is a peculiar sympathy between the beasts and them. Generally, matter is separation between all these animals which we know and the powers beyond. But if one of those animals should be brought within the terrific influence of one particular idea—to call it that— very specially felt through a man's intense concentration on it . . . the matter of the beast might be changed into the image of the idea, and this world, following that one, might be all drawn into that other world. I think this is happening [54].

Because of Mr. Berringer's concentration, a lioness straying from an itinerant show is "drawn" towards him and thence into archetypal "lion-ness", which is the bodying forth of the principle, or Idea, of strength and majesty. If the process were to go on, presumably all lionesses and lions would be absorbed back into the Strength and Majesty that they all embody and exhibit in a sort of apocalyptic return to the unity from which all the dazzling diversity of creation springs.

It will be remembered that Williams is not writing theology here. He is not advancing all this as orthodox Christian doctrine. He is drawing a picture, as all fiction and parable and poetry do, that furnishes us with one way of fancying things. The protest that Williams is teaching cabbalistic or neo-Platonic lore here is as misbegotten as is the protest that Christ was teaching vegetation-cycle myths when he compared the kingdom of heaven to a seed or a field. In this picture we can see quite vividly certain notions that Christians do have about this world, namely, that it all did spring by creative design and energy from a single source, and that appearances do seem to suggest something true about the eternal world, and that it will all be wrapped up and dissolved at the end, with some whole new order of things emerging on the far side of that cataclysm. The Bible does not vouchsafe us more than the most scant and tantalizing hints about the huge and complicated process of creation. We have a great deal of room to imagine how it all might have come to pass. Orthodoxy would seem to bind us only to saying that it was all made from nothing by the

Most High and that he designed and controlled the process by which it all took shape. The question we need to ask about fiction is how well it does the job of startling our imaginations so that we rub our eyes and see, for the first time or the thousandth, what has been staring at us all along. If it takes flying carpets, or the god Pan, or giants named Despair, or Platonic lions, so much the better.

The lion, then, seems to embody the principle of strength and majesty. At one point we see Anthony reflecting on "that immense and royal beast . . . majestic, awful, complete, gazing directly in front of it, with august eyes. And huge—huger than any lion Anthony had ever seen or dreamt of: The lions he had seen had been a kind of unsatisfactory yellow, but this in spite of the moonlight had been more like gold, with a terrific and ruddy mane covering its neck and shoulders. A mythical, and archetypal lion" (38, 39). Later, when it reappears, Anthony and Quentin fall back, "appalled by the mere effluence of strength that issued from it. It was moving like a walled city, like the siege-towers raised against Nineveh or Jerusalem" (67).

Late in the story we come upon a scene which throws light back on the rather bewildering menagerie that troops across the stage in the tracks of the lioness. Snakes and butterflies have appeared, and also an enormous bird which is either a pterodactyl or an eagle, depending on who is looking at it. Besides these there has been a flock of sheep nibbling away innocently in the field. What are they all?

On one accounting they are nothing more than they are in the ordinary world. But then, what *are* they in the ordinary world? What is an animal? If one thinks, as

Williams did, that the great romp we call creation is a solemn pageant and not a mere machine or mess, then one will suppose that all the figures in that pageant are significant. We do not need to flatten out the animals into mere allegories to suspect that what we see in them touches on vast mysteries that zoology has not completely unpacked for us. Our imaginations, if no other faculty in us, will never stop seeing something *regal* in a lion's head and face and mane and bearing. But zoology does not concern itself with the category "regal". By the same token, we look at the faces of sharks, rabbits, eagles, beagles, and fawns, and we will not believe that these creatures are not *like* what we see in those faces. They move across the stage of this world trailing clouds of *something*. To quash this hunch we have to silence every signal that our imaginations put out.

The passage in the story upon which all else turns, and which throws light on all of this business about the animals, occurs in a vision which Anthony has as he gazes from the window of his London flat. We cannot hope to keep track of all these animals, and of Williams' peculiar language, without knowing what this vision means. To deal with it at this point is to jump ahead in the story, but without it we are making bricks without straw.

The vision occurs in chapter fifteen, "The Place of Friendship", and the event which has immediately preceded it is the rescuing of Quentin from his terror by Damaris Tighe, whose effort in his behalf constitutes one of the steps in her own salvation.

Anthony has come to London, to the flat which he and Quentin have shared, to look for Quentin to see if he can help him. Quentin is not there, as we know, although Anthony searches diligently on the chance that Quentin might be hiding. But no. So Anthony sits down in a chair and gives himself up to a reverie. He gets to pondering the meaning of friendship, since friendship touches on the only thing of any final importance in this whole world, namely, Charity. Friendship is one of the ways, along with romantic love and familial love and plain works of mercy, in which Charity presents itself to us. What better place for Anthony to reflect on it than in this room which is so full of all the books and papers and pipes that bespeak the friendship of these two men. It all passes before Anthony's memory, and one of the things that takes shape in his mind is what a good and worthy fellow Quentin is. We readers have not seen much but querulousness and cowardice in Quentin, but love covers a multitude of sins, and through the generous eyes of Anthony's love for Quentin we see a man who has all sorts of gratifying qualities. This itself, of course, is a case in point of what the Divine Love does for every man. It knows what is in him, both the good and the evil that ruins that good, and it will go to any length to rescue a man from ruin. As Anthony sits there and thinks, it occurs to him that this odd thing called friendship, which is so commonplace and at the same time touches on the highest mysteries of human existence, is either truth or illusion. It cannot be both. "Anthony had long since determined on which side his own choice lay: he had accepted those exchanges, so far as mortal frailty could, as being of the nature of final and eternal being" (182). Looking around at all the familiar tokens of his friendship with Quentin, Anthony has sensed that friendship is one of the means of being of use to the troubled world.

That, briefly, is one way of getting at the kernel of the drama in this narrative. Williams is not really interested in bizarre interpretations of Platonic or neo-Platonic notions except insofar as they, like any colorful metaphor, help us to see what lies in front of us.

Presently Anthony goes to the window and looks out. In the intense clarity of the vision that is upon him he is able to see the very bricks and towers of London for what they are, in the same way that he had just now been able to see the books and pipes lying about the room for what they are, namely, tokens. Not symbols, since it is all perfectly concrete and real, but tokens, in the sense that books and pipes and bricks do, in fact, belong to concerns bigger than themselves. Friendship, architecture, engineering, civil life, human life — what categories shall we find to help us arrange our experience?

To Anthony's gaze, the bricks of the London houses suggest strength. The towers and chimneys thrust up with soaring energy, and the noises of London seem to join in a "litany of energy", which itself harmonizes into a "choric hymn, sounding almost like the subdued and harmonious thunder of the lion's roar" (183). The whole thing seems orchestrated with marvelous subtlety, and as he stands there contemplating the man-made pattern in front of him, his vision stretches to encompass two other regions where we can see strength ordered and harmonized with wonderful subtlety, namely, the natural creation and the human body with its "nerves, sinews, bones, muscle, skin and flesh, heart and a thousand organs and vessels. They were his strength, yet his strength parcelled and ordered" (184).

Two vast principles are clearly at work in things: strength and subtlety. For Anthony, those two principles have arrived on the stage of the story by this time in the form of a lion and an immense serpent. But there is more. What shall we call the principle that takes these immense eternal qualities and translates them into "the blue of the sky, the red of bricks, the slenderness of the spires"? Pythagoras suggested that it might be number, but, thinks Anthony, if that is so, then we need a name for the way number presents itself to our senses and our emotions. Aha: beauty. There is the quality we want. There is the name for it. And, as it happens, beauty has long since fluttered onto the stage of the story on the wings of an immense butterfly.

There is yet one more property that seems to be at work along with strength, subtlety, and beauty. "One and indivisible, those three mighty Splendours yet offered themselves each to other—and had a fourth property also, and that was speed" (184).

At this point the vision gets very visionary indeed, and in order to stay abreast of things we must work as hard as we are asked to do with the writings of Ezekiel or Saint John the Divine, and even then we are very far from being sure that we have not fallen altogether by the wayside.

Here is one way of attaching this swirling vision to the action. Anthony has just now reflected that friendship is either true or illusory. He has settled it that he will choose to believe that it is true. Hence he will see friendship as supplying a trustworthy clue to the meaning of life. In his vision the world resolves itself into a lovely harmony, exhibiting properties of strength, subtlety, beauty, and speed. Three of those properties have broken through into the ordinary workaday world in the form of a lion, a serpent, and a butterfly. What creature will embody the fourth?

Anthony reflects that, no matter how mortal he and Quentin themselves may be, or their books and pipes, yet that which stands between them is real, solid, and lasting. It is friendship. That is the real thing in which he and Quentin and all their books and pipes seem to be rather fugitive participants. Friendship is "between" Anthony and Quentin, as beauty is "between" the strength and subtlety of the external world. The knitting together of two people in friendship, or of redness and clay in bricks, or of bricks and mortar in a wall is a beautiful thing, and this knitting, or harmonizing, seems to flash through the whole fabric of everything with infinite speed. There is nothing for it but to include at this point a rather long section from the vision:

> . . . He remembered again that it was not Quentin but the thing that was between him and Quentin, the thing that went with speed, and yet, speeding, was already at its goal, the thing that was for ever new and for ever old—*tam antiqua, tam nova*, that issued from its own ardent nest in its own perpetually renovated beauty, a rosy glow, a living body, the wonder of earthly love. The movement of the Eagle was the measure of truth, but the birth of some other being was the life of truth, some other royal creature that rose from fire and plunged into fire, momently consumed, momently reborn. Such was the inmost life of the universe, infinitely destroyed, infinitely recreated, breaking from its continual death into continual life, instinct with strength and subtlety and beauty and speed. But the blazing Phoenix lived and swept again to its nest of fire, and as it sank all those other Virtues went with it, themselves still, yet changed. The outer was with the inner; the inner with the outer [185].

So we have our creature. It is the eagle, which Anthony has seen soaring at infinite height over the countryside once or twice in the last few days, and which in ghastly parody has thrust its terrible beak into Damaris

Tighe's window in the form of a pterodactyl with rotten breath, because she, like all damned souls, experiences reality eventually as horror and death.

But what is this phoenix? Williams would seem to have muddled two great birds, the one from nature and the other from the ancient myth of the bird that consumes itself in a flash of fire once every 500 years and then rises newborn from its own ashes. But this is not the case. He is taking a liberty that anyone who tries to report a vision must take. Since no human language can quite snare and pin down a vision, we get this puzzling kaleidoscopic quality in visionary literature. Things won't stay put. One thing is always passing into another, only to reappear straightaway under its former guise. Wheels, flames, phials, bowls, heights, depths, noise, silence, light, dark, veiling and unveiling, bread and wine, body and blood—who can keep track of vision and sacrament and transfiguration and apocalypse? What mortal will undertake to give us a chart of it all?

The phoenix would seem to suggest the recurrent and perpetual renewing of what always appears to be fading and dying. Friends grow old and die. Buildings crumble. But friendship does not die, nor the imagination which has erected those buildings. Anthony and Quentin, alive briefly in the twentieth century, enter into the ancient bond of friendship enjoyed by David and Jonathan in their day. The buildings of London, surely not destined to last forever, nonetheless house civil life, as the houses in ancient Sumeria did. The superficial forms recur and recur: the thing itself does not die. The Phoenix gives us a picture of this.

But what of the eagle? Anthony has already seen it high overhead once or twice, and we have been given an early clue to it during a conversation between Anthony and a solitary young man named Richardson who works in a bookstore in Smetham. Richardson has shown Anthony a strange old book entitled *De Angeles*, by one Marcellus Victorinus of Bologna, and published in 1514. The topic of the book is angels. Ancient Tradition in the Church, stemming not so much from the Bible itself as from the sixth-century Pseudo-Dionysius, arranged angelic beings into nine ascending orders, reaching from angels and archangels at the bottom to seraphim at the top. In Marcellus' book the idea is advanced that these nine orders, or "Celestials", correspond to the Platonic Ideas. That is, the invisible and eternal realities lying behind appearances in Plato's scheme may turn out to be intelligent beings. They may be these Celestials of Christian vision. In Marcellus, there is also a dragon, which is not so much a creature as a freak, or even a negative thing—"The power of the Divine Ones arrogated to themselves for sinful purpose by violent men. Now this dragon which is the power of the lion is accompanied also by a ninefold order of spectres . . . and these spectres being invoked have power upon those who adore them and transform them into their very terrible likeness, destroying them with great moanings" (91).

In other words, Marcellus imagines an evil set of "spectres" who are destructive and who correspond to the heavenly hierarchy. We do not need to have rummaged in occult lore to know that for every good there is a corresponding evil: food is good, gluttony is bad; wine is good, bibulousness is bad; sex is good, lechery is bad; money is good, avarice is bad. In each case the evil is a botch or perversion of some good thing, and in each case it is a matter of some human being having subordinated himself to something that ought to be serving him.

This gives us a big clue in *The Place of the Lion*. There are all these great potentialities, or principles, or even Celestials if we will; and we have hints and reminders of them all in the animals in nature—strength in lions, subtlety in serpents, beauty in butterflies, and so forth. But the right order of things is that the beasts be subordinate to us men. If you find a man serving an ox somewhere, something has gone wrong. If you find a cult that worships an ass or a dog, something is topsy-turvy. You don't get wholeness and freedom and intelligence and joy from that mix.

By the same token, all these principles are made to serve us. Adam was given lordship over the beasts in Eden, and that was the sign of the right ordering of things. We humans must bear the yoke of authority. We must rule things, not be ruled by them. The thing that has gone wrong with a drunkard is that he has somehow become the servant of a thing that ought to be his servant. So it is with gluttons, lechers, misers, fools, pedants, cowards, and the rest of us who are tyrannized by things that ought to be our servants.

The eagle is the creature who soars high above all these lower things, and it turns out to be Anthony's special creature, as it were. Several pages are missing from this old book of Marcellus that Richardson and Anthony are discussing, and it is vexing because Marcellus has just embarked on an explanation of the significance of lions, serpents, and so forth, so that Anthony and Quentin are left in the dark about what the rest of the scheme might be. But then they come to a place which speaks of the eagle as somehow at the center point of the whole hierarchy. "For though these nine zones are divided into a trinity of trinities, yet after another fashion there are four

without and four within, and between them is the Glory
of the Eagle. For this is he who knows both himself and
the others, and is their own knowledge: as it is written
We shall know as are known [*sic*: this is a loose quote from
1 Cor 13:12, where Saint Paul, speaking of the final unveiling of things, says, "Then shall I know even as also
I am known"]—this is the knowledge of the Heavenly
Ones in the place of the Heavenly Ones, and it is called
the Virtue of the Celestials" (92).

The eagle seems to represent the proper office of man.
As the eagle poises and balances on its two mighty
wings, so man stands between the world of nature below
him and the heavenly order above him. He must suc-
cumb to neither but rather use both, as an eagle uses its
wings, to fly powerfully and fulfill his unique role in the
creation. The beasts must serve us, not we them; all good
qualities (strength, subtlety, beauty) must serve us, not
we them. Just as the Sabbath was made for man and not
man for the Sabbath, so it might be said that the whole
creation was made for man and not vice versa. Some
time later, Anthony is once more pondering his friendship with Quentin, and his thoughts run thus:

> Much was possible to a man in solitude: perhaps the
> final transmutations and achievements in the zones on
> the yonder side of the central Knowledge were possible
> only to the spirit in solitude. But some things were
> possible only to a man in companionship, and of these
> the most important was balance. No mind was so good
> that it did not need another mind to counter and equal
> it, and to save it from conceit and blindness and bigotry
> and folly. Only in such a balance could humility be
> found, humility which was a lucid speed to welcome
> lucidity whenever and wherever it presented itself.

How much he owed to Quentin! how much—not pride but delight urged the admission—Quentin owed to him! Balance—and movement in balance, as an eagle sails up on the wind—this was the truth of life, and beauty in life [187].

In yet another vision Anthony seems to be peering into an abyss. A great wind is blowing, and Anthony seems to be invited either to quail back from the edge into some safe niche or to yield to impulse and fling himself in. But neither of these options will do. "It was for him to rise above that strength of wind; whether he went down or up it must be by great volition . . . to be then consisted precisely in making an inevitable choice. . . . By a violent action of the will he . . . drew himself back both from safety and from abandonment" (114, 115). At this point he looks up and spies a winged form. "It was a giant of the eagle kind." The eagle's eyes pierce him, and seem to search and reveal his whole being to him. "His whole being grew one fiery shame, and while he endured to know even this because things were so and not otherwise, because to refuse to know himself as he was would have been a final outrage, a last attempt at flight from the Power that challenged him and in consequence an entire destruction by it" (115). Unlike Quentin, who has tried to fly from the challenge of the lion, Anthony knows that the only thing for it is to stand and face the whole reality of things, including the dreadful knowledge of himself (this is usually called repentance). When he does this, he finds that he is suddenly "riding in the void . . . poised in a vibration of peace. . . . Triumphant over the twin guardians of that place of realities, escaped from the lion and the serpent, he grew into his proper office" (115, 116).

It is only when we get this picture clear that we will be able to understand what is going on with all the other characters in the narrative. Anthony faces stark reality—first the lion, then vision after vision—and emerges in the final scene indistinguishable from Adam—glorious, masterly, authoritative, naming and ruling all the beasts. It is because "he had accepted the challenge of the Eagle" (155).

On the other hand we have the rest of the characters, each of whom in one way or another fails to be what human beings are supposed to be. Each one succumbs somehow to something less than himself. We have seen Quentin, of course, who is terrified of the lion. But before we indulge the luxury of pitying and patronizing Quentin, we realize uneasily that his fear is our own: all defenses and euphemisms and dodges and paperings over of the naked truth about ourselves partake of Quentin's fatal fear. It is ourselves that we see scrabbling and cowering under the hedge in the ditch.

Then there is Mr. Berringer. He is the one who paced onto the twilit lawn and was overpowered by the lion. He spends the rest of the book lying in his house in a coma. He has succumbed to the strength of the lion. He knew a great deal about neo-Platonic notions, but his knowledge was idolatrous, and he is overcome. He has long since lost the mastery that was his birthright as a man, and slips into this impotent torpor. Mr. Berringer's house is called The Joinings. This is appropriate, since it turns out to be the place where all the "joinings" between the seen and the unseen take place. "Something very queer seemed to be going on at that house in the country road. The lion—and the butterflies . . . and Mr. Berringer's curious collapse" (44). As far as the tale here is concerned, the point is that a *man* must be the bridge, or the door, or the point of passage for these joinings to take place. That is what is happening as far as the surface of the story goes. But Williams' point is always the moral one: What does it mean to be human? What is the office appointed to man? It is to be the steward, as it were, not only of the creation and of all lesser creatures, but also of all lesser things—passions, appetites, impulses, potentialities, and so on. The lecher succumbs to passion: the saint rules it and is thereby empowered and liberated. It is in the figure of Man that we see the joining of potentiality and intelligent will. An animal functions by mere appetite—lions tearing up smaller beasts at will, monkeys chattering, snakes stealing eggs, and so forth. We and we alone have the power of intelligent choice, and we may choose to sink to the level of the bestial and be ruled, or we may rise by the exercise of that appointed power of choice to our inheritance, namely, the majesty with which our father Adam was invested.

Mr. Berringer's house catches fire during the course of the book, and the fire burns on and on, strangely impervious to the efforts of the local firefighters. It is described again and again as looking like a *nest* of fire. Here is our phoenix imagery again, as though to say that this conflagration, this immolation even, in which Mr. Berringer succumbs, is to be seen as a sign: this is what happens to those who refuse the inheritance of Adam and who choose rather to be overcome by what is less than human. Insight and knowledge may all be very well, but more is needed, namely, the will to rule and not be ruled by passion. Mr. Berringer knew a very great deal, but his knowledge was impotent, and this is his end. But from these ashes hope may spring, as the phoenix rises from its ashes, for any who will behold the spectacle and heed the lesson.

Dora Wilmot, a local woman, is a member of Mr. Berringer's circle, and we see her drawn into the power of the serpent because this is what she is, in effect. Subtlety is a good quality, if we think of the subtlety at work in a Brandenburg Concerto, or a beautifully executed pole vault, or a performance of *Hamlet* by Sir John Gielgud or even in something much closer to home such as the deft and unobtrusive courtesy at work in the way a good hostess notices the smallest wishes of her guest, or the way a well-trained boy might without flourish step quickly to open a door for a lady. But Dora Wilmot, rather than making subtlety serve her, has become its lackey. For this reason she is the first one to sense the approach of the great and archetypal snake when it draws near in the wake of the lion and the butterfly. " 'The snake!' " she screams at a meeting of the circle which is being addressed by Damaris Tighe. The scream interrupts Miss Tighe's lecture, much to Miss Tighe's irritation. Really! These hysterical women who *see* things. It is too much. Miss Wilmot is bundled out, and everyone flees. And the narrative refuses either to corroborate or refute Miss Wilmot's conviction that she has seen a snake.

Damaris, who prides herself on her scholarly ability to study ideas in a detached way and her imperviousness to the silliness and hysteria that incline people to think that there is anything *real* to worry about as long as you are talking merely of ideas—Damaris hears "the sound of a gentle and prolonged hiss" as everyone flies, and then, when they are gone, "The room lay empty and still in the electric light, unless indeed there passed across it then

a dim form, which, heavy, long, and coiling, issued
slowly through the open window into a silent world
where for that moment nothing but the remote thunder
was heard" (33).

Readers will note here Williams' way of refusing to
commit the narrative to anything clearly preternatural. It
is as though we are invited to conclude what we wish
about what is going on, just as we may conclude what
we wish about what is going on all around us all the time.
We may suppose (probably quite rightly) that there is a
very great deal going on, and chase hysterically, like
Dora Wilmot, after all sorts of arcane lore by way of
coming to grips with it. Or we may fly in terror, like
Quentin Sabot, from the sheer significance that seems always to be pressing in on the fabric of life. Or we may,
like Damaris Tighe, haughtily despise any suggestion
that anything means anything.

This is Damaris' difficulty, and it is principally her
conversion that we watch happen in this story. If Anthony is the main character in the sense that his shoulders
bear the weight of the significant action, she is certainly
at the center of the action in the sense that the main thing
that happens happens to her. She is an intelligent young
woman, and very much of a scholar. In fact, she is writing, when she can snatch the time from the vexing clutter
of people and obligations that bedevil her life, a disser-
tation entitled *Pythagorean Influences on Abelard*. It has to
do with a possible relation between quaint Greek notions
about Ideas and quaint Christian ideas about the angelic
hierarchy.

The difficulty about all this is simply that for Damaris,
her subject matter is just that: subject matter. It is her
"field", and she is the expert. Of course none of it has

anything to do with one's real life except insofar as one can publish books and journal articles about it and win a reputation.

In the very first scene of the book, as we have seen, Quentin asks Anthony, after the lion-hunting posse has gone, " 'I hope you still think that ideas are more dangerous than material things' " (12). Anthony answers, " 'Yes, I do. All material danger is limited, whereas interior danger is unlimited.' "

Damaris does not know this. But this is what she must learn. The idea has been put succinctly long before this: it is not things from outside that harm us but what comes from inside, "For from within, out of the heart of men, proceed evil thoughts, adulteries, fornications, murders, thefts, covetousness, wickedness, deceit, lasciviousness, an evil eye, blasphemy, pride, foolishness" (Mk 7:20–22).

Damaris hardly seems to be pouring out frightful things like these, except perhaps a touch of pride here and there. She is an intellectual snob. Here she is, addressing herself to all these rarified scholarly questions, and life has obliged her to put up with all sorts of trifling vexations and inconveniences such as living with her father, who is an amateur lepidopterist. He goes on and on at the dinner table about these butterflies, all the while eating away earnestly at his mutton and potatoes. " 'Really, Father,' she said, 'if it was as beautiful as all that I don't see how you can bear to go on eating mutton and potatoes so ordinarily' " (25). Obviously, beauty in any high and serious sense has nothing to do with mutton and potatoes. How can anyone straddle both worlds? What has beauty, especially in the Platonic sense (which is her specialty), got to do with mutton? Or with anything else that crowds daily life? What a bore it all is.

Her father is not the only irritant in Damaris' life. Anthony is in love with her. "Anthony was always wanting to talk of themselves, which meant whether she loved him, and in what way, and how much, whereas Damaris, who disliked discussing other people's personal affairs, preferred to talk of scholarship or abstract principles" (22). Abélard is one of the great fountainheads of these abstractions, but his exquisitely poignant affair with Héloïse is nothing to Damaris: Héloïse never "appeared to her as more than a side-incident of Abélard's real career. In which [adds Williams] her judgment may have been perfectly right, but her sensations were wildly and entirely wrong" (26).

Damaris is a Manichaean, in other words. For her, only the intellectual realm is worthy: all this emotional and physical baggage is too demeaning.

The account of Damaris has not proceeded very far before we find her being bothered with an awful smell in the air. Anthony also smells it at one point when they are together and describes it as being like the smell of a corpse. There comes a Sunday evening when Damaris is alone in her room with her books and papers. She has just been reflecting that the habit of personifying things is "evidence of a rather low cultural state" (127). Only primitive men suppose that there is anything personal or concrete about ultimate reality. "As education developed so a sense of abstraction grew up, and it became more possible to believe that the North Wind was a passage of air, and not an individual, or that St. Michael was a low-class synonym for—probably for just warfare, and

justice pure and simple" (127). As she is pursuing this
line, she is once more regaled with the smell of corruption. The sky darkens, and suddenly there are an immense beak forcing its way through the window into the
room and great leather wings flapping.

"If only Anthony were here! . . . For the first time in
her life she wanted somebody very badly . . . *somebody
to break this awful loneliness*" (130). She screams for her
father, but he, wrapt in the vision of beauty that has
come to him on the wings of his precious butterflies, is
quite unable to help her, and she seems to be standing
alone in some bog. A visionary figure approaches. It is
Peter Abélard, her favorite retailer of ideas. But this is
not Abélard's ideas: it is Abélard in his flesh and blood.
And he is singing—singing his own hymn, "*O quanta
qualia/ sunt illa sabbata*"—O, what their joy and their
glory must be, Those endless sabbaths the blessed ones
see." Sabbaths? Blessed ones? All these *pictures*? Come.
Those are only quaint and primitive personifications for
abstract ideas. Any intellectual knows that.

Perhaps so. But intellectuals cannot get into the kingdom of heaven. Only children are eligible—children,
poor lambs, who think that a picture or a toy or an Incarnation is better than a speech or a definition. She
strains towards Abélard. Perhaps here is rescue. But the
great shadow suddenly passes over him. He turns, and
his face is like the face of a corpse. He croaks at her the
big words of his philosophy: *individualiter, essentialiter,
categoricorum*, and so forth. What has happened to him?
Alas: the abstract Abélard is the only Abélard that Damaris knows. He has been merely a retailer of ideas for her,
not the man and priest who loves and sings.

She makes one more effort to get help. She tries calling Anthony. " 'An. . . An. . . A. . . A. . . A. . .' " (133).

"And then she heard her name. It wasn't cried aloud; it was spoken normally as it had been spoken a hundred times in that place" (133, 134). It is, of course, Anthony speaking, almost in command it seems, and she responds. She flies to him for succor. It is the beginning of salvation for her. Never before has she acknowledged that she needed anyone. Never before has she obeyed anyone gladly. Never before has she felt other than self-sufficient and patronizing towards others. But all of that is what hell is made of. To enter joy, she must go right back and down to the humility and eager trust of childhood. Anthony is there. The shadow sails over again, but this time the flying creature lands on Anthony's shoulder, and it is not the pterodactyl. It is his eagle. That which had been terror and horror to Damaris in her proud isolation is glorious in its obedience to Anthony. That which terrifies and horrifies damned souls is the very thing which the saints have found to be power and bliss.

In the ensuing few moments everything is changed, the way salvation or transfiguration or apocalypse changes things. Damaris, who has up to this point been a real woman only technically and reluctantly, "received with joy both love and laughter; there went out from him . . . a knowledge of safety would she but take it, and freely and humbly she let it enter her being . . . though she longed for him to gather her and let her feel more closely the high protection of his power, she was content to wait upon his will. As she made that motion of assent she felt the wildness of the desolate plain shut out" (134).

And so on, and on, every phrase of it carrying its weight of glory, opening out from the fetid trap that has been Damaris' milieu to the light vistas of joy given and received, where masculine and feminine bear their appointed roles with agility, grace, and majesty. There is no avoiding the echo of the Virgin Mary's story here, with all this humility and waiting upon Anthony's will, all of it so remote from anything Damaris ever has imagined or known.

When Damaris asks Anthony what has happened, he explains to her that she has now seen what she formerly had only heard (and ignored): "What you wouldn't hear about you've seen, and if you're still capable of thanking God you'd better do it now" (136). This is not an allegory of the Last Judgment, but the same principle is at work in both situations: there is a dreadful and remorseless unveiling. If we will not pay attention to the cues and clues now while it is day, then we will be caught completely off guard when the curtain suddenly goes up. It could all be horrible for Damaris, except that now, having made the one small step of crying out for help to Anthony, she is under his protection, and he is telling her everything. His hand holding hers is "half a chain and half a caress . . . he exposed her to the knowledge of what she had done. Merciless and merciful, he held her; pitiful and unpitying, he subordinated her to the complete realization of herself and her past" (137).

We find here the many-layered quality that Augustine and the Fathers found in the Bible, where any scene presents not only itself but also something about the soul and something about salvation and something about the Last Things. Here is Damaris being rescued from her fright, and every phrase, line after line, turns out to be a description of what happens when a soul enters the crucible of salvation and, beyond that, of what will unfurl itself for all souls at the Last Trump. It is analogy, not allegory. Damaris' experience doesn't symbolize salvation and judgment: all three, being of one piece anyway, look alike.

The one other character who arrests our attention is Richardson, the bookseller's assistant. He is a case in point of the Way of Negation of Images, that is, of the kind of vision which, while granting the validity of all created things as in some way messengers and bearers of the Unseen, yet wishes to press beyond all images to that which they bespeak. The Way of Negation emphasizes the second half of the maxim "This also is Thou; neither is this Thou.

Richardson says at one point, as he and Anthony discuss the meaning of lions and unicorns and so forth, " 'But for myself I will go straight to the end' " (122). And, at the end of the scene, he returns to his rooms, "while his thoughts went out again in a perpetual aspiration beyond even the Celestials to That which created the Celestials" (125). The language Williams uses to describe Richardson's attempt in the spiritual life is the language of apophatic, or "negative", theology, that line of thought that stresses the mystery of God by iterating what he is *not* (he is not high and not low, and not darkness and not light, and not far and not near, and so on), the idea being that all this human language falls so far short of what he really is that it is equally true to say that he is light and not light. A certain line of very exalted Christian mysticism has employed this language down through the centuries, but it has never been the meat and drink of the common Christian laity. We find

Richardson thinking about the Way to God, and this is the language: "But not by books or by phrases, not by images or symbols or myths, did he himself follow it. He abstracted himself continually from sense and from thought, attempting always a return to an interior nothingness where that which is itself no thing might communicate its sole essential being" (139). It is for this reason that Richardson is no more able to appreciate the sparse ritual at work in a Wesleyan chapel which he passes one evening than he would a High Mass: both proceed upon *some* imagery. He thinks, "But no doubt this was proper to them—if it increased their speed upon the Way" (142).

Richardson's end, as far as we may speak of ends who see only a glimpse of the near end of any man's story, comes by his walking voluntarily, and unobserved, into the fire at Mr. Berringer's house to be consumed in this act of self-immolation by the fire which burns, like the phoenix's nest, with the fiery promise of resurrection.

Indeed, that fire stands as the consummation of the whole drama in this tale. It is one of the local firemen who, still struggling vainly to quench the flames late at night, thinks he might have seen the "great shape of a lion leap from the field straight into the flames" (205). And suddenly the fire subsides and dies, leaving only fine ash. The whole thing has dazed him. But Damaris, who is also looking on at the fire, knows she has not been dazed. It has all been an epiphany. She might well say, "For mine eyes have seen thy salvation." And, just at this moment, Anthony leaps over the stile that leads into (or out of, rather) the field where he only now appeared as Adam naming all the beasts and ruling them, and where the sheep so safely graze, and comes to her. The sheer good nature and informality of the last words we hear them say to each other as they go off stage stand at a polar extreme from the brittle and testy formality in which Damaris was trapped at the beginning. She has been saved. She has learned about the rollicking humility and delight that spring up wherever people have learned about co-inherence.

5

The Greater Trumps

More than any other of Williams' seven novels, *The Greater Trumps* depends on our being able to grasp at least something of a highly peculiar and special set of ideas. These ideas are set forth in the pictures found on the ancient set of fortune-telling cards, the famous "Tarot pack". Readers do not, of course, have to master the entire lore surrounding these cards: that would be impossible, since it represents a whole world of semi-scholarly rummaging into medieval, gypsy, Spanish, Jewish, and Egyptian secrets.

The encouraging thing for the newcomer to Williams, however, is that Williams does here what he always does with these apparently bizarre topics: he sketches in enough so that we will be able to follow what he is up to in his story, but then he proceeds to write a story which turns out to be about all-too-recognizable and worka-day attitudes and not at all about remote and smoky mysteries.

The easiest way to come at what is going on in the story is to get a picture in our minds of the Tarot pack. Unlike the ordinary pack of playing cards, this pack has seventy-eight cards in it. There are four suits: swords, cups, staves, and coins. The cups are sometimes called chalices; the staves may be called scepters or wands; and the coins may be called pentacles, since they show a five-pointed star, or else deniers, the name of an ancient coin. In each suit there are fourteen cards instead of the familiar thirteen, since, besides numbers one through ten, there are a page, a knight, a queen, and a king. So far, then, we have fifty-six cards.

But by far the most intriguing thing about these cards is the set of so-called Greater Trumps, or Major Arcana. Here are twenty-two more, numbered from zero to twenty-one. On them we find an unnerving array of virtually all the symbols we have ever come across in any sort of ancient tradition, legend, or lore. The Juggler, for example, is number one. There are the Emperor and Empress; the Hierophant (high priest) and High Priestess; the Chariot; the Hermit; three of the four cardinal virtues, Temperance, Fortitude, and Justice (where is Prudence?); the Lovers; the Wheel of Fortune; the Falling Tower; the Hanged Man; the Sun, Moon, and Star; Death; the Devil; the Last Judgment; and the Universe. So far, then, we have twenty-one of these Greater Trumps. But the most peculiar card in the whole seventy-eight is numbered zero. It is the Fool. Why this? No one can say, any more than anyone can say what it is about life itself that always eludes all attempts to explain it.

There are, no doubt, a hundred theories as to what it all might mean, and occultists have shuffled and arranged and fiddled with the cards for centuries. But the net effect of it all is to leave us mystified, the way life itself does when we try to peer into its riddles. Much learning increaseth sorrow, said the wisest sage of all time, and it is not going to be roadside palmists or rouged and beaded ladies in curtained and perfumed shanties who will give us the answers. If there was one thing Williams was not interested in, it was this latter scene.

In any event, what we find in this tale is that before we emerge at the far end of the events, the characters have found themselves enacting a great deal of what seems to be suggested by the pictures on these cards, and especially on the Greater Trumps. Not that they have set out to become embroiled with the Tarot. Very far from it. They stumble into it, so to speak, the way all the characters in all of Williams' stories stumble into Ultimacy, by tripping over some apparently smallish thing. And the net effect for us readers is to leave us with the unhappy suspicion that no one in the story has stumbled into anything at all that any one of us does not stumble into a hundred times a day. There is nothing in the Tarot, for example, that does not draw its meaning from plain, meat-and-potatoes human life. It turns out, as we might expect, that the one character in this story who is most utterly at home in all that happens is the one who has the least interest in the Tarot.

Her name is Sybil, oddly enough; and it becomes clear early enough that she is indeed a sybil, not in the sense of being a prophetess or sorceress in a murky shrine but rather in the sense of seeing things perfectly clearly. She has this quality, we will find, because she is a simple person. This simplicity, however, is not the simplicity of the ostrich: rather, it is that serene singleness of vision that is the rare fruit of years of courage, suffering, and renunciation such as we see from time to time in people like Saint Francis or Mother Teresa of Calcutta. It is won at fathomless cost. It seems to be synonymous with sainthood, which in its turn seems to be "nothing but" someone's having reached the freedom and health that human beings were made for in the first place, which, the saints would tell us, is a by-product of knowing God, which is the whole thing we were made for to begin with.

It might be worth noting in passing that Williams has waggishly named two of his main characters, Sybil Coningsby and her brother Lothair, after the titles of three of Disraeli's novels: *Sybil, Lothair,* and *Coningsby.* Apparently their father's godmother had liked Disraeli, so to please her he named his children thus.

The first character we meet is Lothair, and the first two words of the book give us our clue about him. " 'Perfect Babel' ", he complains. The Babel is merely the pointless chatter flying about the living room between Lothair's daughter Nancy and her brother Ralph. This is not to his taste: indeed, not very much in life is to his taste. He is a more or less harmless and testy middle-aged man who holds the legal office, or title at least, of Warden in Lunacy. His own view of things, if he were asked, would incline him to see the whole world, and not just the patients at a mental hospital as lunatic. Everyone is so irritating. People are such fools. (We find that we must watch this word in this tale: in the Tarot, as also in the Christian mysteries themselves, the business of being a fool shows up very near the center of things.) And besides this, life generally has always been unfair to him.

"Some people were like that, beaten through no fault of their own, wounded before the battle began; not everybody would have done so well as he had. But how it dogged him—that ghastly luck!" (11, 12).

What we are seeing here, in a word, is a soul en route to damnation. If that seems to be much too abrupt and dire a construction to put on it, we need only chase these attitudes of Lothair's to their ends and see what we get, which is precisely what Williams' novels always oblige us to do. Every single straw in every single wind at least tells us which way the breeze is blowing. This self-pity and irritability of Lothair's have their taproots in egoism and lack of charity, and those qualities have their fountainhead in hell.

Lothair, of course, as any respectable man of us would do, would angrily protest this reading of things: "What are you saying—that I, an entirely peaceable and decent-living Englishman who asks nothing more of life than that he be left alone and not bothered by all the dunces running about the world—that *I* am going to *hell*?"

Well of course (one might venture), that's not for me to say; but what has been said to us all is that all these dunces are the selves made by God and destined for glory and joy, and that, like dancers in a great dance, we've all got to learn the movements, which means greeting and bowing to each other and giving way and linking arms and whirling about and so forth, and this can't be done if I stand there glowering at them all. It is the old question from *Alice in Wonderland:* "Will you, won't you, will you, won't you, will you join the dance?" If I say no, since the dancers are such bores and dunderheads, then I put myself on the outside, and that is what is called hell. Solitude. Irritation. Motionlessness.

Lothair's sister Sybil, on the other hand, is very different. Nothing at all seems to bother her. When Lothair
asks her rather snidely, in this first scene, what she might
have been doing all day, she reports that she has done
some shopping and made a cake and had a walk and
popped into the library, then had tea, and is now reading. Rather a dull day, if what we are looking for in life
is excitement. " 'Nice day,' Mr. Coningsby answered,
between a question and a sneer, wishing it hadn't been,
though he was aware that if it hadn't been . . . but then
it was certain to have been. Sybil always seemed to have
nice days" (7).

He is quite right. Sybil, we learn later in the story, has
learned, through God knows what vigils and renuncia-
tions and ordeals, the lessons of patience and charity,
which is to say, of freedom. Whatever life presents to her
is very well. She would know what the Lady Juliana of
Norwich meant about all manner of things being well.
The Lady Juliana was speaking of the state in which Charity has been perfected and therefore joy perfected. It is
not exclusively a future state, although it is certainly
that, of course. But Sybil knows something of that freedom already.

She is, for example, so much at home with things that
she has the rather rare ability to say simply yes or no, if
that is what is called for, without qualifying and modi-
fying and protesting and apologizing. Whatever this
simplicity is, it seems, says Williams, to be of a piece
with whatever Christ was hinting at when he said, "Let
your yea be yea and your nay nay." It has something to
do with being completely free and unafraid.

It turns out that an old friend of Lothair's, Duncannon, has recently left him an odd legacy. It is a collection

of packs of old playing cards, which Lothair is to keep until his own death and then hand on to the British Museum. It really is something of a bore, since Duncannon had plenty of money and might after all, one would have thought, have left something a bit more.

The company in the room in this first scene has grown to five with the arrival of Henry Lee, Nancy's young suitor, who seems to be of gypsy lineage, although he has the entirely respectable profession of lawyer. They persuade Lothair to get out the collection after dinner so they can all have a look. In the conversation arising over the business of getting out the cards, Nancy asks Henry if he can tell fortunes. He replies that he can—" 'Some by cards and some by hands . . . and some by the stars' " (13). This introduces one of the major images of the story, namely, hands.

All the way through the action, hands stand for the special, voluntary power—authority even—that we human beings have to determine and accomplish what we wish. Animals have only paws. We can manipulate and build and tear down and change and achieve things, and this is an august power that has been given to us alone, of all the creatures here on this earth, and is a sort of sign of the mystery of our having been made in the image of God, the Maker.

Every time we find Williams referring to hands in this story, we may be sure that he wants us to be conscious of the awesome freedom that we humans have to choose and hence to determine our destiny. Shall we wreck, or shall we build? What do our hands reveal about us? Nancy, just lightly and in passing, comments that she has told her father's and her aunt's fortunes by the lines in their hands, and that Lothair's seems to stop abruptly at age forty (he is now in his late fifties), whereas Sybil's goes on forever. The point of course is that somewhere in there, years ago, Lothair ran aground. The psychologists would say his development was arrested. The saints would say that he ceased travelling up the steep slope towards sanctity, preferring to squat down with his petulant complaints and petty irritations.

As the group inspects the cards, we begin to see what the function of these cards is going to be in the story. They have a twofold function, actually: first, of course, they are the springboard for all that happens, the way a casket of gems might be in a pirate story. But second, they turn out to be a silent judgment on everyone's motives and character.

For example, Henry is especially fascinated with Trump number 1, the Juggler, and it turns out soon enough that, just as the Juggler seems to suggest whoever or whatever riddle it is that controls the universe, so Henry would very much like to control things, even if to achieve his end he has to resort to murder. Further, as he lays the card down, Nancy looks into his eyes and sees a great emptiness in them, like tidal pools left to dry up after the ocean has withdrawn. The point here is that Nancy, being in love with Henry, has got some foothold in the mystery of things even if she is not particularly conscious of it, namely, that to love someone else is to know them and to experience exchange with them, which is what the Dance is all about. So that, without being any sort of occultist or adept at the Tarot, Nancy, simply by being a young woman in love, already knows a good bit about the very mysteries that are so enigmatically hinted at in the pictures on the Tarot. But Henry, who, even though he is engaged to Nancy, clearly has his mind full of some agenda of his own, seems to be in touch with nothing. There is nothing in him that answers to the ocean of Nancy's love: just shallow salt pools, soon to dry up (more than one of the Trumps, it may be observed, seem to depict some sort of water pouring back and forth).

For Ralph, the whole thing arouses only a very offhand curiosity. " 'Does one play with them, or what . . . what's the idea of it?' " (18, 19). Ralph is your typical, normal, more-or-less selfish but reasonably nice young man who has not yet been flagged down in life by anything very arresting (love, grief, pain, sanctity, or whatever). His reaction to the Tarot is about what his reaction would be to any attempt to raise the big questions about life's ambiguities: oh, come—let's not get all wrought up about *that*.

It is Sybil, as we might expect, who is immediately and naturally at home with the whole business. She experiences pure delight as she observes the cards. It is, we might say, a matter of recognition: if the riddle of the cards "means" the same thing as the riddle of life, and if Sybil has long since learned to be quietly at home in life, unthreatened by whatever life might bring to her, and believing with all her soul that Omnipotent Love lies at the bottom of all the enigmas—then of course there will be something both familiar and lovely to her about the pictures. Where Henry is maddened by their impenetrability, and Nancy is all agog and curious, and Ralph is only momentarily diverted, Sybil seems to be saying, "Why of course. What else? How absolutely perfect."

The first card we see Sybil looking at is the Sun. To her, it was "perfectly simple; the sun shone full in a clear sky, and two children—a boy and a girl—played happily below. Sybil smiled again as she contemplated them. 'Aren't they the loveliest things?' she breathed, and indeed they were—so vivid, so intense, so rapturous under the beneficent light, of which some sort of reflection passed into Sybil's own face while she brooded" (19).

Lothair is interested in the cards only as historical artifacts of very marginal interest. He says that Duncannon had told him the cards were either a fourteenth-century invention or else perhaps Egyptian. "He stopped, as if everything were explained" (19). This is exactly what he has done with life: stopped, as if everything were explained. Just don't ruffle my feathers; don't get in my way; just let me have my slippers and newspaper and my peace, thank you very much.

Henry comments presently that if you do certain things with the cards, you will get certain results. For example, " 'The shuffling of the cards is the earth, and the pattering of the cards is the rain, and the beating of the cards is the wind, and the pointing of the cards is the fire. That's of the four suits' " (21). Readers familiar with medieval and Renaissance cosmology will recognize the four elements: earth, air, fire, and water. The cards, in other words, correspond somehow to everything. But there is more: " 'But the Greater Trumps, it's said, are the meaning of all process and the measure of the everlasting dance' " (21). This is the old idea that the whole creation, from the highest seraphim and remotest stars right down to the lowest worm and smallest smile or frown, is "choreographed", as it were, and may be imagined to be a great dance, each thing (even the riddles and enigmas and outrages) somehow and eventually turning out to have its place. The Greater Trumps, with their odd pictures, present a set of hieroglyphs, as it were, hinting at bits and pieces of this choreography.

Williams assumed what Christianity assumes, namely, that the "key" to things is love, not knowledge. Or put it another way: the key to knowledge is love. You start doing what is charitable, and things begin to make sense. The riddles will not yield themselves to the ransacking of the occultist or the mulling of the philosopher. Christ hinted at something like this when he remarked that if any man will do God's will, he will know about the doctrine. It has to be in that order.

Hence, Sybil, who has learned to love, finds herself at home. Nancy, who is just beginning to learn to love by virtue of her romantic passion for Henry, is at a good starting point. Henry is hammering at the adamant gates of the Tarot itself, with no success whatever. Lothair has lost the ability to be interested in much of anything at all. And Ralph, nice boy that he is, is still to be waked up, as it were.

When Henry mentions this about the dance, Nancy eagerly asks what the dance is. Henry, who has not made the connection yet between the cards and anything in the real world of human experience, does at least know some of the lore, and he points her to the seventh card. It is the lovers. He tells her that this is the first movement of the dance—unless you go with the hermit.

Here we have Williams' "two ways"—the Way of Affirmation of Images and the Way of Negation. Put in simpler terms, this means that there are, clearly, two ways by which the human soul may reach its goal, which on the Christian view and hence on Williams', means the vision of God. One way is by seeing everything in the creation as a sort of hint or cue of what is true and by treating it all as a sort of ladder, leading up to God. The color red, for example—in a sunset, in a ruby, or in a fire—is a lovely thing and supplies us with some hint about the country towards which we travel. Music, for example—in a Mozart horn concerto, in the song of the winter wren, or in the tinkling of a brook—is a lovely thing and supplies us with some hint about that country. All things do this for us, and if we see them and extol them this way, we are followers of the Way of Affirmation of Images: the frame of mind that says, "This is a hint of That". Or, more radically, "This is a hint of *Thou*", since of course it is the One who dwells in that country that we seek.

Lovers, then, would be followers of the Way of Affirmation. This beauty that we find in each other, and this ecstasy that we find in the knowledge of each other, is a hint of something. What is it? Let us love, by all means, and love splendidly: but let us remember that this splendor is itself only the herald of an overwhelming splendor and bliss compared with which this experience of ours is indeed only a hint, or an image. We are being beckoned along all the time.

The hermit, on the other hand, pursues a different way towards the same country. His is the Way of Negation of Images, which says in effect, Ah: that splendor and bliss are so titanic and unimaginable that no image can quite do them justice, so let me pursue my way, not by *rejecting* the images (they are, after all, appointed to *be* images) but by renouncing them, which is a somewhat different thing. Let me emphasize the "unimaginability" of that bliss by setting these good images on one side and hastening on empty handed, as it were. I love the same reward you lovers do, and we shall meet presently. But for me it will be the fulfillment of the thing which I have anticipated by renunciation, while for you it will be the fulfillment of the thing which you have anticipated by affirmation.

It would be some such idea as this that would be at work in the Christian view of marriage and virginity as two different witnesses to the same thing. The human body is the holy shrine of personhood: it may be consecrated by being attended by a faithful spouse, as a sort of caretaker; or it may be consecrated in solitude, anticipating the great Caretaker.

Henry, of course, knows nothing about all of this. His knowledge is limited to some scraps of lore which he has picked up about the Tarot. For him the great thing is to get a skeleton key which will unlock the power of these cards and bestow some sort of control on Henry. For Sybil, whatever interest may lie in the cards lies there solely because they turn out to be plain pictures of what she has already seen to be true in any case.

In the second chapter we meet the hermit, although he turns out to be a rather misguided hermit. He is Henry's grandfather, Aaron Lee. He lives alone in a house in the country, and his whole life is spent, like Faust's, trying to get the key to the riddle of things. It turns out that the ancient gypsy family of Lee somehow became custodians not only of the Tarot pack but, far more important, of a very strange set of little golden figures which correspond exactly to the pictures on the Trumps. Aaron has these figures set up on a chesslike board on a table in a room in his house, where they move and move and move, everlastingly, by some mysterious perpetual motion, in a kind of golden mist, attended by some ethereal music. It is, of course, the Dance.

The unlucky thing, from Aaron's point of view, is that, many years back, this set of golden figures got separated from the original Tarot pack, which alone would be able to interpret the meaning of this strange Dance. Aaron has devoted his life to the desperate struggle to unscramble the meaning, but without that lost pack of cards there is no hope of success.

Henry arrives with the news that the pack has turned up. It is almost too good to be true. If they can bring the two things together, they will have the secret which has been lost to the world, and of which they, the Lee family, will now be the custodians.

This separation of the cards and the golden figures is a sort of case in point of *all* the tragic separations in the world, which is always the fruit of evil. It is the separating of form from meaning. The cards (which will "explain" the dance of the figures and hence hold the *meaning*) are divided from the figures which are the solid *form* to which the cards are mere witnesses. You have to have both before either makes any sense. The same is true wherever we look: you have to have the form (the body) together with the meaning (the spirit) in order to have a real person. Otherwise you have a corpse and a ghost, two horrors. It is true morally as well: you must have the form (the sexual act, say) together with the meaning (the real union of a man and a woman) in order to have the holy sacrament of marriage. Otherwise you have rape or fornication—both of them horrors.

Aaron's first thought is that if they can get the cards back together with the figures, they will be able to foretell the future. " 'We can tell what the future will be—from what the present is?' " (30).

Ironically, there is some truth in this, but not in the way Aaron thinks. All petty occultists hope that by piecing together this and that—juxtapositions in the zodiac, or sheep's entrails, or cracks in your palm—they will be able to peer forward down the corridor of time. There might, God knows, be some nubbin of truth somewhere in that sad attempt, but it is completely swamped by the more terrifying sense in which "we can tell what the future will be from what the present is", namely, the *moral* sense. That is, we can tell what the crop is going to be by what seeds are being sown now. The future crop is going to be wrath and solitude if the seeds being sown now are selfishness and egotism. The future crop is going to be the impotence that lies on the far side of surfeit if the seeds being sown now are indulgence and concupiscence. Aaron, of course, does not at all see this.

However, there is something to be said for Aaron. He is no mere petty occultist. Misbegotten as his solitary toil is, he feels deeply his responsibility as the heir of the ancient Lee family, to be the custodian of these secrets, and to reunite the cards and the figures if possible. This fidelity and honest labor, then, are "accounted unto him for righteousness", as it were. He does not seem to have the murderous passion that drives Henry—although even Henry has the chance to be "saved", since somewhere jumbled in with his passions there is a genuine, if only intermittent, love for Nancy.

As Henry and Aaron stand looking at the golden figures, they get to speaking of the Fool. Apparently alone of all the figures on the board, the Fool does not move. No one knows why. " 'There are no writings which tell

us anything of the Fool' ", says Aaron (30). Henry wonders whether one can "know the Dance" without being
one of the dancers. The implied answer is no, although
Aaron points out that we are all dancers, because everything that exists is part of the dance. But this does not
satisfy Henry. All those things are, to be sure, but they
don't *know* that they are. Surely it must be possible to
know the dance. What Sybil would remark, if she were
standing by, would be, yes, it is possible to know the
Dance, but you are right, Henry: only the dancers really
know it, and for us humans to know it means that we
have to choose to enter the Dance. No scrutiny from
outside will yield one smallest clue, any more than
watching swimmers in the surf will yield us the pleasure
of swimming in the surf. You have to be in it, and the
only way to be in the dance is to love. Love, not knowledge, is the key.

Henry, all unawares, is protected from the evil that his
desire to know would lead him into by his love for
Nancy. He would like to wrest the cards from old
Lothair, by force and even murder if necessary; but he
won't go against Nancy's will yet, and she would certainly protest the murder of her father. Henry is curious
to see if perhaps the image of the Lovers has some function here. " 'To know—to see from within—to be aware
of the dance. . . . Nancy—Nancy—Nancy' " (32).
Henry utters the words of his own salvation.

During this conversation between Henry and Aaron,
we learn of Aaron's sister, Joanna. She is mad, it turns
out. Apparently, fifty years before this her ne'er-do-well
husband left her and was killed the night her child was
born, and then the two months' premature infant itself
died. Joanna has spent the rest of her life in a wild and

demented quest to find this child. She has even adopted a surrogate, who is now a young man, named Stephen, whom she drags about the countryside with her in her frenzied quest, calling him her son. She has got the whole thing mixed up in her mind with the Egyptian vegetation-cycle myth of the goddess Isis (with whom Joanna identifies herself), whose child Osiris dies yearly with the fall of the year and rises once more as Horus with the spring. In Joanna we have an attempt, misbegotten to be sure but nonetheless desperately real, to find the meaning of the Dance. Unlike Aaron's approach, which is by study and calculation, Joanna's is perhaps half a step closer to the truth of the matter, in that she at at least thinks you have to *enact* the Dance. She *is* Isis, she insists. Well (Sybil might remark), insanity and sanctity have more than once veered fairly close together. The Gospel itself is foolishness to the Greeks, who are the most rational and civilized people ever.

Henry's preliminary plan for reuniting the cards and the figures is to persuade the Coningsbys to come to Aaron's for Christmas and for Lothair to bring along the Tarot pack just as a curio. After that they will see what will be necessary to secure the cards.

Back at the Coningsby house, Henry wants to try an experiment with the cards, with Nancy's help. She fetches them, and Williams describes her approach to Henry with the cards in language that would be appropriate for describing the mystical approach of the bride to the bridegroom, although to any onlooker it would simply be a matter of a young girl coming into a room and handing her fiancé a deck of cards. Nancy notices Henry's hands, for one thing, which in this story are always agents of human purpose and freedom. Whatever his purposes are, though, Nancy does the thing which all archetypal brides have always done in all myths, namely, "disposed herself to meet him . . . with something in her of preparation, as if, clear and splendid, she came to her bridal" (43). Nancy is a young woman in love, and she does what young women in love feel in their marrow is the right thing to do: dispose themselves to the will of their lovers. (This doctrine, ancient and universal though it is, would be incomprehensible to various points of view which attempt the equalizing of the sexes, but Williams died too soon to anticipate any difficulty on this point.)

Henry explains to Nancy as much as he knows at present of the secret of the cards, namely, that their power has something to do with *relation*. " 'All things are held together by correspondence, image with image, movement with movement. Without that there could be no relation and therefore no truth. It is our business— especially yours and mine—to take up the power of relation. Do you know what I mean?' " (44).

Of course she does. It is Henry who does not know what he means. He thinks that he is talking about how you do an experiment with the cards. Fair enough: he is no doubt correct. But what he is really saying, and what Nancy gaily tells him she knows without needing the cards to inform her, is that yes indeed all things *are* held together by correspondence and that unless dawn dances with twilight, and mountain with valley, and summer with winter, and stamen with pistil, and heaven with earth, and man with woman, then of course nothing happens. It is the Dance. Anyone in love knows that. Nancy is no philosopher, but she is in love, and the truth for her and Henry is precisely she and Henry.

The experiment that Henry wants to try with Nancy is the attempt to create, or at least conjure, earth, by means of shuffling the cards. If this is the real and original Tarot pack, then it will work. With his hands over hers, they work the cards over the dining room table, and, lo and behold, a small heap of earth is the result. So: it is the pack they want.

There is a paragraph near the end of this chapter which touches, in Williams' darting way, on matters so vast that it almost defies comment. But Williams has put it there, and readers may be puzzled. After the experiment, when the two of them, Henry and Nancy, the man and the woman, have together "danced", as it were, with the creation of earth being the result, we find Nancy having sunk into a chair, somewhat faint after this act (a woman is tired after parturition: there is no sense pretending that Williams does not have this in mind), then presently throwing her arms up to Henry, who catches her and raises her to himself from her chair. Here is the language of the narrative: "But it was she who was raised from her chair, not he who was brought down to that other level" (50). The language is almost the precise language of the Athanasian Creed, one of whose phrases was a favorite with Williams: "Not by the bringing of the godhead down to man, but by the taking of the manhood into God", speaking of the Incarnation. The scene here, then, we are presumably meant to see as an enactment of the central mystery of exchange in which our mortal flesh (represented here by Nancy: all humanity is, as it were, "feminine" vis-à-vis deity) is taken into godhood, represented here by Henry, who is masculine. Henry lays her down again, and "there was in his action something of one who lays down a precious instrument till it shall be

required" (50). There is something, then, in the love that
obtains between a man and a woman, that echoes the
mystery of the human being "wedded" to the divine—of
masculine initiative and feminine responsiveness.

Williams darts past it with these few phrases, but there
can be no question as to what he had in mind. We may
complain that this is too weighty a business to whisk by
in this manner, but that would be to forget the sort of tale
he is telling. The whole point in every flick of every wrist
in the whole story is precisely that everything means
everything. Glory and mystery lie at our elbow all the
time.

The "chariot" of the title of chapter four turns out to
be the car in which Henry, Nancy, Sybil, and Lothair
drive to Aaron's house in the country (Ralph has gone to
visit elsewhere). Sybil has recognized in Nancy the
opening out of Nancy's being towards love, and Sybil
knows that it will take Nancy farther than merely her experience of Henry, as indeed all human love ought to do.
In the car Henry remarks that Aunt Sybil, as he now calls
her, is strange—a maiden—" 'a mystery of self possession. . . . I think it's too long . . . since you have
wished yourself anything but what you are' " (53). He is
correct, of course: Sybil has learned contentment, but it
has been at the price always exacted by the Divine Mercy
for our happiness, namely, everything. Henry even remarks, speaking of Sybil's tranquillity, " 'You never
seem to move' " (53). Clearly Sybil is the Fool, who also
seems, to the untrained eye, not to move.

On the way to the country they pass a policeman and
Henry comments, " 'Behold the Emperor' " (55). They
are all thinking of the Tarot, so there is a certain appro-
priateness in the remark. But it goes further than Henry

perhaps suspects, since this policeman with his uniform is a case in point of exactly the same thing that all uniformed and robed and vested emperors, caliphs, and kings are, namely, order and law personified. They pass a nurse, and Nancy sees in her the Empress, with "ceremonial robes; imperial head-dress, cloak falling like folded wings" (56). She sees Henry, who is driving the car, as the charioteer—that ancient and mysterious picture of a man driving two sphinxes, the implication being that he may choose which direction he will go. They also pass a roadside crucifix, and Nancy screams in sudden fright, thinking she has seen the Hanged Man, which of course she has.

Just before they reach Aaron's house, they are stopped in the road by the figure of a grovelling old woman, who turns out to be Joanna. Only Sybil is able to meet her with equanimity, since she is afraid of nothing (perfect love casteth out fear, it is said). Her whole approach to Joanna is to grant Joanna all her ravings and to assume that her quest will be rewarded, since she is certainly seeking joy with all her heart.

The point of bringing the Coningsbys to Aaron's house has been to cajole Lothair into letting Aaron and Henry have the Tarot pack, if only as a loan. As a return favor, Aaron has been persuaded by Henry to let them all see the golden figures. As they all contemplate the dance on the board, once again it is clear that they are being judged. Lothair looks for plausible explanations. Henry is keen on figuring out the secret. A small item that attracts general notice is that all of the figures move except for the Fool. He seems to be standing motionless in the middle of the dance—except that Sybil at first cannot see the Fool at all, and then, when she does, she sees it as speeding like lightning all through the dance. This is very disconcerting to everyone, of course. Sybil's usual nonsense, in Lothair's view; but very alarming to Aaron and Henry, who in a conversation a bit later reveal that old tales say that the Fool moves, but no one that they know of—all the generations of custodians and adepts—has ever seen it move.

They are all missing the point. Sybil knows nothing at all of this occult lore. But she knows the one thing in the whole universe that unlocks everything else, namely, Love. Since Love is, in fact, the name and meaning of the whole Dance, and the energy which moves the Dance, then any sample of that Dance, whether in occult lore or in the love of a boy and a girl, will look completely familiar. Indeed, Sybil, in a brief conversation with Nancy just before they all go into the room to look at the figures, surprises Nancy by telling her that she (Nancy) doesn't love anyone. This is an odd thing to say to a young girl in love, but Sybil's point is that the thing that Nancy feels for Henry is just the tiniest clue to the thing that ought to govern our outlook towards all other selves—even, say, old frights like Joanna. Until we have got there, we can barely be said to know what love is.

It is worth noting that much of Williams' phraseology about this dance is very close to what we find in T. S. Eliot's *Four Quartets*, with its imagery of the "still point of the turning world". Williams and Eliot knew each other, but the question of strict or technical indebtedness is outside the scope of this study. The main point of interest would be simply that they were both talking about the same thing. "Worldly" eyes, no matter how informed, cannot see that it is Love that is speeding through all things, enabling and encouraging and making up the blank spaces. To the eye of the saint all the absurdities and pain and imponderables turn out to be, somehow, the motions of Love.

Henry wants to try a bit of fortune telling, so Nancy fetches the cards and brings them to the table where the figures are. In the ensuing minutes, she has a vision, in which the cards, slipping through her hands, seem to be the leaves of some great protohistoric tree—all the aboriginal trees of myth from which great things have sprung. Williams even includes here the olive trees of Gethsemane, that trysting place of love and suffering. Nancy's "fortune", according to Henry, is that she is likely to travel a long distance soon and come under some powerful influence and will find her worst enemy in her own heart. This all happens within the next day or so in which the action, like the action in the latter parts of every Williams novel, becomes almost wholly visionary. But once the reader has grasped the foregoing images and hints, he will be able to follow what seems on the surface to be a bizarre and kaleidoscopic sequence in which it is not so much a matter of one's not knowing whether Joanna is Isis or not, or whether Lothair is the Hanged Man or not, as of its not mattering. As is the case with poetic imagery, one's business is not to sort out a whole list of allegories but rather to take things as they are on the surface and accept the simple face of it.

Henry's plan, which he reveals to Aaron, is to kill Lothair by means of the cards, thus securing the cards for the Lee family, then to marry Nancy, which will of course bring Sybil, who might be useful, into the family. It is a sort of Nietzschean plan: anything is legitimate if it serves the superman's end of power and control. In answer to Aaron's question as to what might happen if

Nancy, later on, discovers what Henry has done, Henry says that by that time she, under Henry's influence, will have enough wisdom (a point worth noting: it is wisdom, not love, that Nancy will gain by marrying Henry, in his view) to know that Henry was right and that anything, even murder, is permissible if it clears the way for the superman. She will know that Lothair was expendable, since by hanging onto his little pack of cards he stood in the way of the release of all sorts of power.

We now come to Christmas Eve, when Christendom anticipates the birth of Love. Nancy, having borrowed the cards again from her father, is standing with Henry in the room in the presence of the golden figures. She is not sure just what is going on, but, like the Virgin Mary in another story, "she was inviting a union between the mystery of her love and the mystery of the dance" (93). She has no way of knowing that it is murder that Henry intends, but that part is irrelevant. The only point for her is to be responsive to the approaches of Love—or, in Nancy's case, of the man she loves. That it is a ghastly parody only makes it the more emphatic, in that it is partly Nancy's love—and Sybil's, and even Lothair's— that rescues Henry from his Luciferean intention of destruction rather than creation, we might say. At least part of the implication here, surely, is that so long as genuinely selfless love is at work somewhere, all is not yet lost. Evil may still be foiled.

As Nancy stands there with Henry and the cards and the figures, she has yet another vision, this time of the whole Dance—of everything from the circulation of the blood to the Himalayas, to law and medicine and music and religion, as being parts of the Dance. "There is noth-

ing at all anywhere but the dance" (95). As she questions
Henry, he suggests that the separation of the cards from
the figures, with the consequent loss of meaning, "is as
if a child were taken from its mother into some other
land" (97). This division, this tragic separation, is what
Joanna feels so keenly, and what any mother of a dead infant feels in her grief. It is not especially occult: it is plain
human experience. Something is *wrong* in the Dance.
This can't be the way it was intended to be—all this death
and separation and pain. Who will make it right?

Presently Henry unwittingly touches on the answer:
" 'There are tales and writings of everything but the
Fool; he comes into none of the doctrines or the for-
tunes' " (98). Of course not: the Fool's tale shows up in
Gospel, not occultism.

At the end of Nancy's vision, during which we have
witnessed with her virtually the entire drama of humanity and redemption, she sees the Fool and the Juggler embrace. So: the enigma of things, and Love, are at unity
after all!

On Christmas morning Sybil and Lothair and Nancy
go to the village church together for the Christmas Mass.
All is vision. As they approach the little church building,
for example, apparently so quiet and immobile, Nancy
reflects that the very serenity and antiquity of these
arches is a whirling and violent "dance" of atoms. The
liturgy is a great unfurling of the Dance, with kneeling
and standing and calling back and forth of responses
from choir to congregation, the way deep calls unto
deep, and the singing of the hymn "Christians, Awake",
with its injunction to "rise to adore the mystery of love",
which is what Sybil does all day long every day in any
event, and which is why she is so apparently unthreat-

ened by all the terrors that are presently to be unleashed
upon them all.

The terrors take the form of a blizzard which howls in
upon the downs that afternoon. Lothair has gone out for
his routine walk, and Henry has conjured up the storm
by means of the Tarot, in hopes of swallowing the old
man up. Sybil thinks it might just be an idea if she
popped out into the tempest to see if Lothair is all right,
and Nancy goes to Henry, whom she finds outside with
the cards. She seizes him in her relief to find him in this
tumult, and in thus doing, causes him to drop the cards,
thus losing control of the blizzard, which may now blow
on forever, since, like the misfortune in the "Sorcerer's
Apprentice", there is no way to recall the spell. " 'You
fool' ", he cries to her—as usual saying more than he
knows, since it is precisely Nancy's intervention, grop-
ing and blundering though it may be, that rescues Henry
from his evil purposes. She must play the Fool for this
part of the Dance, speeding to make up what one of the
dancers is bungling.

Sybil, meanwhile, is out in the snow looking for
Lothair and adoring the mystery of Love, which, she assumes, is no less in control now than it was during the
liturgy in the church. She finds a kitten first and picks it
up, then finds Lothair, whom she manages to convince
that it is *she* who needs help, and could he possibly give
her a hand back to the house—so sensitive is Love, that
it is reluctant even to allow its object to feel the humil-
iation of being rescued. En route home they encounter
Joanna and Stephen, and Ralph, who has been trying to
drive over for a visit; so that as so often happens when
dramas approach their climax, we presently find the

whole cast of characters together on stage—or, in this case, in Aaron's house.

Presently we find Sybil in her bath. The hot water of the bath reminds her of all the lovely opposites and changes that make up the world: drinks and baths, hot and cold; society and solitude; walking and sitting down. "It was all rather like Henry's charming little figures. . . . She knew where the golden light came from among the images; it came from the figure of the Fool who moved so much the most swiftly, who seemed to be everywhere at once, whose irradiation shone therefore so universally upward that it maintained the circle of gold high over all" (134, 135). Put into the vocabulary of Christian theology, this would refer to the same thing that we find in Saint John and Saint Paul about Christ's being the one who made all things and in whom all things "consist" and whose glory fills all.

Sybil goes to Nancy's room presently and finds Nancy almost hysterical over the fact that the cards have been lost in the blizzard when she inadvertently knocked them out of Henry's hands. Sybil is able to encourage her to go to Henry and, as it were, to *be* life between Henry and Lothair, rather than the death that now seems to obtain because of Henry's frustrated murderous intentions. " 'I know the Dance, and the figures that make the Dance. The crown's gold over them, and there's a movement that Henry's not known yet. Do you suppose that storm can ever touch the Fool? . . . Do you think the mystery of Love is only between those who like one another?' " (139). Sybil, in this scene, becomes the Fool for Nancy, holding her and easing her in her agony, as the Fool has held and eased Sybil herself during the crucifixions of her own past. Like the Fool, Sybil has sped to Nancy's side in the Dance to enable Nancy to dance the steps which she is unable to dance. Once again, put into the terms of Christian piety, it is like Saint Paul's remark that part of the point of his own suffering was to enable him to bring to others the same help that had come to his rescue in his need. It is part of the mystery of our "making up that which is behind" of the sufferings of Christ. It is part of bearing one another's burdens and so fulfilling the law of Christ. It is part of entering into the fellowship of Christ's sufferings. The New Testament is shot through with the mystery, the way the Dance on Aaron's board is shot through with the speeding movements of the Fool.

The narrative turns our attention to Joanna now. In her mad quest for her lost child, she seizes upon almost anything, and in this case, it is the kitten which Sybil has brought in from the snow. At least it is a small, warm, living thing, and, " 'It'll grow; it'll grow' ", she says (150). Meanwhile Aaron learns from Henry of the calamitous loss of the cards and of Henry's fear that, since the blizzard was roused by the cards, it will never cease, since only the cards can break the spell. But Aaron reflects that perhaps after all the cards and the images have no power in themselves: perhaps all this mumbo-jumbo is only a passive reflection of bigger things. Perhaps the occult can only peer into things, not create them. Well, then—if this is so, and the blizzard is a coincidence after all, then Lothair is safe. It is a natural snowstorm and will cease presently. Even if (heaven forbid) the cards might be lost, at least they won't have death on their hands— the death of all of them, in fact, if it is a supernatural storm that will engulf them all. Anything would be better than that—even the loss of the cards. "On the very verge of destruction, he cried out against destruction; he demanded a sign, and the sign was given him. Lothair Coningsby came stumbling into the hall" (152).

In this newly tranquil frame of mind Aaron thinks back over the history of the Tarot. He recalls that a time would come when someone would arise who would understand the mystery, and "by due subjection in victory and victory in subjection should come to a secret beyond all, which secret . . . had itself to do with the rigid figure of the Fool" (153). This someone is, of course, Sybil, who, ironically knows nothing about occult lore. All she knows is the simple thing about Love, namely, that it lays itself down for the sake of others. A similar victory is visible to anyone familiar with the Gospel. We find Sybil, presently, at dinner with Aaron and Ralph, able to contemplate the whole drama in peace. Every character, no matter how muddled or frantic or sinful, has "some high virtue, each to its degree manifesting the glory of universal salvation" (156). This is another way of saying what Christians would believe about muddled and sinful humanity, namely, that the selves that God made when he made us were good, and not bad; and it is the business of salvation to retrieve those selves, effaced and lost because of evil. For example, Lothair, whom most of us would long since have written off as a bore and really quite worthless, Sybil sees as "industrious, as generous as he knew how to be, hungry for peace, assured, therefore of finding peace" (156). To us, his hunger for peace looks like the irritability of a dyspeptic old codger who hates noise in the house. But what, asks Love, lies at the root of this wish for peace and quiet? Precisely the wish for peace and quiet, and it is the business of salvation

to bring us to the fulfillment of every longing. Our being ground to powder and melted in the crucible (read
"crucifixion") might have to intervene to transmute and
remake the desire. But whatever trace of the real thing is
to be found there will be smelted out and revealed in all
of its glory. Sybil's thoughts run through the whole cast
of characters this way.

The conversation at this odd dinner, with only Aaron
and Ralph and Sybil present, turns to cats after a bit and
thence to the kitten. Aaron asks whether the Egyptian
sun god Ra is not shown in a cat's form usually. Sybil
doesn't know but ventures, in her gracefully humorous
and demurring way, " 'Perhaps the kitten is Ra, and I
brought the Sun God home this afternoon' " (159). Of
course the kitten is Ra, and of course Sybil has brought
the Sun God from the very teeth of the storm outside
into the very teeth of the storm inside this troubled
house, and all will be well presently.

In the ensuing scene we see the salvation of Henry. He
and Nancy go to the room where the golden figures are,
taking only the cards of the four suits with them, the
Greater Trumps having been dispersed in the mishap
outside. They are going to see what can be done, but
Henry has little hope, since it is always true, is it not, that
the Greater rules the Lesser (trumps always rule other
cards)? No doubt it is true in card games, politics, and
perhaps even in science and the occult. But there is one
realm where the opposite seems to be the case. Unlikely
and inauspicious actions like saying, "Behold the hand-
maid of the Lord", and, "Nevertheless, not my will but
thine be done", turn out to triumph over all principality
and power. What is overthrowing a mere blizzard, when

the citadel of the Prince of Darkness himself was wrecked by this nonsensical strategy?

As Henry and Nancy enter the room, we find that the screaming of the blizzard makes itself heard here, in the presence of the Dance, as music. Also, in the steps which follow presently, we find that Henry must follow Nancy (power and authority—the traditional role of the man in betrothal—must submit to submission itself) in order to discover the saving dominion of Love over domination. It is necessary for the two lovers to be "separated" for a bit, as the legend of the Tarot says, and this is in keeping with the unvarying rule of Love, that we must let go of whatever it is we wanted to keep. His recent mocking at her fear is now changed to fear for her, which is a way of saying that he is beginning to learn some of the rudiments of Love, which is a way of saying that he is stumbling into the first steps of the Dance—he who would have only now wrecked the whole Dance by murder.

Henry's experience in this scene takes him through what seems years of being bound (we may call this Purgatory if we wish) and then of becoming, as it were, one with the Falling Tower: all of his schemes and hopes crashing down in ruins. But through all of this void, one thing alone has meaning for Henry: he hears Nancy's voice saying, as she had said to him when they entered the room, " 'Remember, I wanted to love' " (169). It is as though her desire, so simple and natural, and so good in its purity, holds him and comes to his rescue.

In the next scene we see Lothair's salvation. He is lying in bed after his ordeal in the snow, and his thoughts run back to Sybil. " 'She'd come out to meet him—yes, of course; but which of them—oh good heavens, *which* of them—had really been thankful for the other's presence?

Perhaps it didn't matter; perhaps they'd both been thankful. Reciprocal help' " (172). Ah, Lothair: this is sounding very much like what they call the Dance. Mutuality. The very thing you don't especially like. Of course, if one owes one's life to it . . .

But Lothair's thoughts do not remain thoughts. He thinks it might be an idea to get up and maybe even mingle with the others. " 'I thought I'd rather be among you'. . . . one mustn't be selfish, especially on Christmas Day" (173). We begin to see the testy and querulous Lothair's salvation speeding along in even such a minuscule nuance as the following: he thinks of saying, as he comes down to the others, " 'I thought perhaps you wouldn't *mind* me coming down' ", which carries with it worlds of bogus self-deprecation and snideness; but thinks that a hearty " 'Ha, ha! Well, you see, I didn't need much putting right' " (173) might serve better, the idea being that he doesn't need much help after all. But none of it seems any good, and he simply leaves his room, as though it is better to drop *all* pretenses and clever barbed comments and just appear.

What started out as a simple matter of Lothair's responding to the smallish notion of merely getting out of bed to be sociable on Christmas Day lands him in a huge brouhaha in which he is not only saved but also assists in the salvation of others (which, in Williams' view, is synonymous). It is as though it is said to him, "Right, Lothair, you peevish, funny old man: you've stumbled into Step One of the Dance out there in the snow with Sybil; now here is Step Two—just getting out of your bed and being *nice*. If you can be faithful over a few things like this, you'll be given the chance in a minute here (Love always does this) to be ruler over many. You are going to be a hero presently, you peevish, funny, un-heroic old man."

Lothair, coming into the hall, sees the kitten, Joanna, and Stephen going into Aaron's study. He does not like the look of it: surely Aaron won't want this bizarre entourage creeping about, and suppose Nancy or Sybil blundered into this lunatic? He'd better just see what is going on. (This is a very long way for Lothair from the opening scene of the book, where his whole request of life was simply that everyone leave him alone.)

Lothair tries to expostulate with Joanna, but nothing will turn her back from proceeding on into the inner room to find her baby, she says. Lothair realizes that he must intervene physically in order to turn her back. Surely Aaron won't want her in there fiddling about with his golden figures and no doubt stealing them. There is a scuffle in which it is as though all the symbols of the Tarot are unleashed upon them all. It is lunacy, of course—the whole scene. And our Warden in Lunacy is now called upon to be, in fact, a Warden—to guard the right and keep order. It is no longer a merely honorific title. In the imbroglio, Stephen seizes Lothair and turns him upside down. The Hanged Man all of a sudden—strung up ignominiously like this in the course of inter-posing his body between chaos and order.

Then a smokelike mist seems to be emerging from the inner room where Nancy and Henry are working to stop the blizzard, and at that moment the windows and doors of this room burst and the blizzard rages in. Lothair has just shouted Fire! upon seeing the golden mist from the figures drifting out, but now here is this snow coming in. Apparently chaos and the Dance are to be mingled. Which will overcome which?

At the same moment downstairs, the door has burst open, and Ralph—the more or less normally self-centered Ralph—finds that it is he who must coordinate all the household efforts to get the door shut. No one, not even the offhand Ralph, seems to be exempt from having to dance. Aaron is terrified, and, thinking that the "elementals", that is, the spirits behind the Tarot and the blizzard alike, are calling for a sacrifice, would gladly throw Lothair, or even his own grandson Henry, out for them to consume. But there is no time: the sheer necessity of getting the door shut overrides these dark and passing fancies.

The door is barred, and they all rush up to see what is happening upstairs. Each one's experience of the golden cloud, and of the struggle, is in keeping with the sort of person he is. Ralph cannot pierce the cloud: he has never given one moment's thought to mysteries like being unselfish, and so the golden cloud of Love is opaque to him. Aaron is isolated: having rejected the real Dance in his solitary attempt to wrench the meaning from the mere symbols of that Dance, he has nothing to do now that it is upon him. But then presently the cloud takes on some form for him. It seems to be about the size of a man's hand. Very big things, like the overthrow of principalities and powers like Ahab and Jezebel, come from clouds of this size. Presently more hands seem to be forming from the mist, and it becomes less and less clear to Aaron whether what he is looking at is cloud or human flesh. Translated, this would seem to imply that what he has always seen as only opaque and secret lore turns out to be plain flesh and blood. What he had sought by rummaging through his books he might have learned by turning to the people around him. The glory of this golden mist is "nothing but" acts of love, being done now, heroically, by the hands of these people—Henry and Nancy and Lothair and Ralph. Aaron's response is terror: "Run!" he cries, and makes for the stairs.

At that point the kitten seems to go mad, shooting out of the cloud, then back in, then back out to the stairs, crouching ready to spring at the front door. Apparently there is no more place in this breaking of Reality in upon them all for the illusion the kitten has represented for Joanna. The kitten leaps at the barricaded door, frantic to get out of all of this, and at the same moment Aaron tumbles down the stairs and lands in a helpless heap in the hall. Once more the door gives way, and once more the golden mist and the blizzard are mingled. Apocalypse, it seems, has arrived. But in it we see Sybil trying to give Aaron a hand with his sprained ankle. Love will get on with its quiet and simple business even when the mountains and rocks are falling, and of course it is that quiet and simple business to put those mountains and rocks to rights again in any case.

Meanwhile, back up in the room with the figures, we find Nancy, apparently alone, having become separated from Henry in the cloud. But her experience is one of lightheartedness. She is conscious of being "at the disposal" of whatever good is abroad. Of course nothing is safe or certain; and she is empty handed, with her hands spread out, as it were, offering to do whatever she should, like all hands of service since the beginning of time. She sees, as it were, the figures from the suit of staves, or clubs they seem to be now, raging across the countryside making the blizzard and threatening to engulf England. "Between that threat and its fulfillment stood the girl's slender figure, and the warm hands of humanity in hers met the invasion and turned it" (194). Suddenly the storm abates, and England rests peacefully under "the natural flakes of a snowy Christmas". Carols were sung all over the land, "in ignorance of the salvation which endured among them, or in ignorance at least of the temporal salvation which the maiden-mother of Love preserved" (195). Like the Virgin Mary, the maiden Nancy has simply made herself available to whatever Love wills, and salvation has been the result.

The scene is described as it appears on the Moon card of the Tarot: the moon shining between two towers, no longer falling but serene and firm; and below this two "handless beasts" sit howling, representing perhaps all the yet-unformed desires and aspirations of the creation; and below them a shellfish crawls out of the sea—the deepest and most unformed recesses of the creation, as it were, moving towards the serenity and fulfillment of this peaceful fruition.

But all is not over. Nancy is assaulted suddenly by Joanna, who thinks she hears her baby's heart beating in Nancy and wants to tear him out. Joanna is right, of course—the thing that she seeks, namely, Love, which she thinks is her baby, is indeed living in Nancy. In this struggle, Nancy is torn by Joanna's nails, as another body was torn by nails in its struggle with evil, but Nancy simply offers herself for Joanna's help. In the picture of the Fool in the Tarot, there is a beast rearing against the Fool, although it seems somehow tame: "The Fool and the tiger, the combined and single mystery" (201). Rage and frenzy and all the frantic appetites that tear men, now brought into their proper subjection. The kitten, herself a small tiger, is just crouching to spring at Nancy when it is caught by its neck. Lothair has saved

Nancy. " 'Damn you, woman, let my daughter alone!' " (201).

Many other things happen in the struggle. Lothair encounters Henry as the Hanged Man, appearing upside down by the convex light of the mist—Henry has confessed his murderous intent to Lothair and has hence been delivered from evil. Ralph and Stephen fight—elemental, masculine energy striving with itself, as it were. Lothair sees Joanna is the high priestess ready to sacrifice Nancy; Nancy recognizes her debt to her father, who has saved her from the cat; Nancy desires for Joanna that Joanna shall have all that she seeks—merely locking Joanna in the cellar of a lunatic asylum would accomplish nothing. Joanna grabs the cards and "points" them to create fire, for the thing that she seeks, her child Horus, is said to come from the fire.

The whole thing is resolved in the last chapter as the Sun takes over. Sybil and the servant girl Amabel help Aaron with his ankle; Nancy and Henry come together once again. Aaron sees the cloud the way Israel saw the cloud of God's glory—" 'It's the cloud from which the images were first made' " (220).

Joanna is revealed as a sort of embodiment of heathendom—earnest, full of desire, and misguided. The kitten comes quietly to Sybil, who appears as the Empress, since of course she does wield the greatest power there is, namely, Love. Joanna supposes that Nancy is her child, which is good enough for the time being, Williams would seem to imply, since what better guide out of illusion and into the real realm of Love could Joanna ask for than Nancy? And the Fool (Love) and the Juggler (the mystery of things) come together.

6

All Hallows' Eve

The title of the first chapter of *All Hallows' Eve*, "The New Life", has a snag in it, for we soon enough find that it is death that is being spoken of. But anyone familiar with Dante, or indeed with Christianity at all, will know that *la vita nuova* only follows upon some death or other.

In this case we find Lester Furnival loitering on Westminster Bridge in London just as the bombing in World War II has ended. She had been killed on the embankment nearby when a plane crashed on her and her friend Evelyn Mercer. And here she is now, alone. The main thing that impresses her, and us, about the city is the silence. No one seems to be about. Lester seems to be in some sort of *lull*. She cannot even get time clear in her mind—was she married yesterday, or when? It turns out to have been six months ago, but in the realm of death time does not exist anyway. Things that come to us ordinary mortals in a sequence of days or hours or years are here juxtaposed and superimposed on each other so that we can see how they relate to each other. For example, a fit of sulking when I was a small child might show up suddenly, in the glare of death, to be of one piece with my middle-aged frostiness to someone whom I fancy has insulted me. I have forgotten the earlier incident; but perhaps in death I will be permitted, or obliged, to see that habits built on childhood sulking, and never checked, bore the fruit of sullenness and umbrage in my adulthood. Carried all the way through, of course, this sort of thing will reveal that the dictators' megalomania and territorial ambitions had their roots in the sandbox, with shouting and swaggering and grabbing for toys.

What we witness in this story is Lester's salvation. The angle that Williams has chosen is what we might call a purgatorial angle. That is, Lester, having died, finds that she is in a world of her own making. What she did, and the attitudes she adopted during her life, determine what she finds here. A number of details in these opening pages emphasize this. The reader does not need to accept any special religious doctrine of purgatory, or even of life after death, to feel the force of what happens. The "purgatorial" aspect of things may, if one wishes, be seen simply as a way of casting a special light on human behavior, which is what all novels try to do one way or another in any case. Here a woman's attitudes and actions add up to making her a certain kind of person. How is such a person (or any of us) ever going to be shown what that looks like, much less come to grips with it all? Sometimes a great trauma will bring us to a halt; sometimes it is simply a slow and almost unnoticeable process of maturing and shucking off immature attitudes. Tolstoy and Henry James write about nothing else. In this story we are somewhat jolted to find the same thing attempted by means of Lester's being obliged not only to face but also to relive all her acts and attitudes, as the process whereby she will become a truly free and whole person.

The point is that for any mortal this is the only way to be set truly free from the traps and tangles of what he has said and done. It is never enough, apparently, simply to sweep under the rug what has gone wrong. For things to be set to rights there seem to have to be apologies, restitution, forgiveness, and restoration. Only then will he find himself free from what rankles and irritates. He may, of course, brazen it through, but no one will call that freedom.

It is true emotionally and psychologically, to be sure. But Williams is drawing on notions deeper than this. At the root of this drama is the Christian notion of judgment and the forgiveness of sins. Nothing will be swept under the rug. Nothing will be left over to nag and plague. All will be hauled up and set to rights. If something goes wrong in this mortal life, Christianity directs us to go to the person we have offended and make it straight. Own up. Apologize. Give back the stolen item. Shake hands.

But what about the great list of things left over when we blunder across the border of death? Do they get wafted away by magic? Are we let off of them scot free simply because we never bothered to set them straight in this life? On that accounting it would be much better for us all to sweep everything under the rug, since then we would not ever have to bother with it. No difficult scenes. Just the waving of a wand on the far side of death and all made lovely in an instant.

This picture would not make sense, given the Christian doctrine of forgiveness that lies at the root of what Williams is dramatizing here. Forgiveness may be thought of as the gift which love holds out to the offender. But of course there is nothing magic about it. Nothing is ignored or papered over. The release comes for everyone concerned when confession and restitution and pardon occur. If I have stolen ten cents from you, it is not enough for me to say, Sorry about that! The dime must be produced and returned for the situation to be made right.

Williams draws upon this set of notions in this tale. We may call the picture purgatorial in the sense of its involving this "redoing" of all that has gone wrong, not in a grim and merely punitive way but rather as the very set of steps whereby everyone moves towards joy— towards real release from the snags and tangles still clutching at them. We need not run aground thinking, Oh, but I do not believe in Purgatory. We need only imagine, for the sake of the story, that here is a way of setting to right things that have gone wrong, and of everyone's being set free from the guilt and vexation that selfish and cruel and vain attitudes have left them with.

Some readers, familiar with Christian teaching, will object that all this somehow does less than justice to the doctrine of Grace. Does not Grace take care of all this? Is it not a free gift? Surely one cannot *earn* forgiveness, offsetting guilt by piling up works of restitution in order to balance off the score?

No. Williams' point, however, is that this seemingly laborious way of confession and restitution and restoration seems to be how Grace always brings us along towards joy. It is never magic or automatic. The process never seems to be unconscious.

The drama in *All Hallows' Eve* entails the working out of Lester's (and others') progress either towards joy or away from it.

It does not take the reader long to conclude that Lester must have been an almost wholly selfish person during her life. She has, for one thing, been mainly interested in things, not people. Hence this is what she gets when she is boosted across the borderline of death and all illusion is suddenly whipped away. It is as though it is said to her, There: you wanted, really, a world with no people in it (they are such bores). Well, here it is.

She finds herself marooned in a London with no one in it. She sees shops with their wares in the windows—all the things she used to like to shop for. But no shopkeepers or shoppers. The windows of the city are lighted, but no one seems to be inside. However, her interest in things was at least sincere, and sincerity, even if misplaced, is itself a good thing, and to that extent it comes to her aid now. On its account she is granted "this relaxation in the void" (9). It has earned for her, so to speak, at least some space in which she may begin to work out her salvation.

Presently she finds in herself "a small desire to see someone". Here is a small hatchway open towards salvation. She has not after all really desired mere solitude. There is somehow in her a need and a desire for others. Fair enough. This will do for a beginning. It is a long road from here to that City where one's whole joy is to know others. But one must start somewhere on any journey, and this is a good place. She can't quite *prefer* this silence and solitude, even if most of the time in life she told herself that people were bothering her.

Her husband, Richard, approaches, and Lester falls into her habit of blaming him for being late, or for anything. After a brief exchange, he fades, and with him all the feet, voices, bells, and engines that, come to think of it, she had been hearing while they talked. Because she had had *some* real relationship with Richard and some commitment to him, he, apparently, constitutes the only connection she has with the living world of other selves. He was her spouse, and if marriage is anything at all, it is at least the locale where we learn what knowing another self entails—and thereby what knowing all other selves entails. Charity is the lesson that is learned in marriage—that is, *if* it is learned and not refused. Lester has missed almost all of the cues because she was generally a selfish and irritable spouse, but once again, whatever rag of authenticity clung to whatever fleeting attitude she may ever have exhibited will be made full use of now by the Mercy that is giving her this chance to move along in the direction of the joy that she and all souls want, ultimately. You tolerated Richard? You even had some passion in your attachment to him? Good. That will do for a start. We can build on that.

When Richard has disappeared, Lester begins to cry and realizes that she would like to borrow his handkerchief. So: Richard has something that he could offer you, has he? Something you would acknowledge your need of? Never mind that it is only a handkerchief. Salvation can begin anywhere and will certainly make good use of whatever comes to hand. If it is only your need of this handkerchief that at least brings home to you that you would be glad to be indebted to Richard for even this small thing, then your need of a handkerchief has done its work. Soon enough you will find that you owe everything to others—to your spouse, to your friends, to every laborer who has ever worked in fields or at lathes making the things you ate and used, and, finally, to *the* Other, whose laid-down life puts us all in his debt forever. But of course one can't be asked to learn everything

at once. It is good enough to begin with borrowed hand-
kerchiefs. The saints know that to acknowledge
indebtedness is one of the ingredients of pure joy. Souls
in hell hate it more than anything.

Lester now realizes that she is dead. It is a bore, since,
never having had anything to do with death, she has
nothing now to do *in* it, says the narrative. That is, unlike the old souls who kept a skull staring at them from
a shelf as a sort of reminder that this was their destiny and
that what they did today and tomorrow would somehow contribute to their readiness for this destiny—
unlike these hardy souls, Lester has never given death a
thought. Much too unpleasant a topic, of course. We'll
cross that bridge when we come to it. So, now here on
Westminster Bridge, in this transition, she finds herself
uncertain what to do. She has never prepared herself for
this.

For lack of anything better to do, she begins to move.
Once again, the mere desire to do something rather than
nothing shows that she is very far from the impotence
and inanity that marks a wholly lost soul. If she were
completely lost she would have slipped into a torpor.
Nothing at all happens in hell. All movement is a sign of
at least energy, if not of life, and neither of these is to be
found in hell. So—insofar as Lester simply wants to do
something, or go somewhere, she is, as it were, on the
right track. One would say to a man who had slipped
into a comatose state out on a freezing mountain somewhere, "Get up, man! Jump about! Flap your arms!" It
may seem silly and inconsequential when you compare it
with the movements men make when they are working
at something productive or when they are showing their
skill in feats of gymnastics, but it is at least a sign of life

and a way of fending off death. Indolence and torpor are very alarming signs. So here is another straw in a good wind that is blowing for Lester.

These may all seem to be absurdly small matters—such items as Lester's mere sincerity, and her small desire to see somebody, and her rather desultory attachment to Richard, and her need for a handkerchief, and now her vague idea that perhaps she ought to start moving. But this is the whole point so far: it is ordinarily small matters like this that show the drift of our lives. Very few of us encounter immense and dazzling events that blast us towards holiness or damnation. For most men it is a matter of imperceptible steps. That is what Williams is writing about. It is not Genghis Khan or Michelangelo we have here. It is only Lester Furnival, whose life seems to have been slightly closer to where most of us live than was the life of those titans.

Presently Lester's long-time friend Evelyn Mercer shows up. She also was killed in the crash on the embankment. Lester would infinitely prefer to have Richard for a companion in this vacuous realm, but it cannot be. He is still in the world of the living, and any contact he and Lester may have will only be fleeting. It will be only barely sufficient for the patching up of the frayed places in their relationship. Death has sundered them, and now they must get on with their respective pilgrimages. They had been given to each other for six months of marriage, and they had the chance during that time to learn all that can be learned of Charity, that is to say, of freedom and joy—or at least to begin to learn it. Now they must go on without each other.

It is a bleak irony that Lester must have Evelyn for her companion. Oh, to be sure, they had been friends in life.

But Evelyn is worse than a bore. She is querulous, sniv-elling, selfish, and generally intolerable. But as luck will have it, it is she with whom Lester must travel now. "The second best was the only best." For lack of Rich-ard, who was the best, Lester must settle for this friend, and it is no use protesting. It is to Lester's credit that she sees this and accepts it. She greets Evelyn: " 'So you're here!' "

Immediately she feels cheered, somehow. The point, of course, is that fact is better than illusion, and the ac-cepting of fact is better than denying it. The fact is that Evelyn, and not Richard, is the one who is here, no mat-ter what one's wishes and dreams might prefer. Lester, by greeting Evelyn, acknowledges that she accepts this fact. And not only this, but she *says* she accepts it. In Williams' world, clear speech is better than mumbling inanity. Insofar as anything true gets said, we have got somewhere. If Lester had screamed " 'No!' " that would have been a step backwards. Or if she had pressed her lips in a tight refusal to give utterance to the fact, that also would have been a step backwards. But to see it and grasp it and articulate it: this is forward movement. If she can manage only this much now, she can be trusted with more later.

As Evelyn natters and whines, Lester notices the dark entrance to the London Underground nearby. She real-izes that it leads nowhere for her and Evelyn now, since that world of busy, working, living people is not open to them. But that black hole: "A mediaeval would have feared other things in such a moment—the way perhaps to the *città dolente*, or the people of it, smooth or hairy, tusked or clawed, malicious or lustful, creeping and clambering up from the lower depths" (13).

Given the sort of layered superimposing of times and places that you get in Williams' prose, this is not very far-fetched. Lester is gradually becoming aware, in this lull, that everything matters infinitely. Hence, even a black hole, especially one leading downwards, is a fair enough reminder of the judgment that now hangs over and scrutinizes everything she does. This quaint and picturesque medieval way of fancying things might not be so wildly misbegotten, come to think of it: For after all, what are tusked and clawed demons pictures *of*? The modern imagination has not come up with anything that is any more vivid in reminding us of the horror and dereliction that torment any soul who rejects the exchanges of love. The psychiatrist's couch may incline to a milder and more polysyllabic vocabulary, but no one will pretend that talk about paranoia or psychosis represents much advance on pictures of goblins. After all, "paranoia" is simply a label indicating a state of mind in which we think there *are* goblins lurking about.

As Evelyn babbles and gabbles on, Lester experiences "a slow recollection of her past with Evelyn". Here she is, being given the chance not only to remember, but much more, to re*do*, all that past, which she more or less botched. Readers, especially theologically rigorous ones, will sometimes raise the question as to whether all this is not shaky theology. Where did Williams get all this about our being given second chances and being obliged to live through things again?

The answer is that this is fiction, not theology. It is a way of picturing the thing that our deepest instincts clamor for, namely, that justice be done and that things be really made right and not just swept under the rug. We want to see restitution, and the straightening out of what is crooked, and the evening up of scores.

Christians, of course, believe that some such process will occur before the whole story is over. But since no detailed blueprint has been supplied in the Bible, we are free to come up with pictures as to how it might be supposed to operate. We do this with all doctrine anyway: the Trinity, the Ascension, the Resurrection, the creation itself: everyone has got a mind full of wild pictures about all of these unimaginable and inexpressible notions. For the nonreligious reader, of course, Williams' pictures will present no more problems than do Dante's or Milton's. All may be accepted as merely a way of getting things vivid and concrete.

For example, as they walk along, Lester permits Evelyn to paw her arm. This gives her the creeps, but she permits it out of plain consideration for Evelyn's feelings. She simply puts Evelyn's need to paw someone's arm above her own loathing of being thus pawed. Immediately there flashes through her memory the picture of herself in a taxi years before, permitting some ardent suitor to paw her arm. She had been courteous and had waited for the chance to disengage his hand gently. It is as though that act of courtesy has come to her aid now. As the memory passes, she fancies she sees a taxi race through the park and away, as though to say, "There: you have passed that small lesson with a bit of help from habits of courtesy formed in past days at perhaps some slight cost to your own preferences. You don't need me any more. Farewell!" And the taxi, and that incident, race away.

It is only a fancy, or a vision. But in this world where everything—every act and attitude and memory—is poised, ready to step in and either assist or obstruct, it does not much matter whether it is a fancy, a vision, a real apparition, or even a real taxi just passing coincidentally. The narrative is dismantling these rickety partitions between the various areas of our experience that we keep safely sequestered from each other. Things converge under the tremendous pressure of ultimacy that loads the atmosphere in this realm of judgment. If one supposes that human actions and attitudes matter in any sense at all (leaving aside all reference to any divine accounting), then one will agree that this is a true enough way of imagining what is at stake every day, all day, and not just in some fancied purgatorial realm on the far side of death's frontier. What does this small act mean to me, by way of making me into one sort of person or another; and what does it mean to this other person here, by way of either smoothing or obstructing his path towards joy? The question remains the same whether one prefers to think of human behavior in psychological terms or in religious terms.

Lester, in fact, begins to recognize that she is actually a debtor to Evelyn. They have been friends. Friendship, rightly understood, brings with it immense responsibilities—of trustworthiness, truthfulness, mutual help, and so forth. It is no light thing. Well then, there is no way around it: Lester, for good or ill, has long since become Evelyn's friend. So the question now is not, "How can I get rid of this bore?" but rather, "What is a friend called upon to do with a poor querulous creature like my friend Evelyn here?" For Lester it is one more nudge in the direction of Charity, although she is not at all aware of big considerations like this right now.

In a melancholy refrain Evelyn keeps protesting that she hasn't done anything. That is just the trouble, and her protest begins to sound unhappily like the wail of some ghost in the night, "Where its own justification

was its only, and worst, accusation" (19). That is, what
Evelyn says by way of defending herself (against *what*?
we might ask) boomerangs and turns out to be the worst
accusation that anyone could bring against her. *You*
think you are saying that you haven't done anything
wrong, but you are more lethally correct than you know.
You haven't done anything at all. You should have.
What were your responsibilities in life? To whom should
you have been a friend? Who could have used your help?
What have you left undone that you ought to have done?

Presently Lester, staring in dismay and pity at Evelyn,
exclaims, "Oh my God!" But like Evelyn's, "I haven't
done anything", this is taken at face value in this realm
where the air is very thin. Here every word means exactly what it means. So—she has invoked the Deity. She
need not be surprised, then, if deity comes to her aid; and
indeed deity has already begun to send help—in this lull,
in Lester's need for a handkerchief, and in the arrival of
Evelyn. And again she exclaims, "Richard!" and because
she does know what that means, and because she means
it precisely, she will find that indeed Richard will come
to her aid.

A month or so later we find Lester's husband, Richard
Furnival, going to visit his friend the painter Jonathan
Drayton. Jonathan shows him two paintings that he has
been working on. One is of London after an air raid—in
fact, of the part of London called the City, around Saint
Paul's Cathedral. What strikes Richard about this painting is that the City seems to be suffused, or rather, almost pregnant, with a sort of massiveness of light. Not
only is everything illuminated as though from some
source like the sun: everything seems itself to be full of
this light, and the light itself seems to be massive, sub-

stantial, and full of weight. Richard asks Jonathan how he gets this effect, and Jonathan quotes the eighteenth-century painter Sir Joshua Reynolds in reply: "Common observation and plain understanding" (28). The point is that the artist's eye (Jonathan's in this case) only sees what is *there*. Unlike the dim and vacuous city in which Lester finds herself because of her lifelong preference for things rather than people, a real city is full of substance—people and potentiality and so forth; and, since any city is itself a diagram of *the* City which is the abode of light, the artist who is trying to catch a true picture of a city may see it as full of light. And he perceives this, not by some special insight, much less some occult power, but rather by "common observation and plain understanding". That is, if one will only look at what is there, one will begin to see what it is all about. What are ordinary human exchanges, after all? What is the bustle of commerce and finance and getting and spending about, rightly understood? It all has something to do with exchange, and that is a clue as to what Everything is about. A penny spent for a licorice stick is a tiny case in point of what happened at Golgotha and of what the citizens of the City of God experience as bliss, namely, exchange. The fruit of my labor for the fruit of yours. I need you. Life laid down for another. My life for yours. It takes the murk of evil to keep us from seeing this and to turn it all to greed and mere mercenariness and murder. Rightly seen, a city is a glorious thing—or at least some sort of reminder, no matter how botched, of a glorious thing.

Jonathan's other painting is of one Simon the Clerc, or Father Simon the Clerk, who turns out to be a sort of healer, prophet, and cult leader who has in his entourage Jonathan's fiancée, Betty, and her mother, Lady Wallingford. Jonathan has painted Simon preaching to a throng. The unnerving thing about the painting is that if you look at it closely, not only do all the huddled people in the crowd seem, somehow, to resemble beetles; Simon himself looks like an insect. He is standing in front of a rift in a cliff face and seems somehow to be sinking into it. His outstretched hand seems to spread grayness and weariness and debility over everything. There is something inane, even imbecilic, not only about Simon's influence but also about Simon himself.

Once more, Jonathan has caught the truth of the matter, as he did with the City. As Richard looks at the painting, it occurs to him that perhaps Simon's influence, far from forcing these people back towards mere beetleness, might be beckoning and coaxing them up from beetlehood to the full and free humanity for which they were made. Perhaps they are en route towards real health.

But no. "He saw it was impossible. That blank face could never work miracles; or if it could, then only miracles of lowering and loss" (44). The imbecility that Jonathan has caught is the imbecility that Dante saw in the damned souls: they had lost the good of intellect. Evil has leeched away all the bright vigor of intelligence and left this vacuity and inanity.

As Richard walks home, his thoughts turn to Lester, and he finds in himself a new and lively appreciation of her intelligence and vigor. He becomes acutely aware of how he had not appreciated this while he had her and of how he was guilty of plain neglect of her. He says, almost aloud, " 'Darling, did I neglect you?' " (46).

He is entering his own purgatory, so to speak, but it is not purgatory experienced as pain and labor and horror.

Far from it. Rather, his loss of Lester, and his growing awareness of how starkly and brightly she contrasts in the sheer vigor of her intelligence with the debility apparent in Simon and his influence and the thought that they could certainly use her around here now—all this serves to prod him along towards the true appreciation of Lester, which is what his marriage to her should have been about, but which he botched somehow. Well (the Mercy seems to say), never mind: she's gone now, but let us use her very absence to bring about in you what you missed when she was present. One way or another, your salvation is the main thing for you at any rate. If you won't have it by means of Lester, then perhaps you will have it by means of her loss. After all, the Mercy has been called both Alpha and Omega.

Richard sees Lester coming along the street as he walks, and he feels, as he looks at her, "more like a wraith than a man; against her vigor of existence he hung like a ghost" (48). This seems odd—this talk of her "vigor"—when we have just seen Lester as an apparently weak creature struggling vaguely about in the silent city. But the point, surely, is twofold: first, from *her* point of view she is a very weak and forlorn creature, and indeed, from ours as well. We have picked up some notion of the sort of person she was in life, and it has not added up to much that stands her in good stead now in this time of reckoning. But then this leaves out what is happening to Lester now in her first steps towards the charity and freedom that she avoided during her life. Who is to assess just how strong she is now, especially in comparison to Richard? Perhaps it is that the very things she experiences as weakness come through to him as strength. After all, Saint Paul talks this way: "When I am weak, then am I strong", and "My strength is made perfect in weakness", and his remark that he was allowed to suffer so that he could be comforted, not for his own sake but so that he could then comfort others with the very comfort which had come to his rescue. His vulnerable point became the point at which others received help.

And secondly, of course, Lester did have some strength in life: her common sense, her sheer intelligence, and so forth. All that she ever had that was worth anything is brought into play now; and part of Richard's own progress towards freedom and joy is to learn to recognize, and extol, the excellences in his spouse that he may have inclined to take for granted during their life together. It is as though Death plucks him by the sleeve and says, "Here now: what you overlooked then, you have the especially acute chance to appreciate now, since it is gone."

In the next chapter we find out just who, or what, Simon the Clerk really is. Like all the evil characters in Williams, he is a grotesque parody of the good. Almost every quality that he claims stands in stark and ghastly contrast to what Christ offers. Simon is "the one who is to come". He is a Jew. He is a healer and prophet. He has an entourage. He brings peace. But we do not get very far before it is clear that this is all counterfeit. His followers turn into beetles, in effect: apparently his influence leeches away all real individuality and power, not to say joy, from them. The peace that he gives is like the peace given by narcotics: undeniable but somehow ravaging. Simon cannot tolerate the sight of Jonathan's painting of the City: "No, no; it's too bright' " (60). He makes a bid for Jonathan's loyalty, recognizing in Jonathan something that he can use. We also see here Simon's contempt for the ragtag and bobtail of his followers: " 'They aren't insects, they are something less' " (57). The analogy with Satan is unavoidable—the old notion that he hates those whom he dragoons into his camp. Evil is incapable of love that will face death for others.

The narrative emphasizes Simon's Jewishness. Readers worry about anti-Semitism here, but this concern stems from a misreading of Williams' intentions. Simon is the opposite of Christ, who was also a Jew. He stands in the ancient tradition of Israel, which was the custodian and priest of divine things. But like Judaism itself, Simon does not grant that what happened among the Jews during the time of the Caesars was, in fact, the Incarnation of God. Israel had been the custodian of divine revelation, it was said. "It had been proposed that their lofty tradition should be made almost unbearably august; that they should be made the blood companions of their Maker, the own peculiar house and family of its Incarnacy" (62). That is very Williamsian phraseology, and it simply means that apparently God had chosen Israel to be not merely the recipients of his covenants and the guardians of the Ark but, far more, to be the special bearer of the Incarnation, which is indeed an almost unbearably august calling. The vessel of all this was to be Mary, "the Jewish girl", who, by assenting to what the angel announced to her had, says Williams, "uttered everywhere in herself the perfect Tetragrammaton" (62). Here again, the almost indecipherable phraseology that Williams has chosen means that Mary assented with her entire being (indeed, pregnancy does entail a woman's whole being) to the Lord Yahweh, whose unutterable name was represented in Jewish literature by its four consonants, the Tetragrammaton YHWH.

We find that Simon, on the other hand, springs from an old French noble family of Jews who had been adept in the black arts. His father had been a philologist and as such had had as his special interest the history of languages. But he was most especially interested in the very beginning of sounds and the possibilities of power in words. This is one of the themes in ancient Hebrew literature—this notion that words do, in fact, not only name things but also somehow bring them into being. The universe is described in the Hebrew account as having been created by the word of God, and the special privilege and authority given to man over the animals was to name them. Words and names: What is it all about? Simon is more than curious, and we find that his great experiment is to find the word or words that will furnish the man who utters them with *power*. It is, of course, the attempt of all black art, and indeed it is also the attempt of all science and art. How shall we describe things in order to control them? Einstein with his theory of relativity, as well as Shakespeare with his sonnets, is trying to get a handle on the world by a formula of words. The trouble with the black arts is that they attempt to do this by ripping the fabric of things: obscenities, outrages, perversions—whatever will pry open the world and make it yield up its secrets, even if we have to plunder it and stand it on its head. Simon, a sorcerer himself, had only once had sexual relations with a woman, and that was for a specific end, not to gratify lust but to produce offspring on whom he might test his powers. This offspring, we find, is Betty Wallingford, with Lady Wallingford being Simon's willing accomplice in this depressing parody of the Incarnation. The power which Simon wishes to test out on Betty is his ability to dismiss her spirit from her body and then re-summon it. In other words, he wants the power of life and death over other human beings, Betty being merely the first experiment. As such, she is disposable. She does not matter in the smallest degree to Simon. Nor does Lady Wallingford, for that matter.

The parody is stark. On every point Simon stands at a polar extreme from the Divine Love. His interest in other selves is simply and solely to have total power over them, whereas the Divine Love became one of them and gave itself up for their sakes. Whereas each self matters infinitely to the Divine Love, such selves are mere data, or raw material, to Simon. In his wish for power and control, he is of course guilty of Lucifer's sin: making a grab for what belongs to the Most High alone.

In chapter four, "The Dream", we come upon Betty lying awake in her bed. Her mind is running back over her own history. What we discover, here and elsewhere, is that she is the illegitimate child of Simon and Lady Wallingford, conceived for the single purpose of furnishing Simon with a creature for his experiments in dominion over death. Betty's "father", Sir Bartholomew Wallingford, is an air marshall and away most of the time. For part of each year Betty is taken by her mother to a cottage in Yorkshire, where she is treated as a servant. Lester and Evelyn had been her friends at school, although the friendship took the form mostly of their persecuting Betty. The thought of Evelyn's death (she was the crueler of the two) brings some ghastly joy to Betty as she lies here, and this poor rag of joy, with its reminder that "people die" and that hence all her persecutors will one day die, brings Betty a small suggestion of triumph and hope and therefore of strength. With this strength she is able to manage a weak "Mother, I can't" when Lady Wallingford comes in to tell her that Simon needs her to go out on one of the errands on which he sends her, dismissing her spirit from her body and thus enabling her to scout about, free from the confines of time and space, to gather information for Simon. This scouting takes the form, among other things, of Betty's buying the newspapers from newsstands several months hence, and reading them, and then reporting on her return what they have said about Simon, who is thus enabled to know just how his plan for world dominion is going. The troubling thing, we find, is that these future newspapers have nothing to say about Simon, thus unnerving him with the possibility that he will have sunk out of the news six months hence when his plan calls for him to be dominating the headlines.

But tonight, besides the small surge of strength in Betty herself arising from the mere recollection that her tormentor Evelyn is dead, there is another obstruction to Simon's spell. It turns out to be Betty's memory of Jonathan's hands holding hers. A small thing, it would seem: but, where her mind is now debilitated and confused by Simon, her body still holds, against all of Simon's machinations, the warmth of real flesh and blood holding her in real love. That stark, external reality testifies against this murky limbo of spurious love into which Simon is wheedling her. His murmuring incantations of "love . . . joy . . . peace" seem increasingly to be mere echoes, or parodies, of the real love, joy, and peace she has known with Jonathan.

Simon does dismiss Betty, out into the City. But tonight her journey is marked by a certain buoyancy, even joy. Betty comes to King's Cross Station. This is unmis-

takable: King's Cross is no mere chance name for a railway station. It is the place where omnipotent Love
meets, and fights, hell, even in apparent defeat. In this visionary walk, Betty sees herself, back across months and
years, getting into the train with her mother at King's
Cross, a sad and wilted girl accepting despondently the
dismal oppression laid on her by her mother and Simon—going to Yorkshire to be a mere servant. That
poor creature needs help, and now this Betty, in her very
weakness, but buoyed up by the memory of Jonathan,
calls out to herself, " 'Oh don't *worry*! Isn't it all a game?
Why can't you play it?' " (81). From this vantage point,
where she is just barely beginning to experience help
(Jonathan's love) and therefore salvation, and therefore
the City (where all the happy souls gladly acknowledge
that they have been helped)—from here she is able to see
that "the troubles of this present world" are nothing
compared with the joy that is laid up for anyone who
will have it. The Betty who is beginning to experience
rescue, or salvation, must offer help to the Betty who
was lost in defeat. This is lesson number one in Charity,
as it were, and we may be sure more will follow. Indeed,
soon enough we find Betty offering help to Lester, who
has herself arrived at Betty's house to offer whatever
help *she* can to the beleaguered Betty.

Betty's walk takes her back in time to King's Cross,
then forward to the following January, where she obediently reads the newspapers in order to report back to Simon the news that he hopes to hear, namely, that one
Simon the Clerc is dominating the world (there is no
news), then back to the present October, and then home.
At one point she calls on Jonathan, the only name she
knows that can offer her any help (it is as though the Di-

vine Mercy is saying, "Fair enough for now: you will soon enough learn to call on *the* Name from which all the other names derive their ability to help"), and lo and behold *Lester* hears her cry, across the empty air of the London in which she wanders; and, in a fumbling act of charity, she responds and comes to Betty's house to see if there is anything she can do to help.

But it is an extremely peculiar chase that brings her there. She hears Betty's cry and recognizes it only as the voice of a woman calling to a man, which reminds her that she might try calling upon Richard, the only one she knows who might deign to offer help to her (how, she does not bother to ask). But she finds that all she can do is croak: it is as though, having never really wanted, or called upon, Richard's help in life, she finds that her voice is now unable to do so. It has gone rusty from disuse. (At every point the souls in Purgatory discover that they are getting exactly what they acted as though they wanted.) But Evelyn hears Betty's voice, and it kindles all her old delight in tormenting Betty, and she takes off running towards it. Lester, on some vague notion that she at least ought to follow, follows. But Evelyn outdistances her: "A cruel purpose could outspeed a vague pity" (91). Betty flees home, and when the two pursuers reach the house at Highgate, Evelyn stops outside, foiled in her ugly desire to torment Betty as she loved to do at school and having no other interest at all in Betty. But Lester goes on in, just to see if perhaps there is anything she can do for Betty.

Betty, for her part, has called on Jonathan to be sure: "She had called on something she knew. But that something was more deeply engaged on its work in the world of the shadow behind her [what we would call the plain workaday world] and this world [the shadowy, purgatorial City into which Simon has dismissed Betty and in which she begins to stumble into salvation] would not give her that" (91). It is as though we must learn, first, simply to *call* for help (surely this is the beginning of salvation for any soul?) and then to accept the help that is given; and when we have done that and learned the joyous lesson of indebtedness, we may win the warrant to enjoy greater joys, up the scale of bliss from strangers, to former enemies, to friends, to spouses, to God himself. It is as though the Mercy is saying, "Call for help! If you cannot invoke God himself quite yet, then call on whomever you think might come to your rescue. A spouse? Fine. You may find yourself rescued by someone less than your spouse—someone, say, whom you hated; but having thus learned the primary lesson that your life is indebted to others, you will then be ready for the more blissful experience of that in the exchanges with your spouse. But you can't go on to grade two before you've passed grade one. It is that way in any school, and especially in the school of Charity."

Meanwhile, Richard, out of curiosity, has gone to Father Simon's place at Holborn, just to see what sort of man he is and what is going on in his emporium. He is ushered into a peculiar house by a sycophantic little man—one of those whom Father Simon has "saved". In this house the very corridors and doors seem like crevices in a cliff face (cf. Jonathan's painting of Father Simon). All is "peace", but it is clearly a bogus peace like that offered by narcotics and hypnotism, or even death. At an odd session where they sit in a circle, with Father Simon, Lady Wallingford, Richard, and a window forming an unmistakable mandala, or occult pattern,

Richard realizes that what is happening is that Father Simon, murmuring away, is draining the meaning from words so that they become mere sounds. It is, of course, the same thing he is attempting to do with Betty: drain the meaning (spirit) from her form (her body) in an attempt to gain control; but this is always and everywhere evil, this driving apart of form and meaning. All evil may be described this way. A human being, for example, is the bright crown of the creation, but the evil thing, death, drives asunder this lovely union of form (body) and meaning (person), and you get two horrors, a corpse and a ghost. Or again, language is one of the highest and most exquisite gifts of God, but if you drive apart the form (the word itself) and the meaning (what it stands for), you get a lie, which is evil. Or yet again, sexuality is also one of the most priceless gifts of God, but if you drive apart the form (the sexual act) from the meaning (love), you get fornication, rape, adultery, and all manner of trumpery. It is always the same.

We find that Father Simon is interested in Richard because Richard might be the necessary link with Lester, who might supply Father Simon with an answering commodity for Betty, allowing him simultaneously to dismiss Betty from her body and this world and summon Lester into some body here from the world of the dead. He wants an exchange: that will facilitate his black plans. What he cannot know is that indeed there will be an exchange, but, being an exchange of Love, it will overthrow his entire scheme, just as Love once before, by making itself vulnerable to Death, overthrew that entire scheme.

It will have been observed by any attentive reader that no matter how bizarre and apparently occult Williams' tales may appear to be, he is never writing about anything other than the plain stuff acknowledged by all Christians and counted upon by all men, Christian or not, that it is life laid down which furnishes the seed from which new life comes. We see it in cornfields, and human generation, and the Mass. Very mysterious, and very ubiquitous. Williams' art always seems to be asking the question, how *do* you go about keeping people awake to all of this?

During this scene we find Lady Wallingford recollecting the night of Betty's conception and how, at the time of her copulating with Father Simon, there had appeared in the bedroom mirror two figures identical to him. Apparently he was able, somehow, to multiply himself: After all, what are demons, or even evil men, but tedious replicas of the one fountainhead of evil himself? These "derivations and automata" are sent out into the world to do Simon's work.

Richard, sitting there, realizes that he is being sucked into something. What rescues him is the thought of Lester—a real, external thing, a woman, whom he has really loved, as over against this shadowy world of murmured, wheedling promises. The thought jolts him to his senses. But ironically, it is not the thought of Lester in any of her perfections; rather, it is the thought of her irritating habit of complaining, " 'Why have you kept me waiting?' " But, in these odd and ultimately comic exchanges, this very complaint becomes a sudden summons to Richard, not only rescuing him from this whirlpool here at Father Simon's but also sending him soon enough to her side in Betty's bedroom just in time to save her (Lester) from being almost overwhelmed by Simon as she interposes herself between him and his assault on Betty. Williams has here made his story come to that same peculiar point that you find in the Bible, where we read that God is able to make even the wrath of man to praise him. In these dazzling exchanges of redemption going on here, even Lester's irritable complaint about being kept waiting becomes a summons from Charity to Charity. Deep calling unto deep.

In the chapter "The Wise Water", we return to the house at Highgate, where Lester has arrived to "help" Betty, if she can. Somehow Lester seems protected from Simon, not just because she is a ghost and therefore invisible to him but also by her *intention*, which is an intention of Charity and therefore opaque to his evil eye. The most towering insights of evil become stumpy imbecility in the face of the simplest exchanges of love. It is the one mystery which evil cannot unravel but which any peasant or fool may be an adept in. Lester begins to see many shadows of Betty, and they turn out to be from all the times back at school when Lester had either been cruel to Betty or had at least acquiesced in Evelyn's cruelties. Once again, we find that there is nothing hidden that will not be revealed. The uttermost farthing will be paid. All those times still dangle, so to speak, between Lester and Betty and have got to be made right. Lester cries out, " 'Betty!' " thinking to summon Betty and make her apologies; but, in these flashing exchanges that are speeding along now faster than we can follow them, her very cry offering apologies to Betty turns out to be a cry for help *from* Betty. Lester, in fact, *needs Betty's forgiveness* before she is free enough, and therefore strong enough, to offer any help to Betty in Betty's extremity. All is exchange. All is indebtedness. Nothing can be generated by a solitary soul any more than it can by a solitary body. But the following scene of confession and forgiveness, far from being tense and awkward and miserable, is a jumble of laughter and fun. Lester must persuade Betty to remember every single incident before she (Lester) can feel completely delivered from the guilt left over from every single incident; but it is hard to get Betty to do this at all, so great is her joy now. She consents to do so, for Lester's sake (not, it will be noted, so that she can gloat over Lester's crawling pleas for pardon), but recrimination and retaliation and offense are nowhere to be found. They are as far removed from this happy scene as is the East from the West. Lester "was, and must be now, the victim of her victim" (131). It is like a thousand other paradoxes: *figlia del tuo figlio*, spoken to the Virgin—"daughter of your Son"; and Christ's being the Death of Death and his being both Priest and Victim; and the paradox of the kernel of wheat dying in order to live, and so forth. All wild and implausible—but routine for anyone familiar with the City and its odd ways.

There is one small aside in this scene which might require a word of explanation. At one point Betty, lying on her bed, puts out her hand to touch Lester's lips, "But it did not reach them. Clear though they saw and heard each other, intimate as their hearts had become, and freely though they shared in that opening City a common good, still its proper definitions lay between them. The one was dead; the other not. The *Noli me tangere* of the City's own Lord Mayor was, in their small degree, imposed on them" (133). Williams is referring, of course, to Jesus (the Lord Mayor)'s "touch me not" to the women after the Resurrection. There is a communion of saints, to be sure; but it is subject for now to the laws of life and death. We may not attempt shortcuts like seances, necromancy, and so forth. For now, this communion between the dead and the living must bow to the separation and run along lines of mutual rejoicing, intercession, and hope—nothing more. (If an apparition is ever granted, as at Lourdes, Walsingham, or Fatima, or if the Lord Mayor himself says to Thomas, "Touch me and see that it is I", it is recognized as extraordinary and noteworthy and not the general order of the day.)

At the end of the chapter we find Evelyn "drawn" to Father Simon's house at Holborn by his invoking of the reversed Tetragrammaton, in a parodied and parallel movement to Lester's being drawn to Betty's side, and Richard to Lester's. Like the wizards of Egypt aping Moses' miracles, Simon can do, point for point, the same things that Love is doing. Only the one tends towards dissolution and death and the other towards joy and life.

We now find out in detail just what Simon is up to. He will kill Betty by dismissing her spirit, substitute a mock corpse of his own creating in her official coffin, and send her real body in a case with Lady Wallingford to the cottage in Yorkshire, there to remain as a sort of link between the two worlds that he is attempting to control. But balance must be maintained, so he is obliged to summon some spirit at the same time that he dismisses Betty's, and he thinks that the wife of his new acquaintance, the widower Richard, would be a convenient candidate, since surely Richard would like to have her back (so little does his evil imagination know of the steep and glorious pilgrimage on which Richard is being led precisely by means of this very widowhood that would seem to Simon, and to most men, to be the worst of all fates). Simon knows he has summoned somebody from that world, but we know that it is Evelyn, not Lester, since Evelyn is far more attuned to Simon's beck than is Lester.

Simon's attempt to overwhelm Betty and finally dismiss her spirit is foiled by Lester's standing between them and receiving the force of his power in Betty's stead. She tells Betty she will just stay with her, and this promise reminds her of the business of waiting, which had always been an irritant to her in life, and suddenly she realizes that waiting has been transfigured into a mode of joy for her—just this stillness and acquiescence (it shows up frequently in the language of the saints and mystics). And not only this, but she now knows that she is waiting for Richard, the thing that had irritated her the most. This must be redone, somehow, in this realm where she finds herself, where not one single farthing is lost under the rug. "Oh now she would wait and he would come" (157). The very militancy that had made her such a strong-minded woman now comes to her aid in assisting her simply to stand fast and wait for him.

And as she does so she becomes aware that she seems to be not only leaning on some frame which runs along her spine and out her arms but also to be supported by it. In her fight against the dissolution that Simon's evil influence presses on her, "She pressed herself against that sole support. So those greater than she had come —saints, martyrs, confessors—but they joyously, knowing that this was the first movement of their re-edification in the City" (159). It is the Cross, of course. She is being crucified, with Christ, for Betty and finds this death to be not dissolution but edification. The saints and martyrs have all told us so. Here it is.

Betty, apparently asleep now, murmurs, " 'Lester!' "
and, being *a* name—the one to which she is indebted at
this moment—it will serve for *the* Name, in whom alone
salvation is to be found. Lester has, in effect, become the
bearer of that Name to Betty, as Mary was the God
bearer to us. (It is not a structural flaw in the story that
the imagery keeps changing, with Lester at one moment
being crucified like Christ and at the next being a God
bearer like Mary. Williams would say that this is in the
nature of the case. Imagery itself must dance all over the
place in order to catch even the barest hints of the glory:
witness the parables, where the kingdom of heaven is at
one moment a mustard seed and at the next a woman
with a broom.)

Lester, in the middle of all of this, recollecting that her
being here has saved Betty the trouble of getting up out
of bed in obedience to Simon's summons, recalls the
times when Richard had got up in the middle of the night
to get her a glass of water, to save her the trouble, and
this in turn reminds her of "innumerable someones' doing such things for innumerable someones", and she
says, " 'Darling, darling Richard' " (163).

She has invoked his name, not in irritation now but in
gratitude and indebtedness, and therefore in joy. Now
the frame which has been her cross begins to feel more
like a bed, and Williams cannot resist the pun (he would
say that the City is full of even this sort of merry buf-
foonery) of bedsprings and springs of water (the cups
brought by Richard). Both sorts of spring mean rest and
relief and comfort.

Richard and Jonathan arrive and burst in and interrupt
Father Simon's incantations, to his discomfiture, and

Richard says to the Lester whom he alone can see, " 'Darling, have I kept you waiting? I'm so sorry' " (169). This is his part of the purgatorial exchange whereby both he and she are set free from what was a leftover shackle of irritation for both of them and which had not until now been made right—or, more than merely "made right" in some arid legal sense, transfigured into positive joy.

The action drives on now to its climax—or climaxes, we might say, since we are watching the simultaneous pilgrimages of Lester, Betty, Evelyn, and Simon, and also, marginally, of Richard, Jonathan, and Lady Wallingford, towards either joy or ruin. If we want to say that the vindication and triumph of the City over its counterfeit is the climax, then of course the last page holds the climax, although we leave several of the characters very much en route there, the supposition being that they are at least now on course.

Simon enlists Evelyn, who, because of her querulousness and petulance, finds herself naturally, and increasingly strongly, drawn towards Simon's influence, since he, like all evil, promises gratification. He needs Evelyn to lure Lester into his influence, since Lester (Simon still does not know who this is who has obstructed his experiment on Betty) is the great obstacle to his success. Simon's plan is to cobble up a body (he can do this) and offer it to Lester, since this is the strongest temptation for a disembodied spirit, and ghosts find it nearly impossible to refuse. Simon needs a sort of bridge between the two worlds.

Evelyn does not have to work very hard to find Lester. Other purposes are at work which neither she nor Simon could dream of. Lester has remembered Evelyn suddenly, after all the excitement with Betty, and knows that she must go to her, since she has not yet made right the times back in life when she had "made use" of Evelyn. In the pellucid air of this City into which she is moving, all these leftover bits of selfishness, tiresomeness, and pettiness must be cleared up, not by way of a grim totting up of scores but rather in the merry exchanges of forgiveness, on the far side of which stands the fathomless joy of the City.

Evelyn shows up, dawdling outside the window of Betty's house, and Lester goes with her to Simon's house at Holborn: she is prepared to go anywhere with Evelyn for no reason other than that Evelyn seems to want it. The only thing Lester has in mind is to be at Evelyn's disposal. Love bears all things, believes all things, hopes all things, endures all things, apparently. We begin to see in Lester the agile and almost careless freedom of love that we might fancy, say, in a Saint Francis—a very long distance from the testy and edgy Lester we started out with.

Simon does, in fact, manage to get up a sort of body—it is more like a rag doll or a dwarf than a proper woman—and Lester accompanies Evelyn into it. It is Evelyn who is frantic to get into it, and Lester goes along just to be at Evelyn's service and possibly to coax her back towards accepting the present terms of their pilgrimage, which must be to be without bodies for the time being, until the resurrection. Evelyn, in her egocentric self-pity and irritation, will have none of it; for her, any illusion, even this depressing dwarf body, is better than fact. For Lester, the "fact" of being disembodied, while of course not a state of affairs one might prefer, has nonetheless at least this to be said for it: it is a fact; and the consenting to fact is always, in Williams' world, a step towards the capacity to be at home in the Ultimate Fact, so to speak, namely, the City. Such a consent is at the same time a step away from the Ultimate Illusion, namely, hell, towards which all enticements and frauds and illusions wheedle us.

Lester's whole purpose now is simply "to take and give pardon and courage" (225). She thinks of Richard and of all that she owes him, and in an attempt to get in touch with him she, via the dwarf woman's body, begs two pennies for a telephone call from a kiosk at Charing Cross Station. (It is not, of course, without significance that this is occurring at Charing *Cross*.) Even this infinitesimal detail is not allowed to pass without some notice in the narrative: a nice old man gives her the two pennies, and Lester recollects that she had, at least once, given two pennies to someone who needed it. Exchange. That act of charity comes to her aid now. That very small twopenny seed, as small as a mustard seed, has fructified and borne fruit that she may pluck now. She, or they rather—Lester is stumping about London crammed into this creature with Evelyn, who does not seem to care particularly where they go or what they do just so long as she is feeling the comfort of a body—they go round to Jonathan's flat, where Jonathan and Betty are entertaining Richard, and the last irritants that had been left from her marriage to Richard are dissolved in the glad exchanges of pardon.

Readers will by this time have noticed not only that it is raining but also that Williams is obliging us to pay attention to some idea of *water* in this story. Betty has a recurring dream, or memory, of some lake or river. Jonathan's painting of the City is spoken of as exhibiting some sort of liquescence. And now is it raining. We hardly go a page from here to the end of the book without having this rain drummed into us. What is it?

For one thing we find that Betty's old nurse, Mrs. Plumstead, had baptized the infant Betty, thinking that perhaps it would do no harm and might do some good, since Betty's parents obviously had no such intention. That water has protected Betty ever since. In the worst ordeals to which Simon has subjected her, somehow that water, as a lake or a river, has shown up in her memory and has strengthened her. Betty is somehow being "protected". Christian readers need not run aground on the theology of baptism here. Williams' point (this is a piece of fiction, we must remember) is simply that Grace does, in fact, come to our aid, in ways that are quite out of our grasp or comprehension and for which we may take not the slightest credit; and, more than this, that this Grace is mediated to us in disturbingly material ways: the Incarnation, the sacraments, and so forth. Another way of putting it, on which all Christians, regardless of their view of baptism, would agree, would be to say that somehow the creation itself stands between us and perdition. Simply to *be*, and to be solid, physical selves, is to be somewhere on the hither side of the vacuousness and dissolution of hell. Evil's entire scheme is to unmake what God has made, hence its attempt to spoil, pervert, warp, make sterile, and ruin all good things in nature. The sacraments, and in this case baptism, are pledges, trumpeting to heaven, earth, and hell that the creation is *good*, and that it is being redeemed, and that the promise of this, all hell to the contrary notwithstanding, is to be found in these small, unprepossessing acts like baptism and the Eucharist.

But this image of water has another side to it. What Betty (and Lester, increasingly: the rain seems somehow glorious to her) experience both as protection and as some sort of herald of good things, Simon and Evelyn experience as doom. The rain pours down on them almost the way the brimstone poured down on Sodom. Obviously the reverse side of Grace is Judgment. It is not as though Grace has a hideous alternative face, like some Janus monster. Rather, it is the old business that what goodness experiences as bliss (the fire of the love of God, say) evil experiences as torment (the fire of hell). Our experience of reality as either something glorious or something intolerable is the direct fruit of the choices we have made.

It is worth noting that this climactic series of events is taking place on Hallowe'en—the eve of the Feast of All Saints. It is as though the glorious company of the apostles, the noble army of martyrs, the goodly fellowship of the prophets, and all holy souls are arrayed in a great cloud of witnesses tonight, with all the good influence of their intercessions pouring over Betty and Lester and Richard and Jonathan as they struggle against Simon.

The little party, including Lester and Evelyn in their grotesque body, rides in a taxi to Simon's house at Holborn, ostensibly to take him Jonathan's painting of Simon as a gift.

We find Simon there, worried now over the various obstructions that he is encountering. He thinks he may find a way through to his goal by the simple murder of Betty, since apparently "her body was her safeguard".

Once more we see the hatred that evil has for the good creation. But we know it is the end for Simon. The "single, tiny, everlasting illusion" that he, like Lucifer, has cherished, namely, that he could be omnipotent, is failing him now. Since Betty is not present at the moment, he gets Lady Wallingford to bring some strands of Betty's hair from her hairbrush, and these he works into yet another horrible doll and tries, by the squalid art of voodoo, to kill Betty by stabbing this little mumbo-jumbo with a needle. He botches it and twice stabs the fingers of Lady Wallingford, who is holding the doll. All unbeknownst to her, Lady Wallingford is being interposed between Simon's evil and Betty. She is suffering for Betty, whom she had caused to suffer all her life. Her blood is being shed instead of Betty's. What fugitive, residual scraps of mother love have been gleaned by the Mercy here and put to Lady Wallingford's account? It is as though the Mercy is saying to her, you, too, shall be saved, but sometimes the kingdom of heaven must be stormed. Your entry will be violent.

The final scene, when Lester and Evelyn and Richard and Jonathan and Betty arrive at Simon's house and once more interrupt his magic, rises into almost entirely visionary terms. Simon has drawn a circle on the floor, and it is as though inside that circle lies his evil sway. Evelyn is drawn inexorably into it; Betty follows her in one last attempt to save her, which Evelyn rejects; Jonathan must allow Betty to do this—he must "lose" Betty before she will ever be really his. As it happens, she is perfectly safe, but Jonathan does not know this yet. Both the dwarf woman and the voodoo doll melt in the rain which is now pouring down through the roof of Simon's house into the room; Lester is drawn away into the rain—glad now to go on in her journey, into this rain of glory which now seems to be water and fire and blood and rose. Williams is borrowing unabashedly from Dante's blinding imagery of paradise. The inmates of Simon's "infirmary" all rush out of their rooms like the dead at the crucifixion from their graves, only to discover that all the ills from which Simon had "healed" them have returned. Betty is the one who heals them all presently. Simon is engulfed by the rain and by the return of the two replicas of himself whom he had sent abroad to spread his influence and who now come upon him and destroy him. The evil that a man makes and perpetrates will do this to him, depend upon it. Richard accepts his widowhood with joy now; Evelyn, having rejected joy, wanders off into the vacuum of the city, "there to wait and wander and mutter till she found what companions she could" (269). Lady Wallingford, like an old woman who has had a severe stroke (in fact she has), is given into Betty's care for the rest of her life.

7

Descent into Hell

In *Descent into Hell* Williams came closer perhaps than in any other of his tales to giving us a real novel. The action is all of a piece. There is very little of the clutter that we find in most of his earlier fiction—chases in fast cars for the Grail, African bombers over London, government meetings being called to discuss a talisman, or instant blizzards. There is tremendous pressure here, but it is held in check by the tough fabric of the story itself. If we may think of *Oedipus Rex* as a sort of perfect sample of what all art strives for—namely, the shaping of every single element (in the case of stories, it would be elements like words and actions and setting) into one, seamless whole so that it is impossible to pick out lumps, say, of mere description, excitement, oratory, or whatever—then we may say that Williams has, in fact, managed to arrange an extremely complicated set of elements into a pattern in which we may see that simultaneous

power and serenity that strikes us about all truly successful patterns, that is to say, about all good art. When you
see the finished product—a da Vinci Virgin, say, or a
Brandenburg Concerto, or the Parthenon, or *Oedipus*—
you are quite overwhelmed with the sense of things having come to a point of absolute repose. Each line and
color, each arpeggio and interval, each column and lin-
tel, each speech and gesture, appears in its own highest
perfection precisely because of the relationship in which
the artist has placed it with the other elements of the
thing. And yet this very repose, this very perfection of
serenity, that all good art exhibits, is full of energy and
vitality. It is very far from being entropy or hebetude.

One of the cries that goes up from people who begin
reading a Williams novel is that you cannot tell what is
going on. Things start off nicely enough, but before you
know what has happened you have lost your bearings.
Are these people dead or alive? Is this a vision or the
workaday world? What on earth does Williams mean
when he says that the faces of some people gathered in a
group are "unessentially exhibited to each other"? (This
last is from the first paragraph of *Descent into Hell.*)
Come.

The simplest way to find our path along through this
most complex of all of Williams' novels is to take it as it
comes. Chapter by chapter. And we have no sooner said
that than we find that we may have picked up a key to the
whole thing, for we need only look at the list of chapter
titles to see that there is an unmistakable progress
charted. You start with "The Magus Zoroaster", which
would seem to place things deep in the murky fen of the
occult. Actually you are in a plain London suburb in
broad daylight, but of course this *is* the fen. You move

down towards death and hell with a suicide, a frightened girl, and a man who is going to hell for your companions; past a false Eden, to a sort of crux or junction; and thence, via a "Dress Rehearsal" to apocalypse—"The Tryst of the Worlds", "The Sound of the Trumpet", "The Opening of the Graves", and finally "Beyond Gomorrah". The title tells us what it is all about. Somebody is going to hell. But there is an ascent also. The path splits. The two main characters go in opposite directions, the one towards solitude, wrath, ennui, and oblivion; and the other towards co-inherence, joy, fullness, and liberty.

The whole business occurs without violating the plain world of a rather cultured suburb of London. A newspaper would have very little to report except for an amateur summer production of a play by a local playwright. Williams' narrative, on the other hand, strips away the scrim of routine and lets us see what is really going on. The unnerving thing is that we recognize it all. Nothing unusual or even peculiar is happening. Apparently this business of going to hell, or to heaven, proceeds along almost unnoticeable lines.

The Magus Zoroaster, who supplies the daunting title for the first chapter, is not one of the principal characters. He is only referred to once or twice by way of explaining what is the matter with Pauline Anstruther, who is one of the principal characters. It seems that this Magus, or wise man, who was a prophet in ancient Persia, had a vision in which he saw himself approaching himself; or so Shelley says in two lines which Williams quotes in the first chapter. Pauline has been bedevilled for years with a similar apparition. Her deliverance from her fear on this point is one of the main threads in the action.

But we do not begin with anything so disquieting. The scene opens in Battle Hill, a housing development near London that had been built after World War I, taking its name from the rise of ground on which it sits. The hill itself has a long and bloody history of struggle. It has been the scene of many a battle in the wars that have marked English history, and it still holds those memories. All that has ever happened here is still present as a sort of pressure on the inhabitants of the new houses. Struggle is in the air.

What Williams has done is simply to pick up a commonplace and make it go to work for him. There is nothing especially odd about the idea of history hanging over a given spot. All tourists feel it: walk into Westminster Abbey, and all the kings of England are there. Go to Gettysburg, Waterloo, or Jerusalem, and you find it. Open a trunk in the attic and lift out an old stuffed bear from your childhood, and there it is again. One way or another the past not only clings to things; it haunts them. An exact replica of Westminster Abbey or of the Sea of Galilee would be a farce. The history must actually be there, and indeed it is there and will not go away. We may say that all this is merely psychological, but the phenomenon is no less real when we have pointed that out. And in a sense, it is not merely psychological: the kings really were crowned here, and no one has ever worked out what happens to events once they have occurred. For the purposes of his story Williams merely supposes that everything that has happened in a given spot is still there somehow. It is a commonplace of human imagination.

But Williams makes it a bit more stark, the way any artist does with any commonplace. For example, Cézanne paints a still life. If we had seen this collection of apples and jugs we probably would have supposed merely that someone had forgot to clear the table. But Cézanne says to himself, "Aha: What have we here?" and presently we have, from mere apples and jugs, an epiphany of glory. But Cézanne has not added anything, nor gingered up the scene with gilding and cherubs and scrolls. He has unveiled what was veiled for the rest of us.

Williams does something like this here. He takes the familiar feeling we all have that history seems to hang above places and puts it to work. The story seems to be going on under a great canopy made up of all that has ever happened in Battle Hill. Gradually we discover that what happens among the characters is a sort of echo, or "rerun", of all those prior events. We begin to suspect that there is nothing new under the sun. The conflicts which the characters experience are all variations on the only themes there are: charity, cupidity, jealousy, courage, fear, wrath, and so forth. Whether wrath plays itself out in a battle with horses and men, or in an icy snub in the parlor, the thing itself is the same.

When the story opens we find the poet Peter Stanhope reading a play which he has written to a group of local residents. They are "the dramatic culture of Battle Hill", and they are going to put on a production of the play. It turns out to be a pastoral, which is not exactly what they wanted. They had hoped for a comedy, but Stanhope says this is what he has been working on, and they may use it if they want to.

A number of important items show up. For one thing, we meet Stanhope himself. Probably the main thing that strikes us about him is how relaxed he is. He is very far from being the tumultuous and egocentric genius which one often thinks of in connection with poets. There is nothing here of the artist who is privileged to sulk or be horrid to people or scream because genius excuses all. Stanhope is quiet, courteous, unassuming, and above all free. His slightly offhand manner springs from this inner freedom. He is not agitated about whether they will get his play just right in their production. He seems to feel that the play is in some way theirs, to do with it what they please, as best they can. All he can do is offer to them what he had made. He has no special title to it just because he is the playwright.

Readers will recognize this as one of Williams' favorite themes. His good characters—the Archdeacon, and Sybil, and now Stanhope—seem to be completely at peace. There is nothing brittle or frenzied or shrill about them even when they find themselves caught up in a conflict between good and evil. They seem to have a modest and almost childlike sense of being "at the disposal" of mere goodness. They do not give others the impression that all depends on them, even though they may be very well aware that it might. For them the only requirement is to be obedient to what is asked of them, and in that obedience they are free.

Before the action has gone very far, we will see Stanhope offering himself as a kind of buffer between Pauline Anstruther and a certain fear that haunts her, in much the same way that he is here offering his play for the use of the locals on Battle Hill. The whole point as far as he is concerned is simply to be at the disposal—of anything that needs doing, really. If he has something that can be of service, very well. It does not much matter whether it is a play he has written or some inner strength and equanimity: nothing we have is our own in any case, so we might as well learn what it is for, he seems to say. To let go of what I have is joy and freedom and peace; to hang onto it is fear and solitude and anger.

What we see in Stanhope is, of course, charity. It stands as a sort of pole from which the story takes its bearings. All the other characters stand at greater or lesser distances from this center.

If Stanhope himself stands at the center of the action, his play is also very much at the center. All the characters are judged by their reactions to this play. The point about it is that it is a case in point of the Dance—that perfectly orchestrated and patterned movement in which all creatures move. The name of the Dance is Charity, and only the saints really understand it. All evil represents some violating of the steps.

Stanhope's play is a masque, a special kind of play involving music and dance and rather solemn and elaborate movement and costume. It becomes clear before very long in this story that Stanhope's masque stands as some sort of touchstone: if the characters understand what Stanhope is up to, we may assume that they are on the right track. If the masque seems pointless and opaque to them, it is they, not the masque, who are at fault. As it happens, Pauline Anstruther is the only one who seems to appreciate what Stanhope has done in the masque. The rest of them are bewildered or vexed with it.

Catherine Parry, for example. She is the director, although we get the impression that she is self-appointed. And in a sense this is what her trouble is generally. She is officious. She must run things. Things must bend themselves to her point of view. It is up to her to sort everything out. She is clearly at a very remote distance from the modest and amiable and even amused freedom which Stanhope enjoys. She is above all important in her own eyes.

Not only has Stanhope given us a masque: Williams has as well. We may recall that Williams wrote masques for the entertainment of the Oxford University Press staff. The whole array of characters is like the array in a masque, where we find them more or less lined up quite starkly according to their qualities or virtues or vices. In most masques there is none of the subtlety that we are accustomed to in modern drama. Rather, we find that the characters almost announce who they are: "I am Greed", or "I am Innocence", and so forth. So that, if it seems as though the characters here are too neat and represent qualities that are too pat, we must remember that Williams is presenting his own masque. This plainness is part of his intention. It is not a fault in his art.

We also meet Adela Hunt. She clashes with Mrs. Parry because she, too, would like to take things in hand and organize them. She loves to prattle about how art is symbolic and about contrast of mass and so forth. Neither she nor anyone else ever has a very clear picture of just what she is saying, but it always sounds impressive.

Myrtle Fox is worse yet. The first word we hear her say is "Watteau". This ostentatious reference to the eighteenth-century French painter is typical of her. She thinks things are "terribly sweet" and tells us that she is "rather mystic about nature" and so forth. She thinks that " 'we've only to sink into ourselves to find peace' ". She blunders gaily into more than she bargains for, however, when she allows herself to burble to Stanhope, " 'Nature's so terribly good. Don't you think so, Mr. Stanhope?' " (16).

Stanhope quietly asks her if she really means that and points out that for him "terribly" means full of terror. He does not bother to press the point that he is a poet for

whom words mean something. Miss Fox is puzzled.
" 'If things are good they're not terrifying, are they?' "
" 'It was you who said "terribly." . . . I only agreed.' "

This is one of the major themes of the book. The self-centered fatuousness of people like Myrtle Fox cannot at all see the frightening and bare fact that the good is sometimes the most terrifying thing we can encounter. C. S. Lewis caught something of this in his Narnia tales when he pictured the good lion Aslan as "not a tame lion", and also in *Perelandra*, where we find an implacable otherness in the eldils, who are good spirits.

The idea is that sheer goodness appears terrible to us on at least three counts. For one thing, it is wholly *other*, so to speak, and the wholly other is always frightening: surely this is the source of our fear of ghosts, who do not appear able to do much actual harm. Second, we know that we ought to be *like* this goodness, so we feel naked and forlorn and guilty in its presence. And third, we have the unhappy feeling that we cannot get there. Our helplessness is thrown into dismaying relief. And there may be yet another dimension to it all. The good may be terrible because it will not leave us alone. It crowds in on us, breaking up our little, pitiful defenses and summoning us out to the freedom and perfection that we would at all costs avoid, since it demands the uttermost farthing from us in payment. Williams is simply picking up the old idea that we find in the Bible of men finding goodness to be intolerable. Isaiah cries out "Woe!" and Saul of Tarsus falls to the ground. In neither case was it the devil they saw, but they were nonetheless terrified.

Pauline Anstruther is, if not the main character whose descent into hell supplies the title, then the foil to that character. The very first words she utters give us a clue about her. While the others are nattering on in their fatuous way about what the Chorus in Stanhope's masque might be, she at one point suggests that the Chorus is necessary to the poetry. In her shy way she is closer to Stanhope's intention than the rest of the lot put together.

Presently we find her wondering if perhaps the Chorus might be Stanhope's "effort to shape in verse a good so alien as to be terrifying". She realizes that she has never thought of this notion before — that there might be a good which is also frightening. This reminds her of a terror in her own life. She is pursued by a doppelgänger — a "double-goer", that is, a special kind of ghost which seems to be yourself dogging your own footsteps. If such a thing is an apparition of something that really exists in the spirit world, it must be one of the most unnerving species of ghost about. If we wish to think of it merely psychologically, the terror is not much diminished. Pauline, like almost everyone else in the world, is terrified to face herself and what she has made of herself. Most of us can sympathize. No doubt we all put an immense amount of effort, quite unconsciously, into the business of either papering over or excusing the horrible mess we have made of ourselves. If we were obliged all of a sudden to face squarely an image that was an exact replica of our moral selves, what would it look like? Most of us fear that it would be a goblin.

Pauline's doppelgänger appears when she is alone and at some distance. It is always a bit obscure, but of course she knows what it is and is terrified to look at it squarely. It has not yet come up next to her, much less touched her. But what will happen if and when it does? These are the fears that bedevil Pauline.

It would be a waste of time for us to quarrel over whether this ghost is real or merely a psychological quirk. The plain point about it is that it is a hideous reality. Pauline is terrified to face herself, and in this she is not alone. Williams' interest, here as everywhere, is not at all in occult lore. This is not a ghost story, although we will meet another, even odder, ghost presently. It is about the plain stark reality of human behavior.

In the second chapter, which is entitled "Via Mortis" (the way of death), we hear more about Battle Hill. It seems to have an odd property of pulling men into death. A man might imagine "a magnetic attraction habitually there deflecting the life of man into death" (24). We might at first think that this means that the hill is a peculiar place, spooky and full of strange powers. But then we remember that this might be said of any patch of real estate in the world. Men die. All men die. The people on Main Street and on Fifth Avenue and in the Edgeware Road are all going their way to death. It is impossible to overstate this. Nothing could be more literally true. Like Cézanne with his still life, Williams has added nothing to what is there. He has simply arranged the light so that we will be obliged to see what we might otherwise have glossed over.

Battle Hill, then, is like any town or housing development. It only depends on how we wish to talk about it. We can hardly pretend that the bricks and mortar, and the politics, and the local summer activities tell the whole story of what is going on there. By far the most important thing, there or anywhere, is that human beings are moving along towards death. Any failure to face this is whistling in the dark.

The fact that Battle Hill has had a long and colorful history makes it easier to see this. Lots of death has occurred here: massacres back in Celtic and Saxon times, and feudal sieges, and the Wars of the Roses in the fifteenth century, and a Protestant martyr under Bloody Mary in the sixteenth, and a Jesuit martyr under Elizabeth not long afterwards. "The whole rise of ground therefore lay like a cape, a rounded headland of earth, thrust into an ocean of death" (25). Nothing bizarre or occult here.

As it happens, a fairly recent death finds its way into the story. While the housing development was being built after the war, an unskilled worker had been hired. No one knew his name. It did not matter. He was clumsy and dull and became the butt of everyone's jokes. It seems to have been his lot in life. He had always been unfortunate, even in his marriage to a shrewish wife. Because of some poor piece of work he found himself fired from even this menial job.

As he tramps away from the building site, the hopelessness of his whole existence comes over him. There is not even anything back at his miserable dwelling in London to look forward to, what with a nagging wife and one thing and another. There is no reason to keep on living at all, come to think of it. The whole world has been unkind.

That night he returns to the site, and, by means of a rope which he remembers seeing in one of the half-finished houses, he hangs himself. The scaffold is ready made.

Williams' language is especially vivid here. We follow this man very closely on his *via mortis*. The "republic" has rejected him, that is, the whole world of friendship and fellowship and the normal human contact that we need. Well, then, he will reject the republic. As he goes back in the evening to the site, and to the rope in the half-finished house that looks like a scaffold, the whole area looks like a ruin to him. What builders and prospective home owners and real estate agents, with all their bright expectations, would see as a city a-building, he sees as a city ruined. When you come to think of it, the similarity is indeed disquieting. "Unfinished walls, unfilled pits, roofless houses, gaping holes where doors and windows were to be" (28).

He whimpers a bit, but the universe is indifferent. "It has not our kindness or our decency; if it is good, its goodness is of another kind than ours" (28). It might be a terrible good.

He makes his preparations. The very ladder by which he ascends to an upper story for his jump is "bone-white in the moon". He has reached the end, and "there was nothing more to happen; everything had already happened except for one trifle" (20). He is already dead to the world of human fellowship and has been so for a long time. The trifle is the mere business of jumping. He *wants* solitude, and this, in Williams' point of view, is extremely dangerous, since at the end of that road is hell. If heaven is the place of all good exchanges of fellowship, then hell must be its opposite: total solitude. I will be left alone forever and ever because this is what I wanted. If heaven is the real city, then Sodom, where they reject real, fruitful exchange for a barren and sterile parody, is a sort of reverse city; and, in Williams' scheme, Gomorrah is yet one remove further away, the place of final silence and solitude. (There is nothing in the Bible to this effect, but Williams, by using the strange name

Gomorrah, about which we know nothing except that it seems to have shared the curse of Sodom, has caught in one word the whole idea he wants. An air, not only of evil, but more, of remoteness and silence and impenetrable loneliness, hangs over Gomorrah, since we know nothing about it at all.)

When the suicide falls, the narrative does not leave him, as most fiction would. After all, when a man is dead, what is there to say? Indeed: What *is* there to say? Williams seems to ask. The narrative proceeds right on without batting an eye. The man falls and en route down thinks he sees a sort of rush away from him, as though a huge throng, perhaps of insects, has fled from him into crannies in the unfinished houses. The world of human beings, the ones who will be inhabiting these houses, has nothing to do with him. They are no more than insects to him. He is alone. This is what he has sought, and he has got it.

It will be worth our remembering, in connection with this man, that he has every reason to have wanted suicide. What did he have to live for? Who liked him? If ever anyone had an excuse for ending it all, this wretch did. We do not feel disposed to be very fierce in assigning much blame to him. And yet: despair is a sin. It is a luxury we are not permitted, either by religion or by mere psychological health. And, oddly enough, its root must be found somewhere in egotism: life has dealt *me* a poor hand of cards; they don't like *me; I* am the most unfortunate of creatures. One has at least got to have oneself at the center of one's concerns to reach this point, and this concern stands at a polar extreme from Charity, which is so free and full of joy that you cannot get it interested in itself. This may seem daunting and unapproachably visionary, but it is nonetheless true. From the infant who has forgotten to scream by watching a spider spin a web, to the Samaritan whose attention and effort are directed to this unfortunate in the gutter here, all the way to the saints in heaven who have been set free forever from the trap of self-awareness, it is true. The suicide then, unfortunate though he may be, is guilty.

He begins to wander. He finds himself at leisure. What is there to do? We are reminded of the situation in *All Hallows' Eve*, where the two women who have recently died find themselves in a lull. When all the diversions and baubles have been blown away by death, what have I got left to do? The suicide wanders away from Battle Hill, which is a good thing. He might as well have complete silence until whatever else is in store for him begins to happen.

What is in store for him? He will find out presently, when he is given the chance to "redo" what he had done wrong in his mortal life. He is given first of all the chance to accept a small offer of help and in so doing to begin to embrace the republic which he had rejected in a pique because he thought it had rejected him.

One strange note that finds its way into the narrative here is a reference to the Creed of Christendom, which denies any final separation of soul and body. The suicide knows nothing about these matters, so it never occurs to him that by ending the life of his body he will not end his troubles—or, shall we say, his pilgrimage. The Divine Mercy has joy in store for him, and this destiny will not be frustrated or cancelled by this act of despair which he is about to complete. The narrative has it this way: "The unity of that creed has proclaimed, against experience, against intelligence, that for the achievement of man's unity, the body of his knowledge is to be raised; no other fairer stuff, no alien matter, but this—to be impregnated with holiness and transmuted by lovely passion perhaps, but still this. Scars and prints may disseminate splendor, but the body is to be the same, the very body of the very soul that are both names of the single man. This man was not even terrified by that future, for he did not think of it. He desired only the end of the gutter" (31).

At the risk of pedantry, it is worth glossing that long sentence about the Creed, since it is very typical of Williams' tightly packed prose style. A reader only recently introduced to Williams almost always has trouble staying afloat in this complicated syntax. A long and rickety reading of that sentence might run this way: Christianity always has taught that despite the plain testimony of human reason (how can dust rise and be reassembled as my body?), nonetheless our destiny is not this separation of soul and body, and this dissolution, but rather that "this body of knowledge"—that is, this body by means of which I know my world via hearing and touch and smell—is going to be raised. It will not be an angelic body, made of some "fairer stuff", and it will really be me and no "alien matter". This very body is going to be filled with holiness. Somehow it will be transmuted and glorious in a way that I cannot even imagine now, and the way towards that goal may involve "lovely passion" for me—some intense experience, perhaps of loving someone greatly, which is one way of learning about glory, or the passion of prolonged sickness, which is another way, or perhaps martyrdom. Never mind the particular way. For all of us the end will be the same: glory. And whatever riddles there are en route, the creature that will emerge at the end of the story will be truly me.

The fact that it takes some such expanding as this to say in plain expository prose all that is contained in a given sentence of a Williams narrative shows something of how tightly packed his prose is. It is almost poetry.

This apparently far-fetched commentary, dropped into the narrative here, is very much of a piece with what Williams is up to in all of his fiction. There is very little distance, if any at all, between what seems to be going on in the plain world (a man about to hang himself, say) and the immensities that arch over the world. We have already seen this in the sense of history hanging over Battle Hill. Here we have it again with this reference to the Christian doctrine of the resurrection of the body. If it means anything at all, says this narrative, then it cannot be tucked merely into the archives of theology or the recitations of the liturgy. If it means anything at all, then it splashes out all over the universe and reaches every creature made of flesh, and certainly creatures like this cast-off man who supposes that he can bring his own sad story to a close by hanging. It won't do, says the narrative: but of course you don't know this yet. Never mind. Joy is in the cards for you. It will take a little while, and you will have to begin to undo this despair by accepting some help from a kind lady presently. But it will not hurt much, and then you will be en route to the City for which you have longed and which you have despaired of finding.

In the third chapter, "Quest of Hell", we meet Lawrence Wentworth. His is the title role. It is his descent into hell that we follow. The dismaying thing about this descent is at least twofold for us readers. First, it is not by huge crimes that Wentworth makes this descent; and second, he chooses, quite consciously, every single step down. In each case there is a clear choice between good and evil, or shall we say between thought-fulness and selfishness, or helpfulness and indolence, or growing up and acting like an infant. The steps are very small and very ordinary. The fear that this narrative conveys is not unlike the fear that Aristotle said was a requirement for tragedy: we watch a man *like ourselves* go down into ruin.

Wentworth's quest of hell takes the following form. He is a historian, living as it happens in the very house from which the suicide jumped when it was still only an open scaffolding. We find that Wentworth, scholar that he is, tends to reduce the whole world to diagrams. The things that have happened in history, which form his "field of expertise", had better fit into his schemes, or he will make them fit. He will make the world over according to his own point of view.

There are at least three significant things that we find out about Wentworth. For one thing, he seems to be having a recurring dream of himself going down a rope in the darkness. The rope is knotted, so that at any point there are hand- and footholds by which he might choose to stop his descent and start back up again. But somehow he just keeps going down. The dream is mildly distasteful to him, but he has trained himself to find a pleasant oblivion in sleep by thinking of pleasant things, so he manages to cope with the dream. We will find presently that this theme of thinking of pleasant things as a way of cushioning oneself against hard, bright reality is an important one in the story.

The two other items about Wentworth are connected with this dream. First, there is Aston Moffat, a fellow historian. He and Wentworth have been carrying on a scholarly dispute about a very small detail in the Wars of the Roses. The question itself does not matter in the slightest, and Moffat simply carries on the controversy because he has a real scholar's unselfconscious dedication to truth in every detail. Wentworth, in contrast, has got himself muddled in with the historical question, so that it has become a personal fight for him: *my* reputation is at stake here. If I lose the point, I will be the loser. He is at the point in his life "when a man's real concern begins to separate itself from his pretended, and almost to become independent of himself . . . he identified scholarship with himself, and asserted himself under the disguise of a defence of scholarship" (38).

This is a perilous business, and especially so in a narrative like this where very small attitudes and choices begin to stand out with astonishing vividness the way they would, say, on the Day of Judgment. This separating out of Wentworth's real concerns (his own reputation) from his pretended (the detail in the battle in question) is a kind of fraud. We see him here not only *accepting* a fraudulent division in his being (the pretense that he is interested in the truth about the battle when more and more it is simply his own reputation) but also *choosing* it. By moving in this direction, away from any concern with what is true out there in the real world, towards a solitary focus on himself and his own interests, Wentworth is indeed moving away from the real world of other selves and objective truth and towards the murky illusion and solitude that turns out to be hell.

But of course it is far too early to be talking of hell. Wentworth is a respectable local historian leading an entirely respectable life. If there is anything amiss, it is only the small matter of a scholarly dispute. The disquieting thing is that it is precisely by small and hardly noticeable matters like this that Wentworth makes his descent, knot by knot, down into hell. There is no shouting or any heroic leap into the abyss, only this dreary subsiding.

The final factor in Wentworth's life is the young woman Adela Hunt. He has taken a fancy to her. On the surface of it, this would be a good thing, since any love, even infatuation, represents some going out of myself towards another person, and to that extent I have a foothold, no matter how tricky, in what Charity is about. The trouble here is that Hugh Prescott has decided that Adela is to marry him, and Adela more or less thinks this might be a good enough idea. But she likes Wentworth and likes to come to evenings at his house to discuss history and art and so forth.

Adela and Hugh stop by Wentworth's house to ask for his help on some small matter of the costumes for the Grand Duke's guard in Stanhope's masque. Later that week by a complicated set of subterfuges they avoid Wentworth's Thursday soirée in favor of a date in London. Only Pauline shows up, and she asks Wentworth about doppelgängers. Being a scientific historian, he attaches no importance to superstitions like this and remarks, " 'The uneducated mind is generally known by its haste to see likeness where no likeness exists. It evaluates its emotions in terms of fortuitous circumstances' " (48). Wentworth, being an educated man, is in no danger of seeing any likenesses at all between one realm of experience and another, but at this very moment his own emotions are in a state of tumult over the "fortuitous circumstance" of both Hugh and Adela being absent from his soirée, since this must mean that they are together somewhere. He goes on, " 'It objectifies its concerns through its imagination.' " In a moment we see him decide to creep out into the night after Pauline has left and walk down towards the railway depot to see if he can spy out Hugh and Adela returning together by a late train from London, thereby proving what he has suspected, that they have given him the slip. His imagination of their subterfuges had led him to objectify his concern by moving it out of his mind and into the world of action. He finishes his remarks to Pauline with " 'Probably your friend was a very self-centered individual' " (48). Being an educated mind, he would not, of course, see any likeness between whatever self-centered individual Pauline might be talking about and his own massive egocentrism.

Wentworth's short trip out of the house to spy on Hugh and Adela is described in terms exactly parallel to the suicide's wandering away from this very same house in his quest for solitude, for that is what Wentworth also is in search of. He will not grasp and embrace the hard fact that he has lost to Hugh in the game of love, and so he will seek the furtive and murky world of this solitary spying, finding a ghastly nourishment by feeding on the tidbits of satisfaction that angry souls pick, vulturelike, from successes such as catching their rivals red-handed in a deception. It would be hard to tot up how many removes this sort of thing is from the frolicsome gaiety with which Charity greets all loves, even others' loves, but of course the piquant thing for any reader here is that it is all too recognizable. No one who has ever lost in the game of love will find one strange nuance here. Wentworth is guilty of nothing at all that all of us have not at least wished we could do.

Here is the language we find describing what is going on in Wentworth's mind in this late-evening saunter to the depot. "A remnant of intelligence cried to him that this was the road of mania, and self-indulgence leading to mania. . . . He would not go to spy; he would go for a walk. . . . He desired hell. . . . He walked down the length of his road; if that led towards the station it could not be helped. . . . He was a man, and he had a right to his walk. . . . He was not in ambush; he was out for a walk" (50).

A detail of this is worth noting. It happens that Adela and Hugh are not on the train, so Wentworth must wait for the very last train from London. It is late at night. He is terribly tired, naturally. But "his physical nature, which sometimes by its mere exhaustion postpones our more complete damnation, did not save him" (51). It is our intelligence and will that send us to hell; our poor animal natures, like dogs, can only be hungry or tired or lustful. They coax us in one direction or the other, but like dogs they must wait on our decision. Sometimes, when all else has failed, the only thing we have left to trust is the sheer animal instinct of fatigue, telling us to quit and go to bed. It is the world of decadence that forces itself to stay awake all night for the bacchanal, or for the stealthy ambush, when simply falling into bed would at least fend off the external evil.

This is a corollary to the doctrines of creation and Incarnation, which were central to Williams' imagination. We were made creatures of flesh and blood, and it was evil that introduced the division between our appetites and our will. Only in the Incarnation do we see the perfect knitting back together of flesh and spirit into the seamless integrity that God had in mind when he created man. The way of Charity is the way towards that knitting back up for every man. Wentworth in this scene is rejecting the smallish cues that his body sends out. He is opting for division. He is saying, in effect, Damn my tired body: I will stay here until dawn if necessary to prove my angry point and munch on the ashes of that ghastly satisfaction.

Two other details of this part of the narrative are worth noting. Readers will have noticed the mention of hurrying or pattering feet at various points. Wentworth seems to hear them now and again. Presently we will meet a woman, Mrs. Lily Sammile, who walks this way. She is always fluttering and pattering about. Suffice it to say for the present that the motif has been introduced here.

The other detail is Williams' repeated description of Wentworth's house and of Battle Hill, and indeed of Wentworth's mind, as "the place of a skull". No one can miss the allusion to Golgotha. The suggestion seems to be that all the choices and decisions that we make occur on some such cosmic eminence as this, and that Death and Life wait on what we choose. This way of picturing things would only be true if the small choices and decisions we make in this mortal life contributed in any way to our ultimate destiny. Christendom thinks that they do, and Williams' narratives proceed on this assumption.

In the next chapter, "Vision of Death", Pauline hears from her grandmother Margaret Anstruther about their ancestor John Struther, who was burned at the stake as a Protestant martyr under Mary Tudor in the sixteenth century. His death, like so many of those burnings, seems to have been quite a glorious affair for him, after he once got over his initial fear. " 'It was a terrible thing' ", says Pauline. " 'How he could shout for joy like that!' " (56). " 'Salvation,' Mrs. Anstruther said mildly, is quite often a terrible thing—a frightening good.' "

The conversation turns to Stanhope's play, and Mrs. Anstruther remarks that Mrs. Parry has ruined many a play by "successful production". The trouble with her dramatic work, as with her own life perhaps, is "elocution". She ruins the simplicity of the poetry with laboriously rehearsed effects. Which is a way of pointing out that goodness, in art as in life, is simple, when all is said and done.

The maid announces Mrs. Lily Sammile, and this lady comes pattering in to the garden where Pauline and her grandmother have been talking. The long and short of it is that Lily Sammile is a witch. She does no black masses, to be sure. But she is an evil sorceress whose specialty is telling people nervous and hasty stories that will paper over any fears these people may have, thus making them feel that all is well when perhaps their fears are the very warning they need that all is very far from well. She patters and flutters all over Battle Hill, "like a chicken fluttering round the glass walls of a snake's cage" (58). She is, of course, terrified of the terrible good. Her whole life has been an effort to fly from stark reality and to cover with little nosegays the cracks leading to the abyss. However, nosegays don't keep anyone from plunging down into the abyss. If there is an abyss, and cracks leading down to it, then we had better find out where they are and avoid them. Nothing is gained by refusing to face the terrible truth. But for Mrs. Sammile illusion is always better, because it is more tolerable, than stark reality.

Her name is transparent. Lily is Lilith, the witchlike figure in ancient Jewish lore who was believed to have

been Adam's first wife, and who, because she was dissat-
isfied with things, was exiled from Eden and replaced by
Eve. Since then she has hated Eve and all motherhood
and fruitfulness and has made it her business to come in
from her raging exile in the wilderness and show up at
cradles and christenings and put hexes and curses on infants or steal them away. She is the archetype of all
wicked fairy godmothers and enchantresses. She shows
up as Lamia, and as *La Belle Dame sans Merci*, and as the
crone in Hansel and Gretel and Snow White, and so
forth. The great thing about her is her hatred for plain,
glad, normal life, with all of its fruitfulness and playing
children and family fidelity, and her endless attempts to
wheedle and bamboozle people away from this good
health into the wilderness where they will sicken and die.

Lily's surname is Sammile, which, spelled Sammael, is
one of the names for the devil from ancient occult lore.
From here on, every syllable we read about Mrs. Sammile is to be read in the light of who she is. She is like one
of the evil figures we encounter in a masque.

Presently Stanhope and Myrtle Fox show up in the
garden, and the discussion turns on art and poetry, with
Myrtle Fox plumping for elocution and for art's being
lovely and consoling (obviously Mrs. Sammile has got
to her), and Mrs. Anstruther asking Stanhope what one
needs to recite poetry. He comments, " 'What but the
four virtues, clarity, speed, humility, courage' " (63).
Clarity—as opposed to the murk and illusion scattered
by people like Mrs. Sammile and into which Wentworth
is slipping; speed—not the agitated hurry of Mrs. Sammile's pattering feet, away from plain truth, but the
agility to see and grasp and assent to plain truth; humility
—which is modest and wry and sufficiently self-
deprecating to allow one to accept whatever tumbles

into one's lap; and courage—which is at a polar extreme from the timorous dodging about which we see in Lily Sammile.

We get to know a bit more about Margaret Anstruther in this chapter and discover that she, in contrast to Mrs. Sammile and Myrtle Fox and almost everyone else except Stanhope, is full of clarity, humility, speed, and courage. She knows that she will die soon, and this knowledge, terrible to most people, spurs her to appreciate such a small thing as the evening. She will not have many more of them. Hence her pleasure in this one is intensified. She is content with many or with few, ". . . so long as you accepted what joys the universe offered and did not seek to compel the universe to offer you joys of your own definition. She would die soon; she expected, with hope and happiness, the discovery of the joy of death" (66). Death is merely a terrible good for her.

As Margaret Anstruther reflects on her approaching death, we come upon an important key to what is going on in the story. "If, as she believed, the spirit of a man at death saw truly what he was and had been, so that whether he desired it or not a lucid power of intelligence manifested all himself to him—then that energy of knowledge was especially urgent upon men and woman here [in Battle Hill]. . . . She felt . . . how the neighborhood of the dead troubled the living" (67). This of course is true everywhere, not just on Battle Hill: we may say that the neighborhood of the dead—the fact that all around us people have died and are buried nearby, and hence that the immense fact of death surrounds us—represents some sort of reckoning.

We also find that Margaret is no stranger to the same fear which bedevils Pauline—the encounter with herself.

But she has learned to love and has thereby been delivered from the horror of self-knowledge. "The approach by love was the approach to fact; to love anything but fact was not love" (69).

What Margaret has learned stands over against Pauline's fear and also against Lily Sammile's nervous flight from facts. Because of this, she is in a position to offer help to Pauline, who has not yet really begun to move out of her terror towards the freedom and joy that come in the wake of learning to love. The "vision of death" of the chapter title refers to a vision which Margaret has, lying in her bed, in which she sees herself and all other selves as mountains rising towards light at the summits, with little crawling people scouring about on the slopes. The thrust of the vision seems to be that these great, shining eminences represent the glorious and massive selves that we are to become, and the little crawling figures represent the fears and ordeals that beset us. Margaret sees her own life and that of the others on Battle Hill in this way. She sees Pauline in her vision, but she sees Pauline's situation turned around: the doppelgänger which seems so terrifying to Pauline is really Pauline's true self, which her poor present self is too timid to face. Margaret also sees the suicide, pursued by all of his little troubles like children chasing a stranger with jeers; and she sees Wentworth for a moment, coming out of his house, pursued by a woman. Back to the suicide—their eyes meet for an instant, and there seems to be a start of joy in him; then Pauline again, pursued by Lily Sammile accompanied by the stench of death. Margaret awakes and asks her nurse if she could see Pauline.

In the chapter "Return to Eden", we follow Wentworth in his progress towards hell, which at this point looks very much like the Garden of Eden. The story emphasizes the fact that he and the suicide have inhabited the same house, and that they make their respective decisions side by side, at the same window. Both reject the "republic". Both wish solitude, the suicide because he has despaired of ever finding anyone who appreciates him at all, and Wentworth because life is not giving him what he wants.

What he wants is two things mainly: recognition for his scholarly work and Adela. On the first point he learns that Aston Moffat, his rival, has been rewarded with a knighthood. Bitter pill. "There was presented to him at once and clearly an opportunity for joy—casual, accidental joy, but joy. If he could not manage joy, at least he might have managed the intention of joy, or (if that also were too much) an efforts towards the intention of joy" (80).

Here is a whole theology of salvation and damnation. Salvation for us all consists in joyous assent to fact. Damnation is the refusal of fact. The fact here is that my rival has been honored and I spurned. How on earth is a man to rejoice in that? It is an ordeal for a saint. And that is the very point. It is an ordeal. A sick man is not expected to run a 100-yard dash straight off: but there comes a point, if he is ever to recover, when he ought to begin to flex his toes a bit, admitting that this lying supine in bed is not what he was made for. Perhaps he cannot run right now. But at least he might admit that running is a sign of good health and that good health is better than sickness. That would be a start.

It is very difficult to refuse salvation. You have to insist on damnation. You have to quash all possibilities of joy. Wentworth must refuse very single invitation to accept and be glad in what is. He prefers to hate fact and to embrace illusion.

The form that the illusion takes for him arises from his other disappointment, namely, his loss of Adela to Hugh Prescott. Since he will not accept this loss either, and prefers to fantasize about it, he gets what he wants: fantasy. The fantasy appears in the form of a succubus, which is an odd kind of female ghost who will have carnal intercourse with a man in his sleep. Most appropriate for Wentworth, who has in effect conjured this up by his insistence on having Adela on any terms, even if those terms are wholly illusory. If reality won't give me what I want, then damn reality. I will conjure up my own Eden.

It is very gratifying. It turns out that this Adela, the succubus, is much better than the real flesh-and-blood Adela would be. The voice is "fuller, richer, more satisfying. . . . That truth which is the vision of romantic love, in which the beloved becomes supremely her own adorable and eternal self . . . was aped for him then" (82).

Wentworth's experience of this succubus is very murky, which is to be expected since hell is murky. It is not always clear which one of them is speaking or what exactly is being said. The general drift is that she (or it) will be able to make everything nice for him. All he has to do is to think more of himself, which is what Lily Sammile has been saying all along, and which is what real love knows nothing at all about. They walk out, or, as it turns out, *in*—inside of Wentworth's own imagination, into the darkness and lull and warmth where one is no longer bothered by the brittle and bright edges of reality. It is misty and moist and dreamy, and above all peaceful. In this solitude and vacuousness, at the polar extreme of things from the City, the topography of Battle Hill seems somehow to become the gigantic body of Adam, stretched out along the earth—or Wentworth's own body, the point being that he has reached the point at which, if he will accept a real separation from Adela, and will accept the reality of other selves, as Adam did in Eden when God gave him a real, solid *other* for his companion, then real creation will take place. It will be the beginning of joy for Wentworth.

He is given the chance at least to nod in the direction of *some* other self, even if he cannot quite manage to get rid of this succubus yet, when the suicide comes along the road of his vision. The poor man could use a kind word. Wentworth might offer him one. But no. "He sprang forward and up, to drive it away, to curse it lest it interpolated its horrid need between himself and his perfection. He would not have it: no canvassers, no hawkers, no tramps . . . no City, no circulars, no beggars" (88). These all, of course, represent chances a man might have to go out of himself, if only for a moment, and respond to someone *else*. But Wentworth prefers this illusion and solitude. It is much more comfortable and gratifying. Other people—real other selves—are such a bore. Or so says hell, at any rate. Whatever it is that the saints find so lovely about other selves, it is certainly not anything that Wentworth, or any other damned soul, wants to be bothered with.

We now have all the elements of the story. Battle Hill; Stanhope and his masque; Pauline and her doppelgänger; Margaret Anstruther and her approaching death; Wentworth and his succubus; the suicide; the martyr ancestor;

and Adela, Hugh, Myrtle Fox, and Lily Sammile. It remains only to see how things work themselves out.

In the chapter entitled "The Doctrine of Substituted Love", Stanhope offers to do for Pauline what she cannot do for herself. He offers to bear her fear of the doppelgänger. This strikes her as nonsense, but he refers to Saint Paul's words about people bearing one another's burdens and thus fulfilling Christ's law. But, he points out, one need not refer to Christ. It is a simple fact of experience. If I carry the parcel for you, then you need not carry it. It is I who feels the weight of it now, not you. Pauline demurs. It is too humiliating. " 'Would I push my burden on to anybody else?' " " 'Not if you insist on making a universe for yourself,' he answered. 'If you want to disobey and refuse the laws that are common to us all, if you want to live in pride and division and anger, you can. But if you will be part of the best of us, and live and laugh and be ashamed with us, then you must be content to be helped' " (99).

There is the City. It is at an infinite distance from the hushed and solitary Eden into which Wentworth is slipping by his refusal of all contact with real other selves.

Stanhope's offer is a case in point of what all joy is made of. My life for yours. I owe all to you, and vice versa. The saints know this and find it to be blissful. The souls in hell hate and refuse it.

Pauline agrees to try Stanhope's offer. On her way home from the rehearsal this time, instead of being gripped by the terror lest the doppelgänger show up, she finds herself diverted with a kitten, and some lovely flowers along the way, and a postman who greets her, and so forth—all insignificant pleasantnesses that might make up a day if one is not in the grip of some private terror or grief. She has been set free from that trap by someone else bearing the burden she could not bear.

Three small but significant items occur before the end of this chapter. For one, when Pauline reaches home, she has a few spare minutes and leafs idly through her grandmother's copy of Foxe's *Book of Martyrs*. Foxe's description of her ancestor Struther's triumph in the flames begins to make some sense.

Then she gazes out of the window—usually an act full of apprehension for her, what with the possibility of the doppelgänger's appearing. But she realizes that Stanhope is carrying that burden of fear for her now. "Perhaps, later on, she could give the Omnipotence a hand with some other burden; everyone carrying everyone else's" (107, 108).

Finally, Lily Sammile shows up, in Pauline's first great temptation after her deliverance from fear, offering Pauline tranquillity. It is so appealing. But no. Pauline bids her a crisp goodnight just as she is summoned to a much more genuine test of the reality of this new way of exchange into which she has begun to be introduced.

In the next chapter, "The Junction of Travellers", we see the suicide wandering in his limbo but presently being chased by a light and fleeing through the landscape which seems somehow to contain his entire past, until he sees a face in a window, the first one that he has ever seen without fear. It is Margaret Anstruther, and she says simply, "My dear, how tired you look." It is the first greeting he can remember that has been kind.

What has happened is that Margaret, full of love and therefore without fear of her imminent death, is permitted by the Mercy to assist this soul in need with the su-

perfluity of love and peace from her own experience. She
has seen the man in a vision and has asked the nurse to
summon Pauline. The three of them, Margaret, Pauline,
and the suicide, meet in a junction of travellers, and salvation occurs. For Margaret it is a sort of final salute of
Charity; for Pauline it is a first exercise in Charity. Her
salvation from her own fear has after all not been merely
for her own sake. Everything is always for others. She
has been saved by Stanhope so that by going out into the
night to the suicide, in defiance of all her old terrors, she
will be able to point him towards London. That is all he
needs: just someone to point the way back towards the
city for him so that his salvation can proceed. This is ac-
complished, not without Pauline's undergoing a Gethsemane of temptation to fear.

But this is not the end for Pauline. This itself has been
merely a dress rehearsal for the big test to be undertaken
by Pauline, namely, the offering of herself retroactively,
350 years after the fact, to stand in and carry the fear
which her ancestor Struther felt as he came to the stake.
She does this, and his shout of victory recorded by Foxe
now turns out to have been due to his being delivered
from his fear. Where did it go? Where but onto the
shoulders of Pauline three and a half centuries later. It is
absurd, of course: you cannot jump across time like that.
But if you are talking not about the march of history but
about the region of the Divine Love and of the mystery
of intercession and of substitution and exchange, then
who knows what crisscrossing and shuttling back and
forth might not be possible?

Williams is not imagining anything that is not already
at work in the Christian story. Abraham was saved "by
faith", centuries before the object of his faith became

clear. The sacrifice of the Cross was retroactively applicable to all faithful souls back to the beginning of the world. The humblest prayers sent up anywhere reach across continents and seas in behalf of their objects.

The "Dress Rehearsal" refers, however, to more than one element in the action. On the surface the rehearsal for Stanhope's masque is going on. And we have watched Pauline's rehearsal. But everyone is rehearsing, for whatever part he or she will ultimately play in the Great Dance.

Especially Wentworth. He has chosen to prefer his succubus to the real Adela. It is only a figment of his imagination and hence can come at the summons of his will, in a ghastly parody of real love. She appears to us readers as infinitely old and senile, as old as Lilith and all the tribe of illusionists. But Wentworth can see only the false youth that his imagination wishes. He himself is slipping into an increasing senility. His thinking becomes muddled. He is losing, like the souls in Dante's hell, the good of intellect. He is slipping into increasing solitude also, so much so that he finds the presence of the real Adela intolerable now.

Simultaneous with this increasing murkiness of Wentworth's world we find Battle Hill itself experiencing an increase of luminous power, as though things are standing out more and more clearly in this intensity of midsummer light.

Wentworth arrives at the rehearsal for the masque and is asked if the guards' uniforms are correct. All that is being asked of him is one monosyllable. Yes or no. If any alterations are needed to get them correct, his housekeeper can stitch them up in one evening.

But, it is more than he can manage. He has not even one monosyllable's worth of interest in the world of others now. He knows the uniforms are wrong, but he murmurs yes. They are all right. He has finished with Battle Hill and all its inhabitants. This refusal of exchange—of his expertise for the good of the masque—is almost his final refusal. There remains only for him to refuse joy, or even assent, at the dinner honoring Sir Aston Moffat in London.

Meanwhile Pauline has realized that the very spot on which the masque is to take place is the spot where her ancestor was burned. How can anyone rejoice here? she asks Stanhope. Why not? he asks. " 'Unless everything's justifiable, nothing is' " (149). Which is not to say that everything that has ever been done has been just. It is to say that there is nothing done that cannot be set to rights and *made* just, so to speak. But the martyrdom? It was an outrage. But why shouldn't it be turned into an occasion for joy, perhaps by someone's offering to carry Struther's burden of fear?

And Pauline enters into the glory of Zion, the City of God, via this particular gate of exchange.

The performance of Stanhope's masque, with its joyous solemnity, its rhythm, its exactness and clarity, stands over against the muddle among the inhabitants of the hill, each one of them so busily preoccupied with himself, as most normal people are. The masque proves too much for Lily Sammile, who fears clarity and exactness more than anything else, and she faints dead away at the performance.

In the chapter "The Opening of Graves", we find that Margaret Anstruther has died, and that her son, Pauline's uncle, has arrived to arrange everything, including Pauline's move to London to live and work. Hugh and Adela take an evening walk and happen to pass the local cemetery, where they are hailed by Lily Sammile, who appears from a sort of shed, or dugout, just inside the fence. She makes her usual offer of tranquillity. But presently the three of them are transfixed by what appears to be the graves opening, as though time is moving backwards and dirt that has been shoveled in to the holes is flying back out in small geysers. It is a scene very much like the one described in the accounts of Christ's crucifixion, when the graves in Jerusalem are said to have opened up and the dead in them to have walked abroad. The dead, it seems, are roused when judgment comes to its crux. Certainly Stanhope's play has opened judgment upon Battle Hill, the way all good art ought to do. Adela screams and flees, with Hugh after her protesting that the bizarre phenomenon they have just seen in the confused light of dusk was just the wind blowing loose earth about from the tops of fresh graves. But Adela eludes him and flees to Wentworth's house for comfort.

Alas. Wentworth, summoned at length from his stupor to his study window by Adela's shrieks, will have nothing to do with the real Adela. She thinks she sees a face like her own lurking in the study. It is the succubus, and Adela faints in Wentworth's garden. He drags her outside his gate and along the road and leaves her there. On his return to the womb of his study he finds, however, that he does not now even want the succubus. Ghastly as it is, it is still some rag of a reminder of another self presented to him, and what one wants above all is to be completely alone.

Adela is taken home and is plagued in her subsequent illness with a dream in which she finds herself running from Hugh, which makes sense since if Hugh is to be her husband he will constitute some sort of authority in her life, and she has always resisted the authority of anyone else over her. The great good of marriage presents itself to her in her dream, then, as terrible. A terrible good which she is not yet able to see as good. Another element in her dream is an effort on her part to learn some lines, for a play, perhaps. She cannot seem to manage it, which is very traumatic for her, since managing is what she has thought of herself as being adept at. But now there are some lines that she cannot get right at all.

Pauline visits Adela and agrees to go to Lily Sammile for help, at Adela's frantic urging, although of course Pauline knows that no help can possibly come from this source. But she will consent to go on the foolish errand, trusting that the Mercy will undertake and will translate the effort into the real help that the delirious Adela really wants, unknown to herself. Pauline's trip to the cemetery to find Lily represents yet a further step in her new and bold and joyous pilgrimage into the freedom of love, since to go out alone at all, let alone to the cemetery, let alone to fetch Lily Sammile, would only recently have paralyzed her with fear. But she is learning about the freedom of love. She goes. Lily gabbles meaninglessly, the way the damned do in Dante's hell since they can no longer manage language, the vehicle of meaning. Lily offers help, especially to Pauline, who cannot at all convince Lily that there is nothing that she *wants* help with. (How can a soul in bliss find any way of telling a damned soul what the nature of bliss is?) Finally Pauline laughs gently at the absurdity of it all. This sound is insupportable to Lily, and the whole dugout collapses on her amidst her shrieks and wails.

In the last chapter, "Beyond Gomorrah", Pauline and Stanhope bid good-bye to each other, and Pauline goes off to London to work. At the railway station she sees

Wentworth, who has roused himself enough to go to London to the dinner honoring Aston Moffat. She greets him, thinking they might travel together, but he flees into a compartment by himself.

The rest of the tale traces his final descent into darkness and solitude. Every detail superimposes the small details of his trip to London onto the darker map of a man's final damnation.

For example, Wentworth has lost his watch: time has become meaningless now. He passes Mme Tussaud's wax museum in the taxi and sees himself, in a sort of vision, trying to arrange all the wax figures in some pattern of squares on the floor, unable to get it right. They will not fit his pattern. This, of course, is what he has been doing all his life: fitting all of history and its people into his tidy schemes only to prove his own theories.

Each detail of his progress in London is accompanied by the picture of his rope, and of him going down, knot after knot. Even the coin which he gives the taxi driver is now meaningless to him. He hardly knows what it is, since he has lost all capacity to understand exchange, of which money is the symbol.

When he encounters Sir Aston at the dinner, hate jolts him; and this, says Williams, might even save him, since to hate someone is to care. And even more, if his hatred sprang, albeit wrongly, from a passion for truth (if, say, Wentworth really did think that Sir Aston had falsified history), here also might be some rag of hope. But no. All he can think is, " 'I've been cheated' " (219).

He has completely lost the good of intellect now. Nothing makes any sense to him, and he moves in a co-matose daze. Even the clock on the wall is only "a huge round white blotch, with black markings on it, and two long black lines going round and round, one very fast and one very slow" (220). The men at the dinner in their black dinner jackets and white collars become only black-and-white shapes. "He had forgotten the names of them, but somewhere at some time he had thought he knew similar forms and they had had names" (221). The shape of Sir Aston, bobbing as he acknowledges the applause of the audience, means nothing to Wentworth now. Silence and solitude and entropy and ennui and impotence and inanity and bottomlessness have now closed in upon him. He has descended into the hell which he strove with all his power to enter. He has got what he so fervently wanted.

Afterword

If indeed Charles Williams' work is to find a place, no matter how minor, in the annals of "English literature", then a great deal of work remains to be done. Very little has yet appeared in print on his poetry, which may emerge finally as his most significant work; nor have his critical essays, theological essays, biographies, and plays as yet received full-dress treatment. Studies are appearing little by little, but much remains to be done.

One of the questions, of course, is how much is worth doing. Are his biographies, for example, worth any scholarly attention, or shall we do them the kindest service by letting them sit quietly on the shelf? Are his theological essays to be counted as contributions to serious theology? Certainly they rouse the reader's imagination, as does anything that Williams ever wrote. But may his pell-mell treatment of theological topics properly be called theology in any sense? His small volume *The Descent of the Dove* is a history of the Church, so to speak, which has no doubt piqued the interest of countless historically and theologically literate readers (W. H. Auden read it every year, he said). But may it in any sense be called Church history? His critical essays bespeak an enormously agile mind which could give a reading of Wordsworth, Milton, or Dante that stands quite apart from traditional scholarship and always seems fresh. Are these essays, then, trail-blazing essays, like Tolkien's "Beowulf: The Monsters and the Critics"? Or is it our tact that keeps them in oblivion?

If Williams' name is to find any place among the writers who will be remembered from our century, these questions should be looked at sooner or later.

The foregoing study of Williams' fiction has attempted first of all to assist the reader at points where Williams' singularity makes the going difficult, especially readers coming to his work for the first time. Ordinarily this is not necessary with fiction: a man can pick up a story by Fielding or Thomas Mann or Henry James and, whether he enjoys it or not, at least know what is going on. This is not always so with Williams. Like Blake or Joyce, he demands some deciphering. This study has taken on that task.

The other consideration in my mind during the writing of this book has been to keep one eye cocked on the tradition, as they say, in order to supply some assistance to those who would like to think of Williams' fiction as having some place in this tradition. Or perhaps it should be put another way, since to say that it might have such a place is to beg very large questions: to supply some assistance in *comparing* Williams' achievement in fiction with the major tradition of the English-language novel.

That tradition is to be found generally speaking in the lineage of Fielding, Jane Austen, Dickens, George Eliot, Hardy, James, Joyce, and D. H. Lawrence. Many other novelists are major figures here of course, and the tradition comes further forward in history than the works of Lawrence. But it has been the set of concerns exhibited by these writers that has supplied the major energy in English-language fiction since the rise of the novel. To what extent the currents at work in fiction and criticism over the last twenty years will turn the whole enterprise in new directions, leaving some of these figures in a literary backwater, no one knows. The tides of taste come and go.

We may say with no fear of controversy that this tradition has run along realistic and psychological lines. Romance, fantasy, mystery, faerie—these have not been preeminent, at least in critical esteem. The notion in the major fiction of the eighteenth through the midtwentieth century has been to render scrupulous fidelity to human experience as we mortals find it in the light-of-day world. Even novels of remote adventure like *Moby Dick* or *Lord Jim* derive their interest, at least in the modern critical mind, not so much from their remoteness and derring-do as from the light they seem to throw on plain mortal experience. For the modern mind Captain Ahab's whale furnishes much more than a fishing story: it is a telling image.

This of course has always been true to some extent in all narrative. But we may be sure that the northern kings who listened to the tales of Beowulf and Byrhtnoth did not give the finely tuned psychological reading to these events that we do. Adventure and heroism were virtually ends in themselves. They did not have words like "imagery" and "suggestive" in the front of their minds as they listened. Indeed, we may almost say that our own epoch has come to think of the seriousness of a novel as standing in virtually inverse proportion to the excitement of the external events. Slaying dragons, chasing galleons, creeping into dens of iniquity, dropping ciphered notes into cracks — this is not serious narrative for us. We may thank Henry James for having brought this art to a very fine point, but he was mining the lode already worked by Richardson and Jane Austen and Trollope. Writers of adventure such as Wilkie Collins, John Buchan, Rudyard Kipling, and Ian Fleming are not mentioned in the same breath with these others, although to be sure critics have wondered whether there ought not to be a Kipling reassessment.

The point here of course is that Charles Williams' novels fall into one of these "other" categories of narrative and hence are not to be found among the major works of our century. It is not the argument of this study that they ought to be found there. I myself doubt that they should. Their strangeness is only the most superficial reason for this. The fact that they call upon such arcana as the Holy Grail and the Tarot pack will account for the notion that they are trivial, but criticism needs to dig deeper than this. The fact that vastly urbane critical minds — Eliot and Auden, for example — have found pleasure and substance in Williams' fiction ought to suggest that the question of its worth may be pressed.

At least three elements of Williams' fiction raise doubts in our minds about its final worth, or perhaps we should say its final weight. First is the obvious business of their peculiar matter: the occult would not seem to promise much in the way of serious fiction. I have tried to show in the foregoing study that Williams' novels are never *about* the Grail or the Tarot. These items perform the same function for him as the whale for Melville or the jungle river for Conrad. Melville is not trying to regale us with fishing, nor Conrad with exploring. A novelist chooses his imagery with all sorts of considerations in mind. We might say that Melville and Conrad would plump hard for their whales and jungles in any debate that sought to compare these far-fetched elements with Jane Austen's teacups, say, or Henry James' golden bowls. By the same token, Williams would keep insisting that we pay attention to the *function* of all this arcana in his novels. The focus is always and only on human experience with all of its complexity, ambiguity, and danger. Byzantium, Arthurian Logres, and the Blessed Virgin all appear on stage, so to speak, by way of hailing us with aspects of our experience that we may have neglected, since there is little imagery in the modern world that corresponds to what these images evoke for human experience. They are far-fetched of necessity. The focus that we call realistic and psychological, which is the focus of modern fiction because it is the focus of the modern mind, clarifies certain regions of our experience and thereby blurs others. We do not incline, for example, to talk much of majesty or sanctity or damnation except in a psychological sense, when we probe our experience. But thirty centuries and all their poets would ask us why.

This may bring us to the second element that sets Williams' work apart from the modern tradition. Besides the sheer peculiarity of his matter we find a specific religious frame to it all that strikes us as anachronistic. Not that many modern people are not Christian. Our era extols the notion of pluralism, so that if a writer turns out to be a Catholic or a Swedenborgian or a Hindu, we can accept this with equanimity. And a writer may even write about his Catholicism. Graham Greene is the great case in point here for the English-language novel in our century, and certainly Eliot and Flannery O'Connor and François Mauriac have obliged us to recognize the sacramentalist vision as one of the serious options in our pluralistic array.

But Charles Williams' novels are so unabashedly *Dantean*. It is very impressive, and anyone who has read his Dante (or his Augustine or his Spenser, for that matter) will not be lost. Nevertheless, we cannot quite accept that world as an authentic scheme for twentieth-century experience. All poets struggle to find such a scheme, and some present us with more peculiar schemes than others: Yeats, Joyce, and Flannery O'Connor would all be cases in point of writers who have given us odd and difficult material. Fairies, stream of consciousness, and backwoods Southern freaks are not easy stuff at the outset. But somehow we find that the effort to step across from the workaday world to these other worlds is worth making. Our own world of experience is thrown into fresh light. Perhaps Eliot and his problems, both in *Four Quartets* and in his plays, illustrate more painfully than these others do the difficulties under which a modern writer struggles if he is not at home in the modern world. For all their struggles with philistinism, most of the most disaffected modern writers (Bloomsbury, Gertrude Stein, the early Sitwells,

Pirandello, Pinter, and so forth) have nonetheless shared the modern secularist outlook. It was simply *taste* that they fought. But what do you do if you think the whole modern world *is* in a cul-de-sac? What do you do if the shape of your whole world has more in common with that of Homer and Dante than it does with Ibsen's or Virginia Woolf's, not to say with that of all the critics and literate people who are going to read your work? Eliot not only struggled with this: he made the struggle itself one of the major themes of his later poetry and plays. The fact that these achievements are very far from being accepted as unqualified successes by contemporary criticism would illustrate his point.

But for all of its rigorous Christian orthodoxy, Eliot's vision is somehow significant even for the most modern of us. We may attribute some of this to Eliot's own austerely modern intellect and also to the influence on him of such extremely modern poets as LaForgue, the Symbolists, and Pound. Somehow it is an authentically modern imagination that walks across London Bridge or makes its pilgrimage to Little Gidding. But we are not sure of this with Williams. Despite the fact that he goes to extravagant pains to impress his own scepticism on us, most modern readers find themselves far from home in Logres and Byzantium, or in rooms suddenly full of golden mist in which Tarot figures move or Mass is being said. Is Williams indulging himself, we wonder? Is he more in love with sheer peculiarity than with the texture of real experience?

Who can say? Williams himself was an extremely odd figure. He was loved by many, but everyone who knew him testifies to what an individual he was. This of course may be said of half the world's poets. But if one's individuality reaches further than a bohemian life style, say, then difficulties arise. Williams' individuality did reach further than this: indeed, his life would have appeared conventional, even dull, to an outside glance—plain threepiece suits, off to work every morning early, and so forth. Even if we cannot sort out exactly why Little Gidding or even Yeats' fairies are admissible and Williams' Logres and Tarot are not, nonetheless we may say that this question of his idiosyncratic religious vision does account for some of the difficulty that might stand in the way of his being taken seriously by modern criticism. One of the ironies here is that technically his religious vision was not idiosyncratic. It was a matter of traditional Christian orthodoxy. But his way of *picturing* it all was emphatically idiosyncratic.

A corollary to the plain orthodoxy that animates Williams' work presents a further difficulty to modern imagination. It is the moral implication of it all. In a word, Williams extols a whole fabric of things that appears incredible to our epoch. There is, for example, not a hint of waggishness in his praise of virginity or of elaborate and agile courtesies. These seem somewhat quaint to most readers and hence less than serious. Williams would have held these things to be very close to the center of everything. If a writer's presuppositions are as remote from contemporary sensibility as this, then he is going to find himself out of fashion unless people cannot resist the sheer sound of his lines. The only reason, for example, that Edmund Spenser is now read at all, even in the excessively small corner known as graduate studies in English, is that his poetry is so sumptuous. He is a master of English poetry. Williams is not a master of English prose, so unless some era finds itself taking his moral vision seriously, his work is going to have some difficulty maintaining a space anywhere other than on a dusty shelf.

This brings us to the third major consideration in this matter of Williams' possible place in the annals of English literature, namely, what we may call his style. That is a loose word and hence not a very useful one for criticism, since to set about speaking of "style" as though it were some ingredient separate from "content" is to be guilty of the original sin of criticism. Much of the matter in the foregoing chapters, however, has consisted of very little more than an attempt to decipher some strange sequence of vocabulary or syntax that presents an obstacle to the reader. Once again, on the surface of things we do not find here anything that substantially distinguishes Williams from other "difficult" writers of our epoch: a great deal of *explication de texte* has become necessary in our time. Indeed, this fact is itself an index of our time. With the loss of any publicly acknowledged moral scheme for human experience, art has been obliged to become more and more "private". We welcome this ordinarily. It puts us on our mettle. It compliments us.

But the question about Williams is really a more elementary one. We must ask whether he writes good prose at all.

That is perhaps the most abstruse question that criticism may ask. The questions fan out from it faster than we can follow them. What is the standard? Who are the arbiters? Who are the practitioners? Is there some genius in English itself that constitutes an unfailing touchstone by which we may test writers? Which innovations are legitimate? Which unworthy? What makes prose weak? Strong?

It is too daunting. And yet, even though we can scarcely track down a final definition of good English, we can, like the Supreme Court justice with pornography, recognize it when we see it.

My own opinion is that Williams' prose will never be granted a place anywhere near the center of great English prose for the simple reason that it does not warrant such a place. Somehow or other (and here we are talking about the almost ineffable), when we hear a writer's prose or poetry we must hear more than Jane Austen or John Milton, no matter how colossal a voice is speaking. We must hear *English*. The very genius, the spirit itself, of English, must be summoned. There is no formula, alas. How shall we say what Caedmon has in common with Auden, or Hooker with E. M. Forster? We may talk of economy and evocative power and fidelity to the genius of English until we are all blue in the face, but we will merely be making little rushes at what is *there*. What is it?

Who of us will claim to know? With this flagrant demurral I must allow my guess about Williams' prose to rest. Somehow or other he obliges us to keep saying, This is Williams—this is Williams, in a way that does not obtain when we read James or Eliot, individual though those writers may be. The difference lies somewhere in their power to convince us, at least for the time being, that the world they conjure is *the* world. Their spell works. The external world of our experience becomes indistinguishable from the world they conjure. There is no distance between word and world, we might say.

Perhaps if there is any formula for "great" literature, it would be something like that. In Williams' work we are always peering through the scrim of words. It is a very good scrim, and it permits us to see contours and masses that we would no doubt otherwise miss entirely. But it is always a scrim.

Having thus demurred, we may go on to ask what it is, then, that accounts for the excitement that Williams' work generates even among urbane readers. To say that someone's work stirs up excitement is to say nothing at all: comic books and pornography do that. But when you find that forty years after a man's death his work commands attention and even awe from readers schooled in the whole tradition of English poetry and prose, then you will want to know why.

The foregoing chapters have attempted to answer that question, implicitly if not explicitly. Part of the answer is to be found in the sheer force of Williams' imagination. You cannot stumble suddenly out into Byzantium from a country crossroads, or find yourself hailed with the Blessed Virgin herself when you thought it was only a typist, without being surprised. There is energy here if nothing else. But mere energy is not enough either: comic books abound with lively onomatopoeia and punctuation. It must all somehow crowd you along towards real significance. Your surprise must turn out to be *recognition*. Good heavens! you say: this is true! Why haven't I seen this all along? What could be more obvious? What could be more lucid?

Williams' poetry and fiction do succeed on this point. We are startled awake by the sheer color and brilliance of the imagery, but we are shaken when we see the distance between that imagery and our own experience dwindle.

The vision rushes at us, we might say, and envelops the subdued colors of commonplace experience, suffusing it all with incandescence. Despite ourselves we find that we believe, as it were. Williams overthrows our urbanity. For the moment it does seem that Byzantium is very near.

But it is more than merely momentary. It would be a very rare, and very disenchanted, reader who would insist that reading Charles Williams had not filed the edges of his sensibilities. Only a jade could resist wholly the charting of Lawrence Wentworth's harmless little egoisms as a journey to hell. The trouble with trying to resist is that it is all too clear that if there were ever any hell conceivable in any possible world, it would be made up of just this sort of thing. It is horrifying, and Wentworth's behavior is horrifying. One feels that one will never again be able to indulge in the puerile and egoistic little ruses that Wentworth did without remembering hell. Williams' fiction has done the work that fiction should do: it has clarified and modified my outlook on experience itself. To that extent it is exciting and important.

Is Charles Williams a great novelist? No. Too many questions plague the matter. But his achievement on this front is arresting at least, and his work might possibly attain the crown most sedulously wished for by all artists for their work, namely, longevity.